The journey is everything

Helen Bevington

The journey is everything

a journal of the Seventies

Duke University Press   Durham, N.C.   1983

Some of the poems in this volume originally appeared in *The Archive; Southern Poetry Review; Contemporary Poetry of North Carolina;* and *Southern Poetry, The Seventies.* The following appeared in slightly different form as book reviews or essays in *The New York Times Book Review: Early American Gardens,* by Ann Leighton, © March 8, 1970, by The New York Times Company. Reprinted by permission. *American Place-Names,* by George R. Stewart, © Sept. 20, 1970, by The New York Times Company. Reprinted by permission. *Bring Me a Unicorn,* by Anne Lindbergh, © Feb. 27, 1972, by The New York Times Company. Reprinted by permission. *North of Jamaica,* by Louis Simpson, © April 8, 1973, by The New York Times Company. Reprinted by permission. *Half Remembered,* by Peter Davison, © Sept. 16, 1973, by The New York Times Company. Reprinted by permission. *The Rat-Catcher's Daughter,* by Laurence Housman, and *The Twelve Dancing Princesses and Other Fairy Tales,* © May 5, 1974, by The New York Times Company. Reprinted by permission. *The Great and the Near-Great* (Collections of Christmas books), © Dec. 1, 1974, by The New York Times Company. Reprinted by permission. *The Land Unknown,* by Kathleen Raine, © Oct. 12, 1975, by The New York Times Company. Reprinted by permission. *Love or Nothing,* by Tom Prideaux, © Jan. 4, 1976, by The New York Times Company. Reprinted by permission. *No Laughing Matter,* by Margaret Halsey, © Nov. 13, 1977, by The New York Times Company. Reprinted by permission. *The Life and Works of Mr. Anonymous,* by Willard Espy, © Jan. 5, 1978, by The New York Times Company. Reprinted by permission. *Faeries,* by Brian Froud and Alan Lee, © Dec. 3, 1978, by the New York Times Company. Reprinted by permission. "The Journey Is Everything" (as "A Change of Sky") appeared in the author's book *A Change of Sky* (Houghton Mifflin, 1956); "How to Live, What to Do," *The Collected Poems of Wallace Stevens,* © 1954, by Alfred A. Knopf. Reprinted by permission.

Library of Congress Cataloging in Publication Data

Bevington, Helen (Smith),
    The journey is everything.

    1. Bevington, Helen (Smith), date   Diaries.
    2. Authors, American—20th century—Biography.
    I. Title.
    PS3503.E924Z466   1983   818'.5403 [B]   83-5582
    ISBN 0-8223-0553-4

The traveler takes a notebook and writes:
Should we have stayed at home,
wherever that may be?

—from Elizabeth Bishop, "Questions of Travel"

to Betty and Ted, with love

The journey is everything

The Journey Is Everything

Montaigne believed the journey, in itself,
Was the idea. Yet from this moving plane
I look down on the dazzle of the world,

Conscious of his words but wondering
When, when shall I be there, at journey's end?
The journey, said Montaigne, *is everything.*

Two hours ago the setting out began
With words of love. It is too soon to be
In love with landscape, altering below—

The flight upriver and the dwindling hills—
As if I came for this, a traveler,
And every wisp of cloud were an obsession.

It is too soon! The journey is myself,
Concerned with where I was, where I must go,
Not with the clouds about me (what of them?),

Not with the morning skies—nor would Montaigne
Have noticed them, his mind on other things.
The journey is my heartbeat in this plane.

Yet with more time? Were the excursion longer
To the Côte d'Azur et d'Or, perhaps, La Mer,
The hyacinth fields of Haarlem, Tanganyika,

The river Lethe or the Serpentine,
The Fortunate Isles or Nepal—anywhere,
I might discover what his words still mean:

The journey, in itself, a thing apart.
But no. These words are older than Montaigne's:
The sky is changed. I have not changed my heart.

—

1970

January

There are worse ways to begin a decade. Alone in my house on New Year's Eve, I spend it reading the Rand McNally *World Atlas*. Thank God the planet is still here, full of vast continents and mighty seas. I'm sorry not to have conquered it yet, but my soul is in Cathay, Yucatán, Outer Mongolia, Mount Kilimanjaro, and the Great Barrier Reef. Colette said she didn't like travel but liked to read travel books and wander in her head. Emily Dickinson hid inside her house and announced that paradise is no journey. Elizabeth Bishop asked, "Should we have stayed at home and thought of here?"

So the meaning escapes. I have no second-hand memories of places. With places as with people, you have to see for yourself unless you can imagine Mount Olympus or the Lion Gate at Mycenae, unless you can invent men or gods.

Montaigne was right. The way to take a journey is not to be concerned with arrivals or departures, or in search of something wondrous like Marco Polo or the Three Magi. The journey is everything—to another country, another time, another person's life. And everything is a journey.

The real lady travelers lived in Queen Victoria's reign. As inspirational as the *World Atlas* is Dorothy Middleton's *Victorian Lady Travellers*. About 1870 women started to swarm over the planet, not as missionaries but as tourists with incomparable stamina, courage, endurance, and gentility. The author calls them globe trotteresses. Middle-aged and inquisitive, they went off alone to seek unbeaten paths; they embarked on voyages, bicycle tours, safaris, on mules, camels, elephants, climbed mountains dressed in large hats and long skirts, toting an umbrella. They sought neither love nor romance, and their honor was not threatened. They were upholstered and formidable, with an ideal of womanhood so resolute as to discourage a man instantly. One of them, May French Sheldon, carried to Africa a pennant inscribed *Noli me tangere*. She was not touched. Fanny Bullock Workman bore to the Himalayas a placard saying Votes for Women.

I esteem the Victorian lady traveler Isabella Bird Bishop, a gadabout from Yorkshire, an Evangelical related to Wilberforce. In July 1872 as Isabella Bird she left for Australia for her disordered nerves. By New Year's Eve she was en route from New Zealand to the Sandwich Islands, sailing with gusto through a hurricane. After six months on the islands, where she rode her horse up volcanoes and visited lepers in their huts, she swept on to America. In the Rockies she came across "Rocky Mountain" Jim Nugent, a trapper, holed up in a cabin like the den of a wild beast—a strikingly handsome, golden-haired Irishman about forty (she was forty-two), with only one eye, the other having been clawed out by a grizzly bear. Though it was late October, she made up her mind to climb to the summit of Longs Peak, 14,255 feet, with desperado Jim as her guide, where to reach the top she had to be dragged like a bale of hay. There Jim fell in love with the indomitably chaste lady, who nevertheless refused him. "My soul dissolved in pity for his dark, lost, ruined life," she wrote, and went her way through the snow astride her mare Birdie, running into blue-eyed Comanche Bill, the notorious Indian killer, with whom she rode companionably, agreeing with him in her own words, "The Americans will never solve the Indian problem till the Indian is extinct." She titled her book *A Lady's Life in the Rocky Mountains*. It persuades me that travel is broadening.

On the next trip to the Far East she lived in northernmost Japan among the unwashed Hairy Ainus, where nothing occurred that "could in any way offend the most fastidious sense of delicacy." With stops at Hong Kong that happened to be on fire, Cairo where she caught typhoid fever, Ceylon for the elephant rides, Miss Bird came home battered and bruised and married the family doctor, Dr. John Bishop. After five eventless years of marriage, he died and she resumed her travels among the inaccessible mountains of Tibet, seated on a yak. In her seventieth year she went kiting off to Africa, had herself swung over the ship's side in a coal bucket, and rode thirty miles a day on a black charger so big she mounted him from a ladder. "So I am not quite shelved yet!" crowed Isabella Bird Bishop. She died in Edinburgh at seventy-three, having circled the globe three times, just as she was packing for a journey to China by the Trans-Siberian Railway.

There was a lady and then some. She was a real piece of goods.

February

Three passions claimed by Bertrand Russell—a longing for love, a search for knowledge, an unbearable pity for the suffering of mankind —granted him longevity. Last night he died at ninety-seven. They become his epitaph.

As a young man, Russell wrote, "Good God, what a lonely world it is though there are so many people in it." He tried to lessen the tragic isolation, and he failed. He found the world self-destroying and died certain of the approaching holocaust from nuclear warfare: "Mankind collectively is engaged in the great task of preparing its own extermination."

The last letter I had from him was from an old friend, fond and teasing, with no hint of doom: "I shall never forget the pleasure of the evening when I first met you, which was enhanced by complete surprise. . . . But for you (to mention nothing else) I should never have known of Julia's double chin!" I had showed him Herrick's poem "Upon His Julia" to prove she had one.

March

My review in last Sunday's *New York Times Book Review* of Ann Leighton's *Early American Gardens* carries the heading, "And asparagus provokes bodily lust." When Francis Brown, the editor, telephoned to ask me to write it, I inquired in mild plaint why I'm never invited to review a book whose subject I know anything about.

"A fair question," he said. "What do you know something about?"

A pause. "I can't think of a thing."

It's one way to take up gardening in New England. The first settlers came to found a city of God and survived by faith in herbs. Their gardens were meant not for ornament but for the necessities of frontier life, from the pains of childbirth to the laying out of the dead. The Puritan housewife turned to her garden to feed and dose her family lest they perish. In her kitchen she concocted syrups and distillations, pills, salves, plasters, mixing a dozen herbs together and trusting that one or another would cure the sick cow or croupy child.

A plant like parsley was good for what ailed you—to start the urine, dissolve the stone, break wind, relieve dropsy, draw down the menses, bring away the afterbirth, guarantee virility, and ease the torments of the guts. It was effective for the bite of venomous spiders, said Pliny the Elder, comfortable to the weak stomach, said Culpeper's herbal of 1649. Children were told they were born in their mother's parsley bed. I look on parsley with new respect, not as garnish for a pork chop.

For other griefs, you gathered nettles to relieve fatigue, stir the spirit, stop the whooping cough. You picked a little yellow tansy. It prevented worms and stayed miscarriages, so kind to the female sex that a woman ought to curtsy in gratitude for its powers. Samuel Sewall observed the corpse of a friend long dead preserved in a coffin full of tansy, known as the everlasting flower.

I envy my forebears their cures handy in the dooryard—herbs to sustain life and make the heart merry. Yet the book conveys less the idea that these remedies worked than that people had so many ills to need remedy for. Attacked by black melancholy, they tried apple juice or feverfew. To drive out the lingering sorrows of the heart, there was basil and motherwort. Fifteen peony seeds taken in wine warded off nightmare.

Some plants provoked bodily lust: the artichoke (raw or boiled), fennel, chervil, dill, spearmint, asparagus, or parsnips. Others restrained desire of an immoderate or outrageous sort: lettuce with a little camphire added. The periwinkle was eaten to arouse love between man and wife, the dandelion for incontinence, liverwort for the liver, rosemary for a stinking breath. Wormwood expelled worms, eyebright preserved sight, snakeroot guarded against snakebite. The houseleek kept off lightning. Wild thyme relieved frenzy and madness besides the wambling of the belly.

Able as they were to dispel fear and take away warts, the early gardens fed both the body and the soul.

A test for virginity (from Thomas Hill's *Naturall and Artificiall Conclusions*, 1581):

Burne motherwort, and lette her take the smoke at her nose, and if she be corrupte she shall pisse, or els not. Otherwise take gray nettles while thei bee greene, and let her pisse on them, if she bee no maiden thei will wither forthe, or els not.

After seeing my piece on gardens, a reader of the *Book Review* wrote the editor in vast impatience or in praise. Having the choice, I take it for praise, though he may mean I sound as undiscriminating as My Last Duchess who liked whate'er she looked on: "Mrs. Bevington likes writers. She likes what they write. If you gave her a copy of Napier's Table of Logarithms, she would come up with a review telling how wonderful logarithms were; how much they did for the human race; and what a great man Sir John was."

The film maker Fellini says, "I like everything. Do you understand? Everything!" That may be overdoing a good thing.

April

This is Sophomore Father's Day, one of Duke's least cherishable traditions. I had lunch with a father, because my student Joy asked me to. He was a doctor aggrieved to be wasting his time, who promptly admitted, after Joy introduced us and fled, there was nothing on earth he welcomed less than listening to an English teacher. I softened him up by listening to him, laughing at his medical jokes, proving to his relief less than normally intelligent. By the end of the meal he was relaxed enough to confess he had implored Joy to tell him it wasn't his parental duty to attend my poetry class.

"No," she said. "We're in the middle of a poem about a butterfly."

"No," I said. "A Sophomore Father needn't go that far. Besides, it's a poem about a grasshopper. Fellow named Cummings wrote it."

May

The murders at Kent State occurred today, May 4. Out of student antiwar protest grows finally the death of the young. Four students were shot and killed, nine wounded by the National Guard.

Two major disasters join to overtake us, two wars in one. On April 30 President Nixon ordered American troops into Cambodia, enlarging the Vietnam War to war in Indo-China. Four days later the members of the Ohio Guard confronted student antiwar demonstrators at Kent State. They fired into the crowd. "My God! My God! They're killing us!" cried a student. In that war two girls, two boys are dead.

The shock sweeps the country, and the count is 438 colleges closed down or on strike, the first general nationwide student strike in American history. In this third spring of protest, scarcely a college in the country is without its riots. Nixon is against us and fighting mad. Nixon openly refers to student leaders as bums.

When peace is out of reach including peace of mind, I collect reports of happy people: Dr. Johnson, to a man who declared his wife's sister was perfectly happy, "If your sister-in-law is really the contented being she professes herself, Sir, her life gives the lie to every research of humanity: for she is happy without health, without beauty, without money, and without understanding."

She sounds like Humphry Clinker, a shameless optimist without a shirt to cover his backside. "Heark ye, Clinker, you stand convicted of sickness, hunger, wretchedness, and want."

Yet Dr. Johnson's bouts of black melancholy and Smollett's choler were no sign of greater sanity or courage.

I like Montaigne's story of the loitering rogue who wandered blithe and merry, naked while others bundled themselves to the ears in furs, clad in nothing but rags in the deep of frosty winter. When asked why he neither shivered nor groaned, he answered, "And have not you, good sir, your face all bare? Imagine I am all face."

June

For all I know, Eden still exists on this planet. If so, Hawaii is a place to look. In thirteen hours I reached it by air, traveling first class in an attempt to be worthy of paradise. My neighbor Howard, who drove me to the airport, innocently remarked, "Only a damn fool would go first class."

The loved ones—Peggy and four small brown children—met me at Honolulu, each clutching a lei of scented yellow plumiera blossoms. We picked up David on the campus of the University of Hawaii, where he has been teaching for a week, and began the drive skyward straight up Wilhelmina Rise to the top of the mountain. David and I have rented a house for an outlandish price, since heaven on earth is a victim of inflation. This one includes a Buick convertible, a swimming pool, and a spider monkey named Heathcliff. Far below lies Diamond Head like a brown seashell, tiny high-rise hotels curling around it. Beyond is the blue Pacific with miniature passing ships. At night the view becomes a city of stars.

The two-level house has a roofed-over verandah above the swimming pool. A cocoanut palm leans to study itself in the water. Jungle surrounds us, mango trees laden with fruit, papayas, limes, banana and avocado trees, scarlet hibiscus flowers, plumeria that is called frangipani. Mynah birds squawk and doves mourn. Is this Eden then? The Fortunate Isles? It can't be hell—no billboards, no snakes, thunderstorms, heat waves, snow, or race riots.

From my room on the lower level, I jump out of bed and dive, pajamas and all, into the swimming pool. Three naked children—Stephen, Philip,

Kate—are already there, swimming underwater and surfacing like dolphins, all but Sarah who at five months disdains to wet her toes. "Take your clothes off, Nan," the children yell as we play tag. "You can swim faster." Below us in the jungle, chained on a long leash, Heathcliff swings by his tail in the trees and chatters in fury, black and devilish as a hairy spider.

After only one week, the university professors convey to me what is wrong with Eden. Man is in it. You can't work in paradise, not by the sweat of your brow as man is born to do. Something called Polynesian paralysis sets in. You go to the beach instead of the library, dressed in a loud flowered shirt or muumuu, you become a flower child without anxiety or conscience. Life is effortless, therefore unreflecting. I've strayed by mistake into heaven, too late.

Philip at least is at home here with the gods. At seven he has taken to reading the Greek myths and gained the faith. He declares the gods are still on Olympus, gazing down or wandering free among us in Hawaii. We hear a lot at meals from Pip, the pagan, about the everlasting gods.

Clarification

Now that the boy is seven we discuss
The gods. "They're still alive," he said,
"Like us, on Mount Olympus. In this book I read
There's Zeus and Hera on a golden throne,
Aphrodite on a golden shell—"
Fool that I am I disagree. "The gods are dead."
"NO! There are temples to the gods," he said.
I said, "In ruins." Since he didn't know
What the word *ruins* meant, I had to tell
Him then how temporary altars are.
Why does one need to clarify things so?

July

I asked, "What is the word for love?" "Aloha," of course. If you extend the *o* into aloooooooooha, it means moooooooooore love.

W. H. Auden doesn't belong in Eden. In his new commonplace book, *A Certain World*, he disdains love, expressing strong aversion. The love poems of Dante, Shakespeare, John Donne are "for all their verbal felicities" embarrassing. "When it comes to writing about the relation between the sexes, whether in verse or prose, I prefer the comic or the coarse note." And he offers a list of names for male and female genitals. Yet in his verse Auden writes, "The word is Love. / Surely one fearless kiss would cure / The million fevers."

Today at the beach I glanced up and saw a rainbow forming a complete circle over my head—in Eden at last, beatified by a halo, a nimbus, a divine circlet of light, insubstantial as a seraph. (Christopher Fry: "What, after all, is a halo? It's only one more thing to keep clean.")

A scientist at Duke, an authority on rain forests, told me about them—a place, he said, where it rains a lot. Paradise Park is a rain forest, if indeed it rained in paradise, a green wood where we sheltered under a monkeypod (rain tree) or ran about dodging downpours among blue macaws that lit on one's shoulder and pink flamingoes that did not. It rained every other minute, creating constant rainbows that, as everyone knows, are the sign of a covenant between God and man. They remind me of a metaphor Dylan Thomas got himself hopelessly entangled by:

> And, as we watch, the rainbow's foot
> Stamps on the ground,
> A legendary horse with hoof and feather
> Impatient to be off.

Yes, but Eden is what you have to leave behind. Who could put up with bliss for long? Aloooooooooha only means good-bye.

August

Three days at home were three too many. This morning I set out for Russia by way of Hungary and Poland with my friends Betty and Ted, who have more reason than I to attend the 13th International Congress of Historical Sciences in Moscow. Ted is an historian, Betty is his wife, and I, says Ted, am a camp follower. To improve my image I hastily joined the American Historical Society before filling out forms to tell the Communists why they should let me in ("For culture? For how long?").

At the Kennedy Airport, we met a group of forty historians, wives, whatnots, had our picture taken as proof of a common destiny, and boarded a Pan Am 747 for Paris. I stared into their taut faces as they stared into mine. We speak English, represent a small academic world, expect to spend a month as a company. So far we are strangers on guard. At 3:00 a.m. the sunrise woke me.

"Good morning," I said to the first professor I saw, an elderly gentleman across the aisle. He was sitting upright, smiling into space.

"I was thinking of Napoleon," he said.

At Le Bourget we waited with admirable restraint, considering the restless nature of professors, for a plane to Frankfurt, and that evening for a flight on the Hungarian airline Malév to Budapest. Last night on the immense 747 I said to Betty, "Give me the good old days of the DC3 21-passenger planes," a remark I withdrew as we bounced up and down in a cramped little crate into Hungary. Across the aisle sat the same elderly professor, mounted as on a snorting horse in a merry-go-round. He was still smiling.

"Did you mean Napoleon at Moscow?" I asked.

"Waterloo," he said. He is an authority on Waterloo.

At the Hotel Royal at Budapest, Jean-Claude Dubost assigned us our rooms. He is our manager who joined us in Paris—an excitable Frenchman who becomes demented if one questions his arrangements. To his distress I wanted neither a roommate nor a dark, single room tucked under the stairs.

"I'm claustrophobic," I said in a choked voice. "I get these attacks." It is an infallible way, as I learned years ago, to secure a room with a view.

Jean-Claude turned pale, not understanding the word. But it worked that night and thereafter, though I would catch him regarding me with a wild surmise. Ted calls him Bunny for his way of racing about with ears back like a rabbit.

Budapest. You can spend the morning in Buda and, by crossing one of the six bridges over the Danube, the afternoon in Pest. Or, if a visit to Pestbuda seems logical, you can do it the other way round. Buda is the ancient town of steep hills where the history is, therefore dear to the historians, of whom pretty Julie, the university student escorting us, was tremblingly in awe. They knew far more history of her country than she did. Historians know everybody's past; it's their business. Pest, the flat, modern city, existed separate from Buda till 1873 when the two united and took the double name. What a fake historian I am; I hadn't heard a word of it before.

My contribution was to point out in an old courtyard in Buda a name on a doorplate—Kiss Gabor. One of the Gabor sisters.

Since this is Lenin's one hundredth birthday, a Holy Year, the little man is everywhere with outstretched arm, on posters, monuments, billboards. It was said of Gladstone, "You look up at his statue, and his eye still flashes." Lift up your eyes and Lenin's cold glance says, "You are under scrutiny. Watch out!" I don't mind him, but I mind the huge statue of "Liberation" on the highest peak overlooking river and city, erected in 1945 "to the Soviet heroes by the grateful Hungarian people." It dominates Budapest like a threat, a tremendous female holding above her head a feather of peace, while below the hammer and sickle is the figure of a Russian soldier depicting the Liberator. For this Hungary is grateful? No need to answer.

She has been liberated too often. The Turks came to conquer in the sixteenth century, the Habsburgs in the eighteenth; in our time the Great Liberator Hitler gave Hungary the choice of joining the Nazis or being occupied like Poland. She joined Hitler against Stalin only to be occupied at once and the Hungarian Jews shipped to Auschwitz. When the Soviet victory of Stalingrad prepared for Hitler's downfall, the fleeing Germans retreated from Hungary and on their heels followed the Soviet troops, the new liberators. Hungary became a People's Republic under the U.S.S.R.

It's an oddly irrelevant role to be a tourist, a passerby who sees too little, led into interpretations, assumptions, guesses. After days of sightseeing we gladly accepted nights of entertainment. The fiesta tonight was arranged for our pleasure at the celebrated peak beneath the Liberation Monument. In a high-class tavern we took part in a wine-tasting festival, swaying and clapping without a care to the frenetic gypsy music, fed Hungarian *gulyás* red-hot with paprika, plied with wine till the idea of "tasting" became hilarious. Never ask what a "drinking" festival would be.

Here you found the young professors and the young at heart, forgetful of the facts of history, historians on holiday roaring with laughter. Here were Dick and Nancy from the University of Michigan; here was my new friend Russ; here were Betty and Ted. I liked sitting close to them, touching hands, speaking the same language—convivial, noisy, safe. I liked feeling tipsy and liberated.

Warsaw. In the late 1930s a woman professor I knew, Margaret Schlauch, became a Communist and defected to Warsaw. Her face haunts me as I walk in this sad city. What terror awaited her behind the Iron Curtain? Where is she now?

On September 1, 1939, when Hitler entered Poland Himmler's SS troops began making mass arrests. By spring the Germans had built in the center of Warsaw a brick wall eight feet high to enclose a ghetto of a thousand acres into which the Jews were herded to suffer and die. Others were sent to extermination camps built for their massacre (Auschwitz, ready in 1940). The date set for the erasing of the Warsaw ghetto was April 19, 1943. When the Jews fought back, not to save their lives already lost but for human dignity, the Nazis turned the ghetto into flame. Nothing is left. In the area where a granite slab stands in memory of the murdered Jews, the ground rises higher than its surroundings because so many corpses lie beneath. Its covering is of concrete.

By 1945 Warsaw itself was rubble, since Hitler chose next to eliminate the city. "Level Warsaw to the ground," he ordered, and like Carthage it was destroyed, though the doing took six years. When the Second World War ended, John Gunther wrote, fifteen human beings were found alive. Not even the outline of streets was visible, a vanished city.

A Russian skyscraper, the Palace of Culture, dominates Warsaw. Some impartial historians among us insist that the Poles have reason to be grateful to Russia for coming to their aid. John Gunther asked: Which do the Poles hate more, the Germans or the Russians? There was the tragic partitioning of Poland by Catherine the Great; the German occupation during the First World War, followed in 1918 by the entry of the Soviet armies; the awful years under Hitler when Stalin divided Poland with the Germans; and the final seizing of power by the Communists. Dependent for her life on her historic enemy, Warsaw again picked up the pieces, rebuilding a city brick by brick till next time.

So we historians who come to ascertain the facts have taken the right road, direct and straight, to Russia. It paves the bloody way to the center of power supreme and absolute, the Kremlin.

The heroic figure in Poland, after Lenin, is Chopin. Tonight the festivities took us thirty miles to the village of Zelazowa-Wola, Chopin's birthplace, for a piano recital and a feast of borscht, veal, Polish pickles, and ice-cold vodka. Born in this charming country house in 1810, Chopin studied in Warsaw before his departure at nineteen for Vienna, Paris, and the enveloping arms of George Sand—who described him as her girl-friend, a "highflown, consumptive and exasperating nuisance." He never returned to Poland but died in Paris at thirty-nine.

A young Pole, Teresa Rutkowska, sat at the grand piano in the drawing room and played with style and verve the nocturnes, mazurkas, polonaises, scherzos—not in the least the way my mother played them for me as a child. Only Poles like Paderewski can play Chopin. I heard him once, and that is how I know.

Poem for Adults

The dreamer Fourier beautifully prophesied
That the sea would flow with lemonade.
—And doesn't it?
—They drink sea water
And cry
Lemonade!

— Polish poet Adam Wazyk

Leningrad. We're in Russia. Our hotel the Sovietskaya is new, grand, strictly modern, with no hot water, mended and patched sheets, needle and thread provided to mend one's own tatters.

Lenin is the man of Leningrad. There was Peter the Great, Catherine the Great, Lenin the Great, for whom since 1924 when he died and the Workers changed the name it is the Hero City.

We walk astonished by its magnificence and its youth, younger by a century than New York. It was built in a swamp beside the Neva River by Peter the Great, who in 1712 abandoned Moscow and declared this the imperial capital of all Russia. For two hundred years St. Petersburg remained the glittering heart with its baroque palaces till in 1917 Lenin was smuggled into the city from Finland, arriving as a stoker on Locomotive 293, and with him the October Revolution began. The victorious Soviets moved the government back to Moscow, and six years later Lenin was dead.

"There's your leader," Russ says as we wander about, seeing Lenin, feeling his powerful presence.

During the Second World War, Hitler set out to destroy Leningrad. So sure was he of victory that he had invitation cards printed to a banquet at the opulent Hotel Astoria, marked with the date, September 8, 1941. Such cards were found on the bodies of German soldiers. No other city on earth, in the history of the world, sustained such a siege, bombarded daily for two and a half years when not a building escaped. The people ate vermin and bread made of wood pulp and died by hunger, bombs, freezing to death—some say a million died of starvation alone—a hero city indeed.

I'm sure I don't understand Soviet psychology. To show Russia at its best they reveal it at its worst under the czars. In the terrifying Peter-Paul fortress on an island in the Neva, Tanya, the young Intourist guide, begged us to turn our eyes away. Peter-Paul served as a political prison for two hundred years. Its low buildings hold seventy-two cells, silent, damp, solitary graves. Gorky occupied Cell 21, Lenin's brother Cell 47 before he was executed (an act that stirred Lenin to revolution). In 1849 Dostoevski, condemned to death as a radical and led out to be shot, was sent instead to Siberia for eight years, where he wrote *Buried Alive,* "a man buried alive, nailed down in his coffin." So severe was his torment that he came to believe madly in the salvation of suffering.

Within Peter-Paul fortress stands the Cathedral of St. Peter and St. Paul, its thin gilded spire shining with an angel and a gold cross. Inside the church lies Peter the Great in a marble tomb among the czars, all save Nicholas II, the last one, who didn't make it. At his funeral Peter was likened to Alexander and Caesar. "He was your Samson, O Russia! . . . your Moses . . . your Solomon . . . your David and your Constantine, O Russian Church!" It too is a place to turn the eyes away.

Were this a literary tour I would go straight to the railway station where Anna Karenina said good-bye to her husband, or to the street where Dostoevski lived. But I would lose my historians. Since they came to look at history, at history we look. For this one needs the Cyrillic alphabet that I'm sorry Saint Cyril took the trouble to invent. The historians' favorite character after the unspeakable Peter is the Great Catherine. Born Sophia, the upstart daughter of a Prussian general, brought to Russia at fifteen and married to her second cousin Peter, grandson of Peter the Great and nephew of the reigning Empress Elizabeth—what a mark she made on Russian history. Her marriage to an impotent creature whom she loathed, who played with dolls and kicked her in his hate, taught her to bide her time. With humility she waited eighteen years under the thumb of the childless Elizabeth till, January 1762, Peter became Peter III and prepared to rid himself of his wife. Six months later Catherine had herself proclaimed sole ruler, empress of Russia. Peter was murdered by strangling.

Her reign lasted thirty-four years; her lovelife was the scandal of Europe where she was regarded as a usurper and whore. A lustful woman insatiable in her desires, "I cannot go a day without love," she said, "even one hour without love." The mighty Potemkin, lover and possibly husband, chose his successors himself, some of whom broke under the strain. Countess Bruce tried them out to discover their talents and stamina. Each in turn, always handsome, their average age twenty-three, was installed in an apartment next Catherine's (and she born a Lutheran!). One chosen by Potemkin was an earlier Rimsky-Korsakov, the imperial pet till Catherine caught him in the arms of Countess Bruce. Zubov, a ruthless schemer, was with her before she had a stroke and died at sixty-seven. "I am doing a great service to the State," said Catherine, "by educating young men."

The Winter Palace was the glorious residence of the czars till the 1917 revolution. I love its statistics: 1,050 rooms, 2,000 windows, 117 staircases, 1,000 servants, 15,000 gowns worn by Elizabeth who built it, 100,000 candles burning for her parties, and Lord knows how many mirrors. On the grand staircase I took Russ's picture at his request as Catherine's latest amour. I felt at home among the crowds of Russian people who visit it, to whom these treasures now belong.

In the Hermitage, built by Catherine and including within it the Winter Palace, are two and a half million art objects, plus fifty-one Picassos hidden away downstairs. The Soviets find Picasso embarrassing for his lack of soul, though they can't disown him because of his Party loyalty; the Russian Chagall is not exhibited. Neither conforms to their idea of art, which must be intelligible to the masses. The poet Voznesensky mocks the attitude of a typical Party member: "In a Picasso, to him / Everything is unclear / And Shostakovich has no ear."

Ted wouldn't let me go to the Museum of Atheism (formerly the Cathedral of Our Lady of Kazan), not that he feared for my conversion; he thought it tiresome propaganda, not worth the bother. Since Russia has officially abolished God, the museum is prepared to explain this enlightened development. A Society of the Militant Godless was founded in 1925 but later disbanded.

Instead we went to the Orthodox St. Isaac's Cathedral, a gaudy, savagely ornate church, more baroque than baroque itself. At Easter they used to play a cunning trick when, at the start of the service, the thousands of candles were left unlit, connected by a thread of gun cotton. Exactly at midnight 101 guns boomed from Peter-Paul fortress, the choir sang "Christ Is Risen," and in a flash the candles lighted themselves while the priests poured forth clad in gold robes. And the people believed.

Twice we were taken out from Leningrad to the summer palaces. By hydrofoil the lot of us rode swiftly over the Neva to Peterhof on the Gulf of Finland. There in 1714 Peter the Great built a tremendous yellow palace meant to outdo Versailles. By its fountains alone, Peter vowed to outshine the Sun King and all the world of palaces and kings. (But Versailles had 1,400 of them.)

Everywhere soar Peter's fountains, sixty-four forming the Grand Cascade staircase below the palace. There is the sun fountain with gold dolphins, umbrella fountain, pyramid fountain, chessboard fountain. Tiny fountains rise out of the centers of tall tulips, jets spring from each leaf of an oak—fountains spectacular and fanciful, fountains full of tricks. If you step on a particular cobblestone, it will spray you in the face. If you stop to rest on a nearby bench, streams will leap to drench you. After several such drenchings, I named him Peter the Great Squirt.

He was a startling man in his humor, fond of buffoonery and practical jokes. He cut off the noblemen's beards with long shears to humiliate them, smiling as he worked, or seated them on pierced chairs to test their manhood. At public beheadings he wielded an ax. After forgiving his empress for taking a lover, he placed the lover's head in a jar of spirits and set it beside her bed. He tortured to death his only son Alexei.

Yet all the while, as we stood transfixed by the splendors of Peterhof and the scourges of its creator, who could deny that in our century Stalin was a far greater monster than Peter the Great, Attila the Hun, or any tyrant before him? The two mass murderers of our time killed off humanity by the millions in a new power of evil. Only yesterday Peterhof was obliterated by the Germans, its charred walls left standing. Now nearly restored to its former grandeur, once again the golden fountains play.

Catherine's summer palace at Tsarskoe Selo is a few miles up the coast from Peterhof. The village, renamed Pushkin in 1937, honors the poet who lived there as a boy. Aha, I thought, a literary pilgrimage at last. I should have known better. But the Russians say, "Pushkin is our all," their Byron with a Russian soul whom the Kremlin finds harmless, claiming he was in fact a rebel, defender of the People, though in my opinion he kept too busy being a Romantic. ("Oh Eros, god of youth, your servant / was loyal—that you will avow.") The giddy Nathalie, whom he married at thirty-two, became his 113th love. They settled at Tsarskoe Selo and in winter followed the court of Nicholas I to St. Petersburg. There one of Nathalie's lovers, an officer of the Horse Guards, pursued her till Pushkin challenged him to a duel. It took place February 8, 1837, and, fatally shot, two days later the poet died at thirty-eight. As he lay dying, his doctor asked, "Do you want to see your friends?" Pushkin turned his eyes to the shelves of books in his room. "Good-bye, my friends," he said.

A few days after the duel, the Russian poet Lermontov wrote "The Poet's Death," a copy of which was sent to Czar Nicholas and caused Lermontov to be arrested. It began, "The poet is dead, a slave to honor," and ended with an attack on the court, holding it responsible for Pushkin's death. Four years later Lermontov died at St. Petersburg, killed in a senseless duel with a fellow officer after writing, at twenty-six,

> And life, if you look around attentively and dispassionately,
> Is such an empty and stupid joke.

The sky blue Catherine Palace is, like Peterhof, a distressing spectacle of war, a *restored* palace, gutted by fire and looted by the Germans. It lives again in a majesty of marble, green malachite, porphyry—an immense baroque pile patiently put back together piece by piece by man's insatiable drive to survive and build again. He will work to cover the signs of destruction and death. *And he will forget.*

Glancing out of a palace window, I saw two workers resting with feet up on a marble bench, devouring their lunch—a pastoral scene unthinkable in the Great Catherine's reign. Now the palace named for her belongs to them. Or so they have been told.

Moscow. Like Chekhov's Three Sisters, I thought I would never get to Moscow. But the members of the 13th International Congress finally made it, at least we undaunted Americans are here in the Hotel Rossiya, which claims to be the largest hotel in the world. It looms, a white, glass-walled, incongruously modern slab beside the Moscow River, around the corner from Red Square and the Kremlin.

The hotel is so sparkling new it isn't finished—its elegance meant to shame the Hiltons of this planet, with marble floors, nine restaurants with orchestras, twenty cafeterias, two cinemas, a concert hall, no air conditioning, a few balky and casual elevators. An infuriating ten-minute wait offers a glimpse of one slowly moving up with no promise of return. The Russians shrug and say, "Nichevo," which means "never mind" or "hang in there, comrade."

Outside my window on the eighth floor, the gold domes of the Kremlin blind my eyes. Old women in black with twig brooms sweep the streets below. I have a telephone that answers in Russian, a radio with government-controlled programs, furniture of Finnish modern. The bathroom lacks soap and a sink plug, but the sitting room has a handsome tea service and linen cloth. The question that fills me with panic in this megalomanic hotel is not whether the Russians will threaten my liberty but, in ten miles of corridors and three separate lobbies, will I ever find my companions again.

On arrival Friday, the four of us—Ted, Betty, Russ, and I—went forth to seek Moscow University to register for the congress, where, after meeting with blank consternation (the Russians are so organized, Ted says, they achieve instant disorganization over the simplest plan) we were presented with huge imitation leather portfolios and big silver medallions to wear pinned to our breasts, a badge proclaiming our international mission and our innocence. It reminds me of the Prioress's brooch attached to her rosary, *Amor vincit omnia*. By love alone I hope to win the Russian soul and cow headwaiters.

The university rises up in the Lenin Hills, highest building in the city, skyscraper and citadel with a spire like a Christmas tree, red star on top. Students are enrolled in the scientific and technical faculties, while the humanities make do downtown in cramped quarters. History is scientific in Russia, efficient to train not the man or his humanity but the technician. I signed up dutifully for the sessions in contemporary history, trusting they won't call the roll or invite my remarks while I study it live in the streets of Moscow.

That night, and each night thereafter, we gathered before dinner in one or the other of our rooms to drink vodka bought at the Dollar Store in the hotel where one spends not rubles but dollars, the more the better. Chilled Stolichnaya is lovely stuff in Russia, leading to eloquence and the game of Make Betty Laugh, since she is capable of delighted laughter with her blue eyes in tiny slits. Aware that our rooms were bugged, we hoped to make the monitors laugh too. Once Russ rose and loudly chanted the Gettysburg Address (even that made Betty laugh, but she is very amiable). Again, as a man who in his youth had studied for the priesthood, he settled himself to hear my confession.

"Daughter, have you sinned?"

"Bless me, father, for I have sinned. I am guilty of pride in being an American. I am guilty of anger at all bureaucracy, all dictatorship. I am guilty of greed in loving freedom. I covet liberty. I lust for happiness."

"You are forgiven," Russ said. "These are the petty crimes of capitalism. What else?"

"I'll have more subversive thoughts in a minute."

"Oh sweeties, sweeties!" Ted groaned at our recklessness.

We weren't reprimanded, or reported by those spies, the "Dragon Ladies" who sat along the corridor and doled out room keys, keeping a peeled eye and listening ear—not that night or any other. Nor, decked in medallions, did we expect to be, though Ted is a well-known military historian. The nearest we might have come to discipline was during a noisy argument, one night when Dick and Nancy from Michigan were there, over the merits of *Portnoy's Complaint*. I made my complaint, calling the book one long, boring masturbation, while Dick far from hushing his voice came to its defense, denouncing me as sexist, deaf to the sensitive beauty of Philip Roth's orgiastic exploits and maneuvers, the comedy of his morbid fixations. Later I read that the Communists held Roth in contempt, censoring him as a purveyor of filth, proof of the

Americans' depravity in their willingness to wallow in it. Sex, said Lenin, is bourgeois.

During our stay we were aware of instances of surveillance that are part of the police system. The safe plan was not to speak Russian, visit Russians in Moscow, or deviate from approved itineraries. The two airmail letters I received from home had been slit open, left unsealed. An historian in our group, rambling about alone, found a soldier's hand across his camera lens as he was taking a picture of a railroad station. A priest among us didn't sign himself Father. A young American college student in our hotel tried to mail home a picture postcard of Lenin on which he had drawn an extra mustache. He was arrested, for to deface Lenin or treat him irreverently is sacrilege. Brought up for questioning, he was asked, "Who is the Father of your country?"

"George Washington."

"Would you deface and desecrate in this manner a picture of your George Washington?"

"Why certainly."

They shook their heads and let him go, a harmless fool.

The Kremlin terribly dominates Moscow, its heart and soul, the center of a circular city. It rises like a medieval fortress, enclosed by one and a half miles of battlemented walls, while inside among the gold onion domes of Cathedral Square red stars shine, red flags wave. Black limousines with drawn curtains enter the Kremlin from Red Square by the clock-towered Spasskaya Gate, as in a bad spy novel. Outside the walls, Red Square is a parade ground, railed off and guarded by Soviet soldiers. Whatever the holy word *red* means to the Russians, the square has most often run red with blood, the scene of mass slaughter and gruesome executions. Ivan the Terrible, first czar of Russia, who intended to make Queen Elizabeth I of England his fifth or sixth wife, might well, were history written differently, have ended by beheading her in Red Square.

At the south corner like a Moscow circus stands St. Basil's Cathedral, built by Ivan the Terrible when Shakespeare was a child.

"Disneyland!" Russ exclaimed. "It's awful. Isn't it lovely?"

Some find it sublime, some ridiculous, like a child's toy of peppermint sticks and fat balloons—a central tower with bulbous spires encircled by eight towers. One tower resembles a top, another a pineapple, a crazy design of horizontal zigzags. It has no symmetry and makes no sense, yet arranges itself into something barbaric and gorgeous. Napoleon attempted to blow it up. Stalin threatened to tear it down.

I grew fond of St. Basil's, though its smothering interior frightened me—a dark, cold place of nine chapels no longer sanctified, a prison of narrow passages, dim haunting icons. In there I knew I would never walk in Russia alone.

Two days after our arrival, on Sunday afternoon, the 13th International Congress was formally opened when the Kremlin welcomed us at a ceremony in the Palace of Congresses. We four came early in our best clothes, joined by Dorothea and Len, an historian of Far Eastern studies. Every seat was taken, though Great Britain had boycotted the congress, as had Israel, in outrage at an incident two years ago when more than 200,000 Soviet troops invaded Czechoslovakia for allowing herself to become too liberalized. (W. H. Auden wrote in his poem "August 1968": "About a subjugated plain / Among its desperate and slain, / The Ogre stalks with hands on hips, / While drivel gushes from his lips.") The Americans attended anyway.

At 5:00 p.m. a solemn parade of professors and Soviet officials filed across the platform, sat in a grim row, and rose each in turn to make a stiff long-winded speech. No woman was among them. Next in store was the address, delivered by Professor E. M. Zhoukov on the great god Lenin, his saintly glory, his immortal works. Called "Lenin and History," it went on and on, a doxology of praise, absurd as history, insulting (and meant to be) in its show of Russian magnitude and superiority, defiant in tone. We had to be instructed, put in our place. Even as guests we had to be humbled and rebuked.

The audience responded by removing its earphones and going to sleep. Len snored gently beside me. At intermission the champagne and caviar gave out, we prepared to leave. Then miraculously the real reception began. We returned to our seats for the ballet *Giselle*, performed by the Bolshoi on the shifted stage. The dancing restored our faith and softened our anger, speaking a language we heard and understood—though it's a pity the ballerina dies for love in the first act, requiring her fleshly lover to hoist a very solid ghost.

I couldn't wait another day to have a look at Lenin. While Ted went to a work session of the congress, Betty, Russ, and I sneaked off to join a special queue for foreign visitors beside the History Museum in Red Square. A far longer, shabbier queue of pilgrims gathered in silence below the barrier till allowed to begin straggling inch by inch toward the tomb. These were Russian, the patient and eternal lines. After being sharply scrutinized, we were moved ahead swiftly. The visit took less than an hour.

Lenin's tomb of dark red porphyry is beside the Kremlin Wall. Once the eyes focus on it, it dominates the square, a square itself, rigid and stark. At the bronze doors, where the honor guard is frequently changed, bright gladioli were massed each side of the entrance. Down the thirty steps we went two by two into the death chamber, a refrigerated vault, dark save for a neon light directed on Lenin's face. He lay in a glass sarcophagus, severely guarded. One might not pause or speak while slowly circling the body (though Russian peasants, they say, have to be prevented from dropping to their knees and weeping).

Lenin died in 1924, embalmed and visible these forty-six years. His wife, Krupskaya, had pleaded against putting him on display; he himself asked to be cremated. He was a small man, looking in death like a minor diplomat with a briefcase, less a worker than a clerk in a black business suit. He hardly seemed his age, fifty-three, neat and trim, with slight mustache and pointed beard, scant sandy hair, waxy delicate hands. Emile Vandervelde wrote of him as the "little man with the narrow eyes, rusty beard and monotone voice, forever explaining with exact and glacial politeness the traditional Marxist formulas." Bertrand Russell, who had an hour's interview with Lenin in 1920, would have guessed him to be an opinionated professor. Thirty years later Russell told Alistair Cooke, "I think he was the most evil man—and certainly the most imperturbable —I ever met."

They sought to make him imperishable, and the paradox is strange. This is their god in his shrine, the mummified god who replaces the icon. When the Soviets denied belief in God and life hereafter, they substituted Lenin ("Lenin Lives, Lenin Will Always Live"), God the Father of Communism, immortal *in the flesh*, more real than Phidias' gold statue of the Olympian Zeus that the Greeks took for Zeus himself.

Russian orthodoxy says a saint's body does not decay. Many assume this is a wax model; others that the corpse of Lenin survives but suffers rapid decay and will soon betray its mortality; others that what is exhibited is but the skull covered with layers of wax and paint. On his visit to Russia in 1931, E. E. Cummings was enraged by what to him was clearly a hoax, "a fanatical religion of irreligion." "I view the human god Lenin; I ascend; I emerge—and then (breathing fresh air once more) I marvel. Certainly it was not made of flesh." He had seen better waxworks at Coney Island.

For eight years after his death in 1953, Stalin lay beside Lenin, till Stalin's star fell and he was removed to a grave at the Kremlin Wall beside astronauts and revolutionaries, Gagarin and Gorky and the American John Reed. As we walked in the garden afterward among the graves, a university student stopped to chat. We had been without news of the outside world for the last three weeks. Her mind was full of lurid tales of the American Manson murder case, reported with wide eyes that Manson in an orgy had killed a mother of five and eaten her heart. She rejoiced to be Russian: "*You* have to worry, but *we* don't. We're taken care of." In Russia students were lucky because no mind-destroying drugs were allowed in her country: "In America *all* students take dope, all are hippies with long dirty hair and no morals, no souls." But she was puzzled: "If it is true only the rich can afford to go to your universities, why do they dress and act like hippies?" She didn't believe a word of our astonished denial.

To reveal what was unsavory about Russian orthodoxy and the worship of the Christian God, or to show Soviet tolerance, a daylong trip was arranged for us to Zagorsk, the holiest spot in Russia—a village forty miles north of Moscow, where at the St. Sergius monastery Orthodox priests are in residence.

The choice was peculiarly effective: it was a saint's day and it poured rain. Under Lenin's portrait we slopped about in the mud, aware of the grinding poverty of a town of thirteen churches, three of them cathedrals, and inhabited it seemed only by priests and toothless old women in black shawls. At morning service in a chapel of the Cathedral of the Assumption —where Boris Godunov is buried—we stood among old crones with broad fat faces who moaned and crossed themselves while the black-robed priests chanted the Mass in the stupefying odor of incense. Following the service these same bent, black-shawled women toiled on to the next ritual and lined up at the town privy, where they climbed groaning onto a long wooden platform. Teetering side by side, they hoisted their filthy skirts over holes that emitted so choking, sickening a stench I could neither breathe the foul air nor stop running to escape it. Later, when we found a place where it appeared possible to eat lunch, Ted and Russ praised the thick, steaming cabbage soup, with its penetrating smell, as the best they ever tasted. But I was gagging, as was Betty, at the memory of Zagorsk.

The New Maidens' Nunnery (Novodevichy Convent) gave its own testimony, a queer name for a convent used as a fortress, enclosed by a high wall and bloody history. Russ said the idea was you renewed your virginity inside the walls and lost it as you departed, though no maidens were on hand, no signs of a life devoted to chastity. Peter the Great had confined his sister Sophia there when she tried to seize power, while the two hundred soldiers who supported her were hanged under her cell windows and left to rot; a thousand more were beheaded in Red Square with a tree trunk used as a block. In the cemetery of the nunnery, Stalin had buried his wife Nadezhda, the one who shot herself.

Betweentimes we made a habit of studying Russian icons in Moscow museums and cathedrals, fascinated to see how the simple devout paintings on wood of Christ and the Virgin, introduced from Byzantium in the tenth century, had become with time relentlessly ornate and lavish. In Peter's corrupt century, only the frames mattered, adorned with priceless jewels, encrusted with gold and silver. The holy picture had shrunk, till dirty, blackened, it had been removed altogether.

If this was not the proper way to attend an international congress, Ted assured us we didn't miss a thing. No exchange of ideas was possible with the Russians who demanded agreement with their views. Attendance was scant during the week of meetings, the discussions angry or languishing. I remained a delegate who never went.

Ted bought me a volume of *Fifty Soviet Poets*, recently published. It begins in the chilling voice of the Kremlin, "Considering the almost universal loss of interest in poetry in this age of scientific progress, the demand for books of verse in the Soviet Union appears as a somewhat unusual phenomenon." The volume contains safe poems, no banned poets, nothing incendiary except (at least for the Finns) Yevtushenko's theatrical attack on Finland: "Every nation has its own vermin. / So I'll talk about vermin. Here goes."

Mandelshtam is missing, the greatest Russian poet of the twentieth century ("My beautiful pitiful century"). The Soviets viewed him with implacable fury, defamed him, destroyed him. Entering his Moscow apartment, the secret police found his bitter poem on Stalin's love of torture: "He rolls the executions on his tongue like berries." Mandelshtam paid with his life for this poem of fourteen lines. He was imprisoned as a nonperson, exiled at hard labor, attempted suicide and died, possibly murdered, in 1938 ("Help me, Lord, survive this night. I'm afraid of my life"). His wife, Nadezhda, wrote of his torment in *Hope Against Hope*, published in America in 1970. Stanley Kunitz quotes Mandelshtam as saying there is no denying the importance of poetry when people are killed for it.

A few poems appear by Anna Akhmatova, who died in Russia in 1966 after years of persecution. Her husband was executed, her son imprisoned ("You are my son and my terror too"). A woman in a Leningrad prison asked, "Can you put this into words?" She replied, "I can." In 1946 she was denounced, forbidden to publish, her poems banned ("And if they shut my tortured mouth / Which shouts with the voices of a hundred million"). She wrote of fear too paralyzing to remember. In the last decade of her life she was given limited official recognition, but her books can be bought only on the black market for many rubles.

The poem of Anna Akhmatova's I like best is not included in this volume.

The Muse

When in the night I await her coming
My life seems stopped. I ask myself: what
Are glory, freedom, or youth compared
To this cherished friend holding a flute?
Look, she comes! She tosses back her veil
And watches me, steady and long. I say,
"Was it you who dictated to Dante the pages
Of Hell?" and she answers, "I am the one."

I was honestly sorry to leave Moscow because of being happy there. Among the perils of staying in the biggest hotel in the world, in a city claiming the longest bridge, the largest swimming pool, the highest television tower, *Pravda* the largest newspaper, the hugest bell, Lenin himself, and who knows what else of superhuman proportions, in a self-exalting city boastful of its power and greatness, I was happy and my heart sang. *Bolshoye spasíbo*, as the guidebooks say, "thank you very much."

Moscow meant the Kremlin, rigid dictatorship, police terror, tight controls, the constant element of fear, threat, Siberian labor camps, suppression of human rights. It meant rules that might not be broken or anxiety forgot. I knew why the impassive Russians, obedient to authority, couldn't treat us as friends or trust us as a people. Once a waitress at the Hotel Rossiya, with hate in her eyes, turned to spit on us. She didn't quite dare.

But I was happy to outfox the Soviet by knowing myself, at least in their terms, dangerously free.

Berlin. There was one more city. I didn't want to go to Berlin, not after weeks of witnessing Germany's murderous role in our time. Russ said, "It's an elegant city. You'll be won over." I said, "*No!*" stunned by his tolerance. Then the charm worked after a fashion, at least in West Berlin.

We left Moscow by Aeroflot early Sunday with breakfast on the plane of caviar and red wine, landing hours later at the Schoenefeld Airport, East Germany, still Communist territory. With obvious intent they were rude at customs, held us at the barrier, questioned the validity of our passports as pretext to detain and frighten us. A customs officer sneered, "You don't recognize our government. Who cares about you?"

Released at last, we rode in a bus into West Berlin. Back in our world the air cleared, the Parkhotel Zellermayer was a *small* hotel, nowhere to get lost in walking from one's room to the lobby and into the quiet street. My friends had rooms next to mine. Having left Russia behind, I was unaccountably thankful to be gone. But I had forgotten that West Berlin, encircled by the Wall, is a little island 110 miles inside East Germany. Though the way out is kept open by the Allies—America, England, France—by means of the Berlin Air Corridor, West Berlin in its isolation has no countryside, only gardens and parks within the city. If you could ignore the Wall . . .

Nobody can ignore the Wall. On August 13, 1961, 40,000 East German soldiers with orders from Moscow sealed off the city, using tanks, barbed wire for the first hasty barrier. Gradually the Communists built the permanent Wall of bricks and concrete, fortified with watchtowers, gun implacements, searchlights, killer dogs, electric fences, a mined death strip. Anyone trying to escape was shot, though Ulbricht had trouble finding border guards who would kill their own people.

This Monday morning we went sightseeing, which meant going straight to view the Wall from wooden platforms built by West Berliners for looking over. So far the Wall is fourteen feet high. We climbed a ladder to peer wordlessly across the barbed wire into the death strip, beyond to the sullen faces of tower guards in East Berlin. After climbing down we walked beside the gray Wall studying its height and thickness, its graffiti, stopped often by markers dotted along the base with their flowers and crude crosses, each signifying the spot where someone died trying to escape, one an eighty-year-old woman, Olga Segler. It couldn't be true —you can't sunder a city into two armed worlds. But there it is and nobody guesses when, or if, it will be torn down. The tensions are always there, the threat of a shooting war. Russia doesn't want a unification of Germany.

We saw three extraordinary sights this morning—the Wall, the parade of prostitutes, and Nefertiti. The streetwalkers were a surprise, a number of well-dressed, attractive women ranged in broad daylight along the tree-lined Kurfürstendamm. They looked like models for a fashionable dress shop, and they inspired to ribaldry our German guide, who made merry with a few jokes.

"Well, gentlemen, how about that one?" he asked with a wink, slowing down the bus to cruise beside a delectable blonde. "Some class! Wouldn't you like to take her home with you? How about it?"

The heavy silence in the bus should have warned him. Later he received such a dressing down from our leader Jean-Claude, to whom the complainers loudly complained, that next day a crestfallen guide came dragged by the ear, and, following Jean-Claude's indignant apology, begged our collective pardon. He hadn't known he was in the company of high-minded historians and (I once heard a professor say) ilk of that sort.

We nearly missed Nefertiti, because the guide had it in mind to omit her from the tour and show us the Olympic sports stadium. By sheer luck Ted caught sight of the Staatlichen Museum and stopped the bus. We four would get out and find our way back to the hotel. At that a vote was taken: to the guide's chagrin and blank amazement everyone chose to visit the queen.

She stands on a pedestal, alone in a room of the museum. No statuette or postcard can do her justice, an exquisite lady in her mid-twenties, with full red mouth, shapely nose, flawless skin. Beneath her top-heavy royal crown, the black-lined eyes are hypnotic, though one eye is missing. Both ears are cracked. She is beautiful, I think because she looks truly loved, a woman in love. Her husband called her a lady of grace, mistress of happiness, wife endowed with his favor. They rode through the streets of Amarna locked in each other's arms.

Nefertiti, Egypt's queen thirty centuries ago, was married at fifteen to King Akhenaton and bore him six daughters. He became the Sun King, she the Sun Queen, since the sole god they worshiped was the sun. They lifted their faces to the creator of life, the Aton, each sun ray ending in a tiny hand to bless them. In the sixth year of his reign Nefertiti's heretic husband had changed his name from Amenhotep to Akhenaton (he who serves the Aton) and moved his capital from Thebes to Amarna, in Middle Egypt on the Nile. It became a magnificent city of thousands, its temple open to the sun, a place of peace. And it lasted about twenty years, only to be abandoned and cursed. The Egyptians could not grasp the concept of a single deity. They could not, did not, accept this dangerous religion or allow it to survive.

Gazing at her with love, I thought of Wallace Stevens' poem "Sunday Morning," the Sun day for worship of the sun. Stevens imagines a future race of men who in their greater wisdom having rejected Christianity, a religion of death, will choose to follow this shining star. They will adore the sun as a source of life, "Not as a god, but as a god might be," with the faith of men that perish yet loudly rejoice in the bright day before the dark.

As for the Impressionists, they had already made luminous their belief, *"Le soleil est Dieu."* Long ago, so had the sun-worshiping Incas.

Louis XIV too was a Sun King, whose temple was Versailles, his father's hunting lodge that in 1661, aged twenty-three, Louis began to transform into a palace, the largest in the world, with its illusion of shedding beams of sunlight. It was not the sun, though, that became a god, but Louis himself, *"Le Roi Soleil."* The sun served as blazing emblem, adorning his gilded beds and gold plate, gold coaches ornamented by sunbursts, the sunflowers in his garden. During a reign of seventy-two years, he was *the* god in a gallery of mirrors, whom his courtiers and 5,000 servants treated as deity. In his chapel, Louis XIV knelt and worshiped God from whom came his divine right, while the courtiers turned their backs to the altar and worshiped the king.

Visit to Nefertiti

The only lady I've ever seen
With two cracked ears and one eye missing
Is Akhenaton's luminous Queen

Nefertiti. What girl would risk it,
Wearing upon her head a crown
In shape like a wastepaper basket?

Whose other eye is pure rock crystal,
Painted a shade of brown like Swiss
Chocolate or a female kestrel?

And yet the lady glitters gold,
Flawless as apricots in sunshine,
So young at thirty centuries old

That, named "The Beautiful One Is Come,"
Is how she struck me—blindingly
Herself in the Staatlichen Museum.

For the journey to East Berlin, the point of entry was the notorious Checkpoint Charlie at Friedrichstrasse. We had been warned by the U.S. Department of State we went at our own risk. Our West Berlin guide left us at the barrier, after which a stern female inspector in Communist uniform appeared with a checklist, frowning as she compared our faces with those on our passports. That took a while. The idea was to make us feel unwanted, on sufferance.

Checkpoint Charlie is desolate, an area a hundred yards long consisting of a series of red-and-white candy-striped steel barriers to zigzag through as in an obstacle course. A busload of tourists waited beside us, the words *Sans Souci* across the side of their bus. A few cars in the opposite lane were being inspected by an officer using a flat cart covered by a mirror to roll under the car and reveal the mechanism. At his curt order each car was opened up—the engine, the trunk—and the seats taken out in a search for escapees or contraband to West Berlin. We waited in a no-man's-land of tension and dread.

Ignoring us, an East German girl guide entered the silent bus with a new driver, and we crept slowly forward. The girl was cold and arrogant; nobody asked her any questions. For two hours she pointed out the sights we were permitted to see. In spite of her boastful attempt to impress us, we saw poverty, bombed-out buildings, almost no cars on the street, soldiers on guard, few people. Not even a child gave greeting.

The heart of East Berlin stretches from the Brandenburg Gate (where the horses atop the columns have been turned to present their rear ends to West Berlin) through Unter den Linden. We passed a huge monument of Lenin, a Karl Marx Avenue, the square of the Nazi book burning, and the mound where Hitler's bunker was, now a bare grassy expanse reminiscent of Warsaw's ghetto. Departure followed the same harsh routine of scrutiny. We sat mute till they chose to release us.

Bertolt Brecht lived in East Berlin, a longtime Communist sympathizer who adhered to its ideology though he considered himself a Marxist. In 1949 he returned to Germany after exile during the Nazi regime, settled in the East Sector ("The city of my fathers, how can I find it?"), and died in 1956, five years before the Wall. Brecht was a close observer of evil, a man isolated in the savage world around him. At least he was spared knowledge of the Wall.

> On my wall hangs a Japanese carving,
> The mask of an evil demon, lacquered in gold.
> I see with sympathy
> The swollen veins on his brow, showing
> How exhausting it is to be evil.
>
> —"The Mask of Evil"

But his most poignant words are "To Posterity": "Alas, we / Who wished to lay the foundations of kindness / Could not ourselves be kind."

On the last night in Berlin, Betty, Ted, Russ, and I celebrated with a light heart. I learned long ago the lesson of the light heart, which is that the feeling is at best intermittent and should be made the most of. "Madame," wrote Catherine the Great in old age to a friend, "you must be gay, only thus can life be endured." Since Catherine required love by the hour, her joy was less intermittent than mine.

We went to the Inn of the Zither Player, where we were ushered into a leather-lined private room belonging, it seemed, to a mad collector of objets d'art and junk. There we ate so long and drank champagne so expansively that at the end I emptied my purse of its remaining Deutschemark and fled with Betty to the rest room. Not till we were leaving the charming inn did the thought occur that something was missing. The Zither Player.

"What happened to him?"

"Ach! nicht hier."

He had taken the night off.

From Berlin to Frankfurt we flew out of East Germany through a narrow strip at a prescribed height the Communists have set. It must be deliberately vindictive. The ride was so turbulent, like flying in a kite, that the pilot ordered the stewardesses to remain strapped in their seats. Yet during the Communist blockade, a record day on this air corridor was 1,383 flights.

A few hours later we were aboard a Pan American Clipper to London, where in the bustling airport Ted had a sudden urge to book passage on a plane being announced for takeoff to Johannesburg, a city he loves.

"Why not?" I said, meaning it, jumping up to follow him. "Let's go now!"

I wanted to go anywhere to keep this journey from ending. Instead we obediently stayed with our homebound historians, none of whom during the past month had disappeared, died, or been detained for espionage or heretical views, and crossed the Atlantic that night to New York. The elderly authority on Napoleon made his retreat from Moscow unscathed.

So I prate of freedom and come home to surveillance. With the highjacking of planes to Cuba, a passenger is frisked for hidden knives and machine guns. To board a plane for North Carolina, we walked single file three feet apart. Big Brother was watching us all the way.

The Traveler Who Never Went

"Approve the traveler who never went"
— James Reeves

Past the dooryard and the triangular cedars,
The world is small. As anybody knows,
It consists of a cloud or two, a countryside,
A road to elsewhere, nothing grandiose.
A few trees like Cézanne's, the blue of Memling
Appear, a misty morning by Corot.
But to visit the monuments, tombs, shrines, and wonders,
The Objects of Interest, you have to go
Beyond these applepink-and-Turner sunsets
To wider landscape. Night is by Chagall
With halos on the moon. And yet so narrow
A view and so uneducational
Has little to do with planetary travel—
Culture, museums, tombs—little per se
With global matters, guided tours and tourists,
Or the state of the world.
                              Or with hating one's enemy.

September

My essay on "Speaking of Books" in the *New York Times Book Review* is about George R. Stewart's *American Place-Names*, which is a dictionary, and I love a dictionary. This one, by title concise and selective, contains 12,000 entries to show how Americans have named America, honoring our pioneers, heroes, postmasters' wives, and the ordinary man named Jenkinjones. Or how a father flattered his daughter by christening a summit Clara Bird's Nipple.

It is a story of native inventiveness to make one proud. Granted, the country still belongs to the Indians, with names like Punxsutawney, Pa., Pongokwayhaymock Lake, Me., and Itchepuckesassa River, Fla. (Seminole for "tobacco blossoms are there"). Chickiechockie, Okla., commemorates the twin daughters of a Choctaw who married a Chickasaw wife; it was shortened to Chockie in 1904. Podunk isn't merely a funny name: it's Indian.

The endearing places are those labeled by Mr. Stewart commendatory, from Benevolence, Ga., to Welcome, N.C., from Friendly in West Virginia to Happy in Kentucky. Texans live in Security, Joy, Comfort, Blessing, Utopia, and Paradise, though Eden is in Arizona and the Promised Land in Arkansas. As a spot to spend the rest of my life I lean toward Delightful, Ohio, or, as a solution to existence, Frostproof, Fla., or Heavenly Valley, Calif. Equality can be found in two former slave states, Alabama and Kentucky. Liberty is all over the map (my grandmother was born in Liberty, N.Y.), with lots of towns called Union, Freedom, Hope, Amity, Harmony, and New Harmony. But no Honesty and precious little Peace.

On the other hand, the derogatory names make one ask who lives with a faint heart in Total Wreck, Ariz., Troublesome, Colo., Accident, Md., Worry, N.C., or Anxiety Point, Ark. What goes on between the neighbors in Hostility Branch, Tenn.? Sodom, N.Y.? Or, for that matter, Intercourse, Pa.? Hell as a habitation, a name freely bestowed during frontier days, has been abandoned. God scarcely appears but Devil often.

Right away I looked up my own beginnings, vastly relieved to find them literary and classical, since I was born in Robert Burns' "flow gently sweet" Afton, N.Y., and reared near (James Fenimore) Cooperstown. At a tender age I traveled to Athens, Rome, Syracuse, Troy, Ithaca, Sparta, not to boast of Nineveh and Carthage, all in New York State. I was familiar with Ovid, Cicero, Homer, Hector, Ulysses, and Vergil, since I hail from the famous "classical belt" created in 1790 by a board of commissioners in New York City with a classical turn of mind.

True, we Americans have a flair for place-names, the more outlandish the better. Part of the pioneer story is Pizzlewig Creek, Calif., formerly Sweet Pizzlewig, in memory of a whore who flourished there. Or Ticklenaked Pond, Vt., Cheesequake, N.J., Mousie, Ky., for a girl named Mousie Martin; Pluck, Tex., because it took pluck to settle there; Jackass Flat, Calif., where in 1885 a jackass was hit by a locomotive; Big Bug, Ark.; Jo Jo, Wyo., because two settlers were both named Joe; Snowflake, Ariz., honoring a Mr. Snow and a Mr. Flake; Smackover, Ark., that grew mysteriously from *Chemin Couvert*.

Tesnus, Tex., spells itself backward for Sunset. Pippa Passes, Ky., was named by a schoolteacher to signify God's in his heaven, all's right with the world! Yum Yum, Tenn., and Twain-Harte, Calif., reflect the literary scene, though Mark Twain hated Bret Harte and anyway he hailed from Hannibal, Mo., named for a Carthaginian general. Whittier bequeathed his name in a poem: "The Love I felt, the Good I meant, / I leave thee with my Name," and then Whittier, Calif., turned around and heartlessly identified itself with Richard M. Nixon.

Altogether it's more than a dictionary. It's a book of travel, a winding journey through America. By our pride of heritage and origin, as by our funny bone, can we be recognized.

October

Leonard Woolf's fifth and last volume of autobiography was written at eighty-eight. That is too old, he was too old. The title from Montaigne, *The Journey Not the Arrival Matters*, sounds like my own book title but not nearly so good. What he means is, the journey is everything.

The sins of age are repetitiveness, long-windedness, and lapse of memory, as Woolf demonstrates. He repeats the distressing fact that he figured he had spent in his life 200,000 hours of useless work, accomplishing nothing in the end. Might as well have played a game of darts. Lost and melancholy are his reflections on old age, "It is regrettable that the impotence of the aged body results in my inability any longer to play cricket, football, squash rackets, hockey, or lawn tennis, and to function in still more important ways."

The trueborn Englishman is speaking from the heart. He places *five* sports in that order ahead of making love.

November

The Nygards had a faculty party that they called "a drift of hogs," meaning an outdoor barbecue in this nippy weather. I marvel we dared show ourselves—how can you tell the professors from the pork? A conversation I had with a professor, licking his fingers and grunting a little, went like this:

"You know, you must take up the study of Coptic."

"Why?"

"Because I have done so and can recommend it."

Coptic is extinct, a dead liturgical language spoken in a chant that is said to be monotonous, just what I need. I could become a lady Copt.

In Chicago with my family for Thanksgiving, I couldn't help

noticing how sex has gone downhill since I was a student at the University of Chicago. A copy of the *Maroon*, the college newspaper, contains a drama review of a student production of Arthur Schnitzler's *La Ronde*. The actors, it reports, "seemed lost and embarrassed by the necessity of copulating on the stage in full light: a task difficult for experienced actors —impossible for tyros."

La Ronde is Schnitzler's *Reigen* ("merry-go-round"), which he first called *Liebesreigen*, a series of ten dialogues spoken by ten characters before and after the act of sex—but sex without tenderness or meaning, seen as sham and observed with detachment, a light sense of the absurd. They meet, couple, and separate. It has nothing to do with love.

Schnitzler used dashes to indicate a brief lowering of the curtain at the exact moment of the olde daunce. Not a word is obscene or lewd. Yet none of the characters is honest, no one is faithful to a vow. You know without witnessing it that to satisfy lust the prostitute sleeps with the soldier, soldier with housemaid, housemaid with young gentleman, young gentleman with young wife, young wife with her husband, husband with girlfriend, girlfriend with poet, round and round as poet sleeps with actress, actress with count, count with prostitute on the same old merry-go-round. (I don't know why I say "sleep." Back in the seventeenth century, John Webster asked in *The Duchess of Malfi*, "What pleasure can two lovers find in sleep?")

From the start, *Reigen* created uproar and scandal. Published first as a book in 1903 it fell like a bombshell in Vienna, and a public reading was forbidden by the police. In Germany it was confiscated. Schnitzler opposed a presentation on the stage, but it appeared anyway, causing mass meetings, riots, a court trial in Berlin, a storm in the Austrian parliament. At last he gave his consent, and every effort was made by changes in forty-one pages of text to tone down the action, make the gestures more discreet.

When it was performed in Vienna in 1921, a group of young men moved into the theater shouting "Pfui!" and "Schweinerei!" throwing stink bombs and eggshells filled with tar. Men were clubbed, ladies slapped in the face, the stagehands turned on the hose while police blew whistles. Words were hurled at Schnitzler's head like *gemein, frech, unverschämt, schmutzig*.

In America, published in 1920 as *Hands Around*, its performance as a play was prevented by the Society for the Suppression of Vice, and under the ban of John S. Sumner suppressed as a book. By 1950 the film version of Max Ophuls' *La Ronde*, with expert actors Danielle Darrieux, Simone Signoret, Daniel Gélin, ran into trouble with censorship and had to be cut. It sounds fine in French. Roger Vadim directed a film version in 1964, *Circle of Love*, and cast his wife, Jane Fonda, in a leading part. In 1969 a musical appeared in New York as *Roundelay*, a vulgar failure.

La Ronde seems tame now, except when students think the plot requires them to copulate on the stage. Schnitzler didn't mean that. As the prostitute says, "Who knows whether we will still be alive tomorrow?"

In the Personal column of the *Maroon* was another item reflecting the state of college morals, "Liberated young woman with fantastic physical attributes desires meaningful relationship with male, female, or both." In contrast the Quadrangle Club, where the professors go for amusement, contains a bookcase in the parlor with a matched set of twenty-six volumes of Bulwer-Lytton.

At 2:15 p.m. before the holiday, I met Kate at the Lab School, where she is in the first grade, and we walked home through windy streets, my hand-in-hand child. Kate, who knows 7 times 10 is 70, is writing a book called "All About Everything." We passed Saul Bellow on the street but didn't ask him, though the question interests Kate, why he has had three wives and three sons, one apiece by each wife. Sounds like a nursery rhyme.

I'm reading Saul Bellow's new novel, *Mr. Sammler's Planet*, which says, "New York [and Chicago?] makes one think about Sodom and Gomorrah, the end of the world. The end wouldn't come as a surprise here. Many people already bank on it. It is in the air now that things are falling apart, and I am affected by it, suppose it to be so." My mother would say he is a bit previous in his remarks.

December

Fanny Patton invited me to see the film of Henry Miller's *Tropic of Cancer*. Shuddering to recall the novel I said, "Sure, if you like." By the time I reached her house to pick her up, Fanny had got cold feet and suggested a quiet talk and a cup of tea.

"No, ma'am," I said. "Henry Miller or nothing."

We went to the matinee, which was singularly devoid of patrons. Since the picture hadn't started, Fanny felt the need of a cigarette. As we stood in the corridor beside an ashtray, the manager came hurrying up, a kindly middle-aged man with a paunch. He looked flushed and agitated.

"Ladies," he said, "I am obliged to ask you to leave. This is a dirty picture. I don't believe nice ladies like you ought to sit and watch it."

He offered to refund our money, a noble gesture considering we were practically his entire audience.

Fanny thanked him with her southern charm. "We truly appreciate your concern, sir, and your courtesy." I told him it was my fault. I had read the book and knew the mistake we were making, we would take the risk. The manager bowed his head at such prurience and walked sadly away. Fanny doused her cigarette, clutched my arm, and we slipped into the darkened theater, where I counted two customers both male.

Well, the picture *was* literary. Its obscenity was not only visual but auditory, orgasmic in word and act. Miller himself said the book wasn't a book but a prolonged insult. With its randy language intact, it struck me as more than usually moral, a lesson in the boredom of sin. If sex isn't any fun, I said to Fanny, what good is it?

1971

January

Newspaper headline: "1971 May Not Be So Bad."

Apollo 14 dashed off to the moon for the third landing. "Really a nice place," they said, "but unearthly." The irony of the moon trips is that they regularly coincide with news of disaster on earth. We keep one eye on the moon, one eye on Indo-China, and pray. The descent of the astronauts nine days later with bags of rocks prompted an earthquake in Los Angeles. The Manson case swelled with the report of ten murders. The invasion of Laos brought nearer the threat of large-scale war.

We are tampering with something, and nobody listens. The confessional poets in their rejection of life frighten me. John Berryman frightens me. His new book of poems, *Love and Fame*, was conceived by a wounded man who wants two things more than love or fame: to wound others against whom he has a grudge, and to die. Stabbing away like Pope, he tells Robert Creeley: "Sir, you are trivial. / Pray do not write to me again. Pitch defileth." He "dispatches" his former teacher at Columbia, Professor Emery Neff, who was my teacher too, a mild, shy, honorable man and scholar.

> Not only did I give him hell in class;
> I saw my nine friends did. With ironic questions
> & all but insolent comment & actual interruptions
> we made Professor Neff wish he was elsewhere
> rather than in English 163.

(Wallace Stevens: "That prose should wear a poem's guise at last.")

Berryman sounds like a man signing off. His references to suicide are constant; how can they be read but as the cry for help of a desperate man? The poem "Of Suicide" considers his father's suicide when Berryman was twelve. In "Despair" he says, "I certainly don't think I'll last much longer."

He ends with eleven addresses to the Lord, in which he trusts his son and daughter will fend without him. But "Strengthen my widow." The last words are "I pray I may be ready with my witness." Will no one *listen* to this man?

[John Berryman committed suicide by jumping off a bridge in 1972. A poem in *Love and Fame* referred to a friend who "killed himself, I never heard why / or just how, it was something to do with a bridge."]

February

Mollie Panter-Downes, inspired by Max Beerbohm's essay "Number 2, The Pines," has written *At The Pines*—the house where Swinburne lived for thirty years in the care and keep of Theodore Watts-Dunton. The account may bring about, God forbid, a Swinburne revival of galloping anapests and purple diction (when Swinburne meant "long ago" he wrote "long since in old time overpast").

The Pines was named for two marble pineapples carved into the gateposts of the lugubrious mid-Victorian villa in Putney. When B. and I made the pilgrimage in 1950, we saw the carvings and laughed. "Number 2, the Pineapples," we said, assuming they stood for the former residents, Swinburne and vigilant old Watts-Dunton, chubby and deaf in his crumpled frock coat and walrus mustache. Swinburne had collapsed and was dying of alcoholism when Watts (he then called himself) rescued him from a wrecked and shattered life. That was in 1880 when Swinburne was forty-two, his friend forty-seven. Till he died, Swinburne had a benefactor.

Max Beerbohm arrived for lunch one day in 1899. Swinburne, now sixty-one, cured, restored, was living becalmed and domesticated in Putney, deaf as a doorknob—deafer even than Watts-Dunton—having to be roared at. While his keeper carved the boiled mutton and the apple tart, Swinburne, allowed a small bottle of Bass's ale, burst into soaring monologue. One subject was his morning walk on the Heath, another was babies, with whom he was infatuated. His voice, said Max, rose "like the sound of someone singing in the distance." He was like a bird or an elf, the red curls gone from the huge bare dome, like a child with short arms, jerky legs, swan's neck, tiny fluttering hands, and the skittish air of a fey but lovable, weird but well-bred little fellow. You expected him to pirouette in his carpet slippers.

Max said, "There was not a minute nor a second that I did not spend with pleasure." But Max was an extraordinary guest.

With the second day of an ice storm, our winter specialty in North Carolina, which festoons the perishing trees in a glazed countryside, I didn't go to the mailbox till evening. When I did slide down to the road, risking the possibility of no return, I found a copy of my new book and thawed it out at the kitchen stove. The artist had read the title, *The House Was Quiet and the World Was Calm,* and drawn for the dust jacket a tall, dark-brown, formidably gloomy New England dwelling full of ghosts, house of the seven gables. It might be described as "Type of domicile in which author does not live." My house is white, one storey high, perched like a cloud on a little hill.

Years ago on reading Wallace Stevens, I dreamed of a book for which this title from his poem would be light and fitting. I wrote the book, and the title is *not* light but ironic, and the world is *not* calm. Still, it might be worse. Among Stevens' poems I might have fallen for "The Desire to Make Love in a Pagoda," or "A Dish of Peaches in Russia," or "The Woman Who Blamed Life on a Spaniard."

March

I've been to Washington, D.C., fifty times but never before in the company of four small children. Peggy and I took them about—Stephen, Philip, Kate—while Sarah, aged one, rode her mother's hip and I toted a large green bag slung over one shoulder. It was a time of crocuses and green willow. We ate Senate bean soup each day for a week.

Peggy had obtained tickets for a private tour of the White House one morning at 8:30. We zoomed through the place like UFOs as the children plunged from East Room to Green Room to Blue Room, climbing into marble fireplaces, rattling the crystal chandeliers, joyously ignoring the portraits of our presidents and first ladies—seven presidents and a crystal chandelier in the Blue Room alone. A cluttered little house. And all the while the guards smiled on our romp and didn't report us to the present occupant, Mr. Nixon. Just a week ago a bomb exploded inside the Capitol. You would think our visit might have alerted them, but nobody showed concern for my green bag worn on my back like a peddler—not till 2:00 p.m., that is, when we toured the FBI. There I was put under instant surveillance and searched.

"Let me have a look at that bag," said a guard.

"Help yourself," I said, handing it over.

He reached in and poked about, his face struggling to stay impassive. He returned it gingerly without a word.

"Diapers," I said. "Wet diapers."

At the FBI they warned us of the Red menace that so upsets J. Edgar Hoover. As we listened crime increased tick by tock—a murder every twenty-nine minutes, a rape every seventeen, a theft twice a minute. Afterward in the crowded elevator, Stephen asked, "Mom, what is a rape?" In the silence twenty passengers strained to hear while Peggy leaned down and gave a clear, simple answer, which we followed as if we hadn't had it explained before. Sarah began to scream.

"Mom, speak up, Mom!" cried Philip. "Can't hear a word you're saying."

April

I think this is a funny story. I found it first in Anthony Walker's *Life* of his friend Mr. John Bois, one of the translators of the King James Version, 1611. John Bois's good friend was Sir Henry Savile, also a translator. Savile had become famous as a scholar, secretary to Queen Elizabeth—who favored the handsome gentleman—warden of Merton College, Oxford, provost of Eton, maker of a monumental edition of Chrysostom, in which he was aided by John Bois.

A brilliant man, Sir Henry Savile was not a witty one, nor did he suffer levity in others, especially students. According to John Aubrey, "He could not abide Witts." "Give me the ploding student," said Sir Henry, and no doubt got his wish.

The story is, so sedulous in his study of great works was this scholar that his wife felt neglected. Coming to him one day, she saluted him plaintively: "'Sir Henry I would I were a book too, and then you would a little more respect me.' Whereto one standing by said, 'Madam, you must then be an almanack, that he might change every year.' She was not a little displeased."

About that time, 1607, Thomas Dekker (popular for his plays, *The Shoemaker's Holiday, The Honest Whore*) published a joke book, *Jests to Make You Merry*. Jest #23: "A gentlewoman coming to one that stood at a window reading a book, Sir (says she) I would I were your book, (because she loved the gentleman). So would I, quoth he, I wish you were. But what book would you have me to be (said the other) if I were to be so? Marry, an Almanack (quoth the gentleman) because I would change every year."

In 1608, Samuel Rowlands, writer of satires (*'Tis Merrie When Gossips Meete*) put the anecdote in a poem:

> A scholar newly entered married life,
> Following his studies, did offend his wife;
> Because when she his company expected
> By bookish business she was still neglected.
> Coming into his study, Lord (quoth she),
> Can papers cause you love them more than me?
> I would I were transformed into a book
> That your affection might upon me look;
> But in my wish withal be it decreed
> I would be such a book you love to read.
> Husband (quoth she) which book's form should I take?
> Marry (said he) t'were best an almanake.
> The reason wherefore I do wish thee so
> Is, every year we have a new, you know.

A half century later along came John Dryden, displaying the same nimble wit or lack of it. ("I am none of those who endeavor to break jests in company or make repartees.") He married late, in 1663, and unhappily, the reluctant husband of Lady Elizabeth Howard:

> Dryden has himself told us that he was of a grave cast and did not much excel in sallies of humor. One of his *bons mots*, however, has been preserved. He does not seem to have lived on very amiable terms with his wife, Lady Elizabeth, whom, if we may believe the lampoons of the time, he was compelled by one of her brothers to marry. Thinking herself neglected by the bard, and that he spent too much time in his study, she one day exclaimed, "Lord, Mr. Dryden, how can you always be poring over those musty books? I wish I were a book, and then I should have more of your company." "Pray, my dear," replied old John, "if you do become a book let it be an almanack, for then I shall change you every year."
>
> —Sir James Prior, *Life of Edmond Malone*

It's a good story even when (sick of it by now) you find it in *Poor Richard's Almanack* in the next century, December 1737:

> Are women books? says Hodge; then would mine were
> An almanack to change her every year.

May

Wallace Stevens was a connoisseur of my state of North Carolina. I assume he liked the sound of Carolina, since the letter C intoxicated him. In his autobiographical poem "The Comedian as the Letter C," written in the key of C, he is merely a cipher—Crispin, the comedian, the clown, whose career like Candide's is somewhat circular. Being at sea with himself in an age that left him behind, Crispin stops cultivating his garden to take a journey by sea, and, by peering in a sea-glass as the sound of C accompanies him, sees himself as he is, "the merest minuscule" or lowercase letter. He is a voyager reduced by storms, a trifling poet close to catastrophe, saturated by gales on the sea of life, from which as the storm subsides he gains a new vision of himself ("Crispin beheld and Crispin was made new").

From Bordeaux he travels to Yucatán where, for a while following naively this new vision, he mistakenly finds "a new reality in parrot squawks" and seeks the exotic in green barbarisms and the savagery of palms. Too consciously liberated as a poet, more capacious in this lush climate, he hears the rumbling of a different kind of thunderstorm, a clarion wind that threatens him with extinction. Crispin takes flight.

As he approaches North Carolina, he begins to see where he natively belongs, not in the sultry tropics nor yet in the Arctic moonlight but north, "A northern west or western north, but north" (which seems to eliminate South Carolina). In the commonplaces of the earthy reality around him, Crispin conceives a couple of solutions—one, to form a colony of contemporary regional poets, a kind of local-color literary movement (an idea that comes to nothing); the other, to build a cabin and marry a beautiful prismy blonde, which he does. Fate has clapped her in his hands. She brings him a variation of c's —contentment, comfort, and children (four daughters with curls). Like other men, Crispin reaches a conclusion to his dreams—a compromise, of course, for a poet but a choice with compensations. He is no longer "content with counterfeit." Common sense has won: the quotidian way is the price he pays for love and happiness. He has undergone conversion, lost his colossal ego and conceit, complacent now to stay at home and write his yearly couplet to the spring. Like Candide who took Cunégonde for bride, Crispin ends where he began, cultivating his garden yet infinitely wiser, "A clown, perhaps, but an aspiring clown." He has found himself not heroic but comic; whatever the cost it was worth it. So the story comes "benignly, to its end." In North Carolina.

[Neil Simon in an interview showed the same attachment to the letter C. Cupcake is a funny word, he said. Tomato and lettuce aren't funny. Cucumber is.]

His letters show that Wallace Stevens visited North Carolina several times but gave no hint of conniving to live here. He told Harriet Monroe of finding among the people of this state something "integrally American." He loved the South for a quality of being "beautifully and sedately the early and undefiled American thing." His poem "In the Carolinas" calls her the timeless mother whose "pine-tree sweetens my body / The white iris beautifies me."

On February 11, 1923, he wrote his wife Elsie from Greensboro, N.C.: "This hotel is named after O. Henry, the writer of short stories who came from Greensboro. Such is fame. Fancy having your name on the soup ladle, on all the linen, shrimps O. Henry, salad O. Henry, parfait O. Henry. There's an O. Henry cigar, an O. Henry drug store and so on." He closed by endorsing North Carolina: "She is one of the great states or will be."

That was high praise from a Connecticut man.

Actually O. Henry was a shy, self-effacing writer who shunned publicity, somebody said, with the timidity of a child, and clung to his anonymity. An admirer of his stories once wrote enclosing a stamped return envelope to ask whether he was a man or a woman, yes or no. He didn't reply.

June

One way to live unhappy (let me count the ways) is not to keep a journal. Not that I attach value to my journal's opinions, but this is no world to face alone. Mine is a companionable quoter, turning up entries from other entries from earlier entries still.

From A Jacobean Journal:

June 26, 1604: Edward de Vere the 17th Earl of Oxford, who died on this date, was in former times one of the Queen's favorites among the noble lords of her Court. He departed abruptly for the Continent, the occasion for his departure being this: while making his ceremonious bow, a low obeisance, to the Queen, he had the misfortune to break wind. He did not return to the Court for seven years. The Queen welcomed him back, saying, "My Lord, I had forgot the fart."

February 13, 1608: The old Countess of Shrewsbury, whom they call Bess of Hardwick, is dead at last in her 90th year at Hardwick, greatly flattered, seldom deceived, and without a friend.

Dead at last, without a friend—Bess of Hardwick, the infamous Bess with the tongue of an adder, the richest, meanest woman in England. She liked being told no one dared look her in the face. She had four rich, miserable husbands, dominating and outliving them, taking care to inherit their estates. Her last, the earl of Shrewsbury, made her a countess and came so to loathe her he tried to obtain a divorce. In revenge she accused him to Queen Elizabeth of a scandalous love affair, resulting in two bastards, with Mary Queen of Scots, the poor lady ordered by Elizabeth to Shrewsbury's care as jailer for more than fifteen years. Of the many prisons during the nineteen years Mary was held captive till her execution, this prison in the dank medieval castle at Tutbury she hated most of all, under the thumb of the proud and furious Bess, who nearly destroyed her before Queen Bess succeeded.

Till she was ninety, Bess of Hardwick built one imposing castle after another, confident she wouldn't die so long as she kept building. On February 13, a heavy frost in Derbyshire stopped work. Stopped too was the redoubtable Bess. She had a splendid funeral and was declared by the archbishop of York who presided to have been a virtuous woman.

July

E. B. White has a piece in the *New Yorker* about geese, a letter from his barnyard in Maine. Whether he writes about chickens or chipmunks, I wait to hear the news. But the witty tone of the country man reminding the city man what he is missing has changed, with charges that geese are hecklers, contentious and sarcastic, guilty of ingratitude and false accusation: "Geese are friends with no one, they badmouth everybody and everything."

(From *The Complete Country Housewife*, 1770: "Except when they [geese] are fatting, it is not necessary to pay any great attention to them.")

He ends his letter, " I don't know anything sadder than a summer's day." It's time we both reread Thoreau, who has served as Mr. White's conscience "through the long stretches of my trivial days," whose summer afternoons were laced with serenity and content. Thoreau liked to heckle too, but he wouldn't take it from geese. And there's the other Mr. White —Gilbert White of Selborne—to remind him to count his geese and his beatitudes that I may count mine.

August

James Dickey, poet, appeared tonight on William Buckley's program on public television. There was a doomsday pair.

Dickey, middle-aged and puffy, with a South Carolina accent (try him on the word *important*), hammered home this theme: introspection has eaten us up in America. Eternal questioning saps our spirit, increases our guilt. We have lost simplicity of motive.

"Go out and do something simple," he told a group of college students sitting at his feet. "Do some kind of simple act and don't feel guilty about it or self-conscious, as if you had had sexual intercourse with your mother." (Here Buckley looked scared, but then he always does.)

"You mean like drinking Coca-Cola?" a student asked to clinch the point.

"Sure," said Dickey. "I like Coca-Cola. I like gin too."

Thirty years ago tonight, August 14, 1941, I heard Koussevitsky and the Boston Symphony Orchestra play the Mass in D, the *Missa Solemnis*, at the Berkshire Music Festival. It was so momentous I made a note of it:

> I came for Koussevitsky and the moon,
> Beethoven vying with the Pleiades,
> For the sweet lusty evening . . .

But I couldn't tell the whole story in twenty lines, given the compressed nature of verse. By the time you get yourself into a poem along with the moon and impassioned stars, the thing is done. It takes saying twice. Fourteen of us drove over to Tanglewood from the Flanders farm where we were spending the weekend. Sally Flanders organized the party on the lines of a camping trip or scout jamboree, equipping us with army blankets, sweaters, two smoky lanterns, the musical score, and a huge picnic basket, whose contents she spread over the lawn beside the open-air auditorium where the fashionable concert would take place. We did everything but pitch a tent and build a campfire; we looked like an encampment of gypsies. As patrons drifted by, dressed in evening clothes, they stared in outrage and disbelief. Who had opened the gate and let in these tramps?

Our supper done, the lanterns lit, the score spread open, we lay on our blankets awaiting the arrival of Koussevitsky. Sally sprang to her feet. "All right, one and all! We'll start with a round." Nobody could stop Sally. She divided us into three protesting groups and led off in her deep husky voice:

> He that would an alehouse keep
> Must have three things in store:
> A chamber and a featherbed,
> A chimney, and a hey nonny-nonny . . .

Cringing at the spectacle we made, we obeyed her. It was wonderful how we obeyed her. On she led through the soberer canons of Haydn ("Tod ist ein langer Schlaf"), Mozart, Bach, Lawes, Purcell, Cherubini, Schubert, that she had taught us. We sang like the village choir for an ungodly time, closing with "Dona nobis pacem." Give us peace. We never knew whether Koussevitsky was late for the concert because he was detained or unwilling to show his face. Nobody applauded. Nobody threw us out or drew a gun and shot us.

I wished I was dead. I wished it was the end of the world. At the same time the thought struck me that were the world to end tonight, I would meet it singing my life away with Sally. She should have been on the *Titanic*.

Sally's favorite motto (by which she justified these performances) was "Anything worth doing is worth doing badly." After believing it for years, I've concluded she was wrong. It doesn't apply, for example, to making love or making Irish stew.

Homer said as much in his lost comic poem *Margites*—if he did write it as Aristotle said. Margites was a fool who did everything badly. The gods had taught him nothing, neither to dig nor to plough. By the time he was grown he didn't know whether it was his father or his mother who gave birth to him. He wouldn't lie with his wife for fear she would tell her mother the kind of husband he was. Margites failed at every skill. So he remained a fool.

September

My course in modern poetry begins with Gerard Manley Hopkins. You would think his strain and stress might discourage all but the dogged few. Anyone might give up the struggle to unravel to the end "The Wreck of the Deutschland":

> Let him easter in us, be a dayspring to the dimness of us,
>   be a crimson-cresseted east,
> More brightening her, rare-dear Britain, as his reign rolls,
>   Pride, rose, prince, hero of us, high-priest,
> Our hearts' charity's hearth's fire, our thoughts' chivalry's throng's Lord.

Yet a century later, Hopkins hurls them half off their feet. Some believe in his God-centered world, others believe in him. Their faith is unrelated to the new Jesus movement with its vulgar rock songs ("Me and my friend Jesus," "Put your hand in the hand of the man from Galilee, O yeah!"). Or to Billy Graham's latest crusade for Jesus, where he told of a Salvation Army lass to whom God had spoken. "'Hey!' said God. 'Are you O.K.?'"

October

A constant joy of reading is to come across the coincidences—the same story turning up big as life in strange places. My neighbor Howard's mother, who lived all her days in Tennessee, saved everything. She made little cloth bags to hold pieces of string, each bag carefully labeled as to length of pieces. After her death in the 1950s, they found one little bag labeled "Too short to save."

The poet Donald Hall, who was born in Connecticut, published a book of prose pieces in 1961, *String Too Short to be Saved*. To explain the title he wrote: "A man was cleaning the attic of an old house in New England and he found a box which was full of tiny pieces of string. On the lid of the box there was an inscription in an old hand: 'String too short to be saved.'"

The Evening Star (1945), a diary Colette kept in her seventies, told of the neat, ordered drawers she meant to leave behind at her death. But, she said, "I haven't gone as far as the drawer containing 'little bits of string no good for anything' which Robert de Montesquieu [poet and critic, who died in 1921] claimed to have seen at one of his female relatives."

At least Henry King knew what to do with the string:

> The chief defect of Henry King
> Was chewing little bits of string.

> — Hilaire Belloc, *Cautionary Tales*

From a letter to the editor in the *New York Times*: "Bits of string are appreciated by nest-building birds."

November

So far an unmixed good in my life is not to live in opulence in Texas. The Neiman-Marcus Christmas catalogue contains the gift for the man who has everything (including murder in his heart). For 1971 they offer a His and Her authenticated mummy case, $16,000 apiece, two thousand years old. From the land of the Nile it comes empty of its former occupants or, the advertisement says, "gratefully vacant." How or with whom you fill it up again is a matter of personal choice. I've read that Mrs. Jack Gardner used to greet her guests from the depths of an open Egyptian sarcophagus, where she lay more or less like a mummy. Everything has happened before.

December

From Enid Bagnold's *Autobiography*, published aged eighty:

Who wants to become a writer? And why? Because it's the answer to everything. To 'Why am I here?' To uselessness. It's the streaming reason for living. To note, to pin down, to build up, to create, to be astonished at nothing, to cherish the oddities, to let nothing go down the drain, to make something, to make a great flower out of life, even if it's a cactus.

Of course I agree. I don't blame her at her age for boasting of her lovers, the conquests and holy pleasures. At eighty it's time to tell or be forever still. But if my first lover had been Frank Harris, who deflowered her in an upper room of the Café Royal in London, I would have kept the secret. What abominable luck.

"Sex," he told her, "is the gateway to life." Whether Enid Bagnold appears in Frank Harris's *My Life and Loves* I don't know; his loves are anonymous. In my junior year at college, someone lent me volume 1 to keep overnight, the first book of explicit sex I had read, not counting *The Sheik*. By skipping the life and concentrating on the loves, before breakfast I had got through most of the affairs. I didn't believe him, an obvious embellisher. Besides, he was sixty-seven years old; the girls to whom he dictated the fantasies addressed him as "Sir." The book revealed superhuman prowess and sounded unreliable.

One seduction, I remember, occurred on the running board of a car, an impossible feat without somebody's falling off. After these tattlings I never tried the second volume, which he finished at seventy. The five volumes, published in 1964, contained over a hundred chapters. He kept a card file of the 2,000 females he had seduced and insured the list with Lloyd's of London.

Frank Harris, braggart, fraud, said Casanova wasn't worthy to untie his bootstrings. But young Enid Bagnold, who worked in his office, went to her Uncle Lexy's for dinner that night chanting to herself, "I'm not a virgin." A pretty thin boast sixty years later.

1972

January

On the Comedy Hour on television: "If you think last year was bad—wait!" (Gilbert White of Selborne: "I made this same remark on former years, as I came this way annually.")

Tonight in Chicago David and I appeared on ABC television as "A Literary Family." Mr. Lincoln interviewed us as part of a series called "Perspectives," a hearty man full of becks and nods, groping his way through the half hour though clearly without a clue as to what we were doing there or why literary.

David and I also were without a clue. I was told not to wear white, since the program was taped in color, so I wore a broad smile. We laughed and kept on talking to each other. Afterward neither of us could recall that we had been literary or even literate. Mr. Lincoln drove us home in silence, his labors over and done.

A few days later a grateful letter came from the Vice-President of Public Affairs at the University of Chicago, addressed to Mr. and Mrs. David Bevington, warmly thanking them for the stimulating program, a treat for television viewers. He found it refreshing that a married couple who lived six hundred miles apart, one at Duke University, one at Chicago, were dedicating their lives less to each other than to English literature. Peggy said I could keep the letter.

So far David and I have been taken for brother and sister, aunt and nephew, husband and wife—never for mother and son. It's too literary a relationship, like Mrs. Trollope and Anthony.

Morton Zabel was an eccentric professor, writer, critic at the university, who died in 1964. This year I am a Morton Zabel lecturer at Chicago. Since I chose to hold a writing seminar rather than give a public lecture, I've acquired a class mostly of graduate students, two of them candidates for the Ph.D. Their creativeness, in prose and verse, tempts me to take the next flight home. One long story by a Ph.D. candidate describes the trauma of her first menstruation. A second tells of a torrid homosexual encounter between two college students, one of them the author. A third is about a gorilla who reads English. The poetry is surrealist, full of tangled images. "My rose Picasso is an apple," writes Cathy, whom I visualized from these words as a married woman with a fat baby son. Turns out she was praising her lover, a tempting rose-red apple from the forbidden tree.

Each day I've plodded through snow to Ida Noyes Hall (where as a student I took lessons in Advanced Diving), meeting with these wonderfully opinionated writers. At the final session I invited them for sherry in David's study on the third floor of his house, where the congeniality seemed destined never to stop. By the fall of night, all had survived save Curtis, the youngest, who unaccustomed to strong drink fell headlong down two flights of stairs. God knows whether he ever reached home.

Christine's stream-of-consciousness confession of fifty pages baffled me to the end. But love and sympathy prevailed, faith triumphed, leaving only wisps of mystification behind.

February

I liked reviewing Anne Lindbergh's volume of diaries and letters, *Bring Me a Unicorn*. It's one of the great love stories of the century. Besides, she and I are contemporaries, same age, same size; on the same night in Town Hall we heard John Masefield read his poems, a shy man with a small voice introduced by a shy man with a small voice, Stephen Vincent Benét. I fell in love the same year she did, married, had a son. But I could never have summoned up courage to reveal the drivel I wrote at sixteen, the gush in college, the ecstasies when I found the man I wanted. "Let her speak for herself," says Anne Lindbergh of young Anne Morrow. At first I thought it too bad to leave the girl struggling with words, with transport and exclamation points, rapture and despair. At Smith College, she is given to calling clouds "great archangel wings," has an understanding with some lavender sweet peas, is smothered with joy when praised for an English theme, and permanently hounded by final exams. It seemed ironic that, having become the writer she yearned to be, Mrs. Lindbergh should refuse to rescue Anne Morrow from her youth.

I was wrong. In a self-portrait to label "before and after meeting Colonel Lindbergh," she reveals herself as more than girlish, a complex person strong-willed yet meek, a poet fond of unicorns, a girl falling in love. Born and brought up in Englewood, New Jersey, one of four children in a family of Presbyterians and educators, Anne felt isolated in her walled garden protected from the real world in a household of family prayers, family reading, family travel, family love. Her mother, Elizabeth Morrow, was a crusader for equal education for women. Her father, Dwight Morrow, became ambassador to Mexico under President Coolidge, then senator from New Jersey. Anne was sent to Miss Chapin's School and moved on obediently to Smith, though for one rebellious moment she considered breaking with family tradition and bolting to Vassar.

In her senior year she went with her older sister Elisabeth to Mexico City for the holidays. To Anne's annoyance her father, the ambassador, had arranged for Charles Lindbergh to fly the *Spirit of St. Louis* down from Washington, D.C., "all this public-hero stuff breaking into our family party." She hated the fuss, the sound of his odious name Lindy. Then she met him, an abrupt, embarrassed boy, around whom crowds swarmed, worshipful and terrifying. He was a hero after all. Against her will he gave her the distinct impression of divinity. Yet during the two-week stay at the embassy, he did nothing but gaze at Elisabeth till Anne was sick with envy.

From this distance, how could Mrs. Lindbergh retell the love story? She had no need to try. Anne Morrow pours out the exalted tale as she lived it. Her first flight in an airplane was with Colonel L. as pilot ("God, let me be *conscious* of it! Let me be *conscious* of *what* is happening, *while* it is happening.") He swept from sight the other men she had known. "All my life, in fact, my world—my little embroidery beribboned world—is smashed." He didn't hear her as she thanked him. He hadn't noticed her.

The next year she spent dreaming of him, watching birds as they mounted on wings. At the dentist's the drill roared in her ear like a plane overhead. Yet "fool, fool, fool," she told her diary. "You are completely and irretrievably opposed to him. You have nothing in common. You don't even sincerely care a damn for his world."

By July after graduation, feeling fat and old, she knew she wanted to be married and wouldn't be asked. Colonel L. was seeing Elisabeth in New York, "Elisabeth of course again." Her dream of heroes was dead. Then on a Wednesday for no apparent reason he telephoned her home in Englewood and offered to take her flying. She set down that crowning day like a young Fanny Burney, pages of polite dialogue between them, recalling every word. Afterward there were secret meetings. He taught her to fly.

When a Mexican newspaper reported, "Lone Eagle no longer lonely—courts Elisabeth Morrow," she wept with rage.

It crossed her mind "How absurd this will sound in fifty years." It doesn't sound absurd. Anne is an honest witness, bewildered by contradictory feelings comical and touching—the dilemma of a sheltered introspective girl in love with a Lindbergh. She writes her sister Constance, "Lord, that man is cold, always on guard, with a one-track mind, and his coat doesn't fit." She analyzes him in her diary, "Why is he a great man?" and lists his shortcomings: he never opens a book, he plays practical jokes, he clings to facts, facts, facts. "I don't want to marry him—God forbid. I don't even want to go up in the plane!" But there he is, "the biggest, most absorbing person I've ever met." He has no sense of humor, he *has* a sense of humor; he is overwhelming, forceful, and "we are utterly opposed."

Only one letter in the book is written to Dear C[harles], a demurely noncommittal one. Shortly before her marriage in 1929 she wrote Corliss Lamont: "Don't wish me happiness—I don't expect to be happy, but it's gotten beyond that somehow. Wish me courage and strength and a sense of humor—I will need them all."

March

Newspaper headline: "World Today Full of Clenched Fists."

This is untrue of my writing seminar, which is full of tolerance and good humor. We fourteen, in a space limited to twelve, crowd around the table drinking tea. Marjorie brings a roll of pink toilet paper for blowing her nose, not for tears. My motto for the term is "strive mightily, but eat and drink as friends."

Nobody shakes a fist, though Jill, nineteen, tries the patience of her contemporaries by writing stories consisting of "shit, man, shit." Yesterday my telephone rang in the midst of her dialogue of a couple quarreling to the music of Henry Mancini, and Jill stopped reading. When we were ready to take a deep breath and resume, she said, "Where was I?"

"Somewhere after the last shit," I said, for which I am ashamed.

"That's the way people talk," Jill said. "I have to tell it like it is."

She submitted a three-page poem titled "Sex," which she called a rough draft. "A catchy title," we said, "but too sweeping." In it Jill, the aggressor, played on her lover's body a crashing melody. "She has turned me into a piano!" he cried. Our elder statesmen, Keith and Winslow, both married—one with a baby son, the other with a brown dog they bring occasionally to class—advised Jill where she went wrong. "It's naive," they told her. "No man alive ever said a thing like that."

They drift into my office a half hour before class time. Today Joey said, "Tell me about bastards." He is mulling over in his mind a story about one. "Which kind of bastard?" I asked. I recommended Plautus, Terence, and T. S. Eliot's *Confidential Clerk*. "A bastard," I said, "is a child begotten on a pack saddle."

Joey laughed. "You're putting me on." That's what the word means, a chancechild, a merry begot.

My poet Harry writes a love poem about two ripe tomatoes, big, red, and fat, lying together on the windowsill. They remind him of his present love affair, when "we are laid close for one short, ripe hour." I tell him "Ripeness is all."

Harry clears up the mystery of what happened to Romantic poetry. When Keats wrote "Isabella," his suffering hero Lorenzo, sick for love, languished for months before working up enough courage to kiss the lady:

> So said, his erewhile timid lips grew bold,
> And poesied with hers in dewy rhyme.

I've never been able to visualize that dewy salute. Or Endymion's moist one either: "Thy lips oh slippery blisses."

But when Harry takes a notion to kiss his girl, he says,

> Darling,
> Would you come here please
> Just a second so I may
> Nuclear-blast you
> With a fusion of our lips?

The atomic age of poetry.

Since the subject of kissing occupies our studious minds this spring, I've been rereading the *Kisses* of Johannes Secundus to see how accurately he dealt with them. He was a Dutch poet (Jan Everts) noted in his time for amorous Latin lyrics, who died in 1536 before he was twenty-five. Montaigne listed as the books he found especially stimulating Boccaccio, Rabelais, and the *Kisses* (*Basia*) of Johannes Secundus—whose curious name the poet took because he had an uncle named that.

A Spanish girl, whom Secundus called Neaera, inspired the short collection of nineteen poems, Kiss I through XIX, none very wanton or original. At least three—VI, VII, and XVI—are close imitations of Catullus:

> Kisses told by hundreds o'er;
> Thousands told by thousands more!
> Millions! countless millions! then
> Told by millions o'er again.

Of kisses, said Secundus, "I'm the bard." In an opening epigram he was more specific, "Moist kisses are my theme," which his translators, notably George Ogle (who died in 1746), made the grave mistake of translating into *humid*:

> Whene'er with mine thy humid lips unite
> Then humid kisses with their sweets delight.

Humid is a worse choice for a kiss (that flows or pours from the mouth, "a fragrant shower of balmy dews") than Keats's *slippery*. Humidity suggests water vapor rising like steam. *Damp* is bad, and *wet* would imply really sloshing about.

April

Some years ago I used to teach an essay by Stuart Chase written in 1931, "The Luxury of Integrity." This appeared in a collection of modern essays meant to stimulate thinking. For some reason it gave the students a lot to think about besides making a lasting impression on me. I thought of it tonight as I watched the television commercials—a woman in flutters over the effect of Secret, a deodorant, another fulfilled for life by a gentler laxative or stronger detergent. These were women guilty of opportunism, selling their souls for Alka-Seltzer. Their children too were freely exploited, TV's little shills for Oscar Mayer's bologna.

Stuart Chase found integrity a luxury we can't afford. We can be bought, out of greed, necessity, fear, conceit. The cost of honesty is so high we give up human dignity and self-respect rather than pay the price, which is, in the present idiom, escalating. He made a list in descending scale—arbitrary if you like but not whimsical—to include us all as losers of integrity. You could see the students wondering where their parents fitted the picture, apparently not conscience-stricken about themselves. Those on the list with highest marks were the least tempted, removed from the marketplace. The housewife held an honorable place below the farmer. The professions followed in strict order, doctors at the top, lawyers at the bottom. In my notes I had copied out, "Professors, like canvassers, must eat."

The list then took a deep plunge to the salesman, the clerk, the office worker who to keep on the payroll blink at corrupt practices. Below them in impenetrable darkness lurked the politician, of whom Chase said, "To expect integrity from an elected public servant is almost to expect a miracle." We seemed to touch bottom, but no, there was one lower still: the corporation executive, the brazen advertiser of his product, willing to say or do anything not short of killing off his competitor to sell it.

As I sat there I felt sorriest for the housewife, who, with limpid eyes, finds joy in a liquid soap and happiness in a hairspray. She moves with such complacence in the marketplace.

May

I set off with Betty and Ted this morning, closing the door of my house with a prayer and a light left burning. From Kennedy Airport by Alitalia it was seven hours to Milan. A wrestling team on the 747 made us feel safe, though a swimming team would have helped more. As we flew over the Alps to Italy a woman across the aisle sobbed, "Oh God, oh God, I am so happy!"

Milan. I have thousands of liras stuffed in my purse, unspeakably rich. Thirty thousand of them are enough to buy me a hat, appropriately, since the word milliner comes from Milan. Though I haven't been here since 1950, the *Bevete Coca-Cola* signs haven't changed or the *Vota socialista* banners. The traffic is frantic, infested with scooting bugs that jostle and dart, "Beep, beep, beep." People park them on the sidewalk, hoisting them by hand. This afternoon we three went to the showrooms while Ted bought a Fiat in avocado green. Proceeding by leaps and beeps, we reached the Hotel Rosa, where Ted placed the little Fiat in storage till we leave town to avoid certain destruction on the swarming streets of Milan.

This Sunday is *Festa della Mamma*. The shops feature heartshaped boxes of candy with a sign in English, Love—a touching tribute to my mother tongue. Round the Cathedral Milan's traffic beeps and curses. I disliked the Duomo twenty-two years ago when I was here, pleased with my intolerance like D. H. Lawrence who called it a hedgehog of a cathedral. I called it a frosted birthday cake with 4,440 candles. Now I see it takes detachment to appreciate a Gothic pile sprouting delicate spires like icicles. In the Piazza del Duomo little girls stepped among the pigeons in wedding dresses for their first communion, little brides of the Lord who will soon wear such white veils and bouquets to marry a man. Across the way in the Galleria Vittorio Emanuele, the immense arcade roofed by a dome of glass, we sat at a pink-covered table at Biffi's and drank Milanese beer while the lovers passed, the babies were wheeled by, a sinister group gathered (those who cry "Vota communista"), and a knot of police stood near. Nothing happened, not on Mother's Day.

Tonight we rushed through the Galleria clutching three tickets to La Scala for Gluck's opera *Alceste*. Stendhal, who fell in love with Milan (and with Angela and Matilde), called La Scala the universal salon, which he attended each night partaking of a lemon ice. Later exiled from Milan yet faithful to the end, he ordered his tomb to inscribe him not Parisian but Milanese.

Alceste is delightfully morbid, a German wail from a Greek lament with an Italian libretto. Gluck said his work should make one weep, but I was full of unsuitable joy. Who can weep at operatic plots, even one inspired by Euripides? The god Apollo made an unseemly bargain to give life to mortally ill Admetus if another took his place in death. So we swooned at the gates of hell with Alceste till Apollo got around to relenting and all was saved by love, or what passed this night for love. Posturing regally, the singers must not have been introduced and so were careful to keep their distance.

We couldn't stay forever (why not?) staring at Raphael's *Marriage of the Virgin* at the Brera. We couldn't linger in the Dominican refectory gazing at Leonardo's fresco, where the friars used to sit at supper as if actually eating with the disciples, while Christ uttered the words to them all, "One of you shall betray me!"

After extricating the Fiat, Ted gritted his teeth, roared at Betty for God's sake to watch the map, and maneuvered through Milan traffic to the Pavia-Genoa road. Like the early travelers, we followed in style the route of the Grand Tour.

Pavia. Before I left home, I memorized Dr. Johnson's lapidary statement: "A man who has not been in Italy is always conscious of an inferiority from his not having seen what it is expected a man should see." Dr. Johnson never got to Italy, but this is true if a man hasn't seen the Certosa of Pavia, what Stendhal unkindly called "that frivolous and undignified marble *bonbonnière* known as the Charterhouse of Pavia." Sixteen miles south of Milan we stopped in the courtyard of the famed

Carthusian monastery, dedicated to the Virgin in 1396. Its multicolored marble facade, laden with plaques and medallions, flaunted one of Alexander the Great. The locust trees were in bloom, so were several hundred schoolchildren mooning at us while being lectured to by harried priests. The church sumptuous as a palace was cold and lonely, since long ago the monks were expelled and the monastery closed, leaving twenty-four empty cells each with its flower garden. The austere Carthusians believed along with serving God in a riotous garden of one's own.

The town of Pavia, five miles farther, boasted another treasure at San Pietro in Ciel d'Oro—the body of Saint Augustine of the *Confessions*, who told in them how he was converted in Milan one day in a.d. 387 when he flung his unworthy self weeping under a fig tree. A Lombard king, Liutprand, brought the body from Sardinia four centuries later that he might lie in death at the feet of the saint. My favorite confession of Saint Augustine's is "Make me chaste and continent, but not just yet."

We gave stricter attention in Pavia to buying bread and cheese, not a light undertaking in Italy. You can say "Formaggio," or cry "Un morso di pane per amor di Dio," which doesn't work, or roll your eyes and act out the menu. With bread and cheese under Lombardy poplars beside the avocado green Fiat we saluted spring in Lombardy.

Piacenza. On December 16, 1816, Stendhal wrote in his *Journal*: "This morning as I drove out of Pavia on the road to Piacenza, I found myself embarked upon one of the liveliest highways that I have known in all my life." But Piacenza annoyed him with its pair of equestian statues in the main square. Two bronze horses with invisible Farnese dukes on their backs reared so high that all I could see was their testicles.

Hannibal swept down from the Alps to Piacenza, leading his Carthaginians on his way to fail at conquering Rome. Here he fought Scipio, trampling the Romans with his thirty-seven elephants, and in defeat Piacenza (then Placentia) offered a gold thunderbolt to Jupiter. The god was not appeased. Nor were the divine powers placated, I think, when in 1754 the foolish monks of San Sisto sold Raphael's *Sistine Madonna*, which he had painted for the church in 1515, to Frederick Augustus III for 20,000 ducats. So the town lost its soul.

Parma. In a city of Parmesan cheese, violets, and Correggio, our hotel is the Jolly Stendhal, not an adjective meant to describe the morose Stendhal or *The Charterhouse of Parma*, but the name of Mr. Jolly who owns a chain of hotels. Actually no charterhouse ever existed in Parma, nor have I seen a field of violets, only plastic ones in shop windows. In the Giorno, Ted introduced us to the despicable dukes of Parma, sporting their enormous codpieces. And to Marie Louise and her carnal lovers beside Correggio's Magdalen with the golden hair. Marie Louise had a beauty definitely sheeplike, though after divorcing Josephine Napoleon wooed and married her. With his downfall, Marie Louise was awarded the duchy of Parma, to which she proceeded cheerfully, took herself a lover, then another and another. Napoleon in exile made threats to abduct her.

Salmon-pink Lombardy lions guarded the Baptistery. In the mighty cathedral with frescoes by Correggio, the holy candles were standing in rows of Gerber babyfood jars. Strained prunes and apricots.

Mantua. Forty miles across the poppy fields is Mantua, to which Romeo was banished after murdering Tybalt. Virgil, born a true Mantuan (whom Dante logically chose as guide), loved this countryside where his father had a farm in 70 b.c., and wrote of it in the *Eclogues* and *Georgics*. Praise great estates but farm a little one, he said. "Break the dull clods with a mattock, and call loudly to Ceres for help." Here the fierce dukes of Gonzaga ruled for four hundred years, celebrated for all I know from his unintelligibility by Ezra Pound in the *Cantos* ("with usura / seeth no man Gonzaga his heirs and his concubines"). In the vast palace we lingered deep in Gonzagas to escape the dripping rain, which reminded Ted of a threat more frightful than any Gonzaga—the watery Italian gasoline that causes the Fiat to stutter and stall, enough to drive a man nuts with two women on his hands.

Verona. What more could anyone ask than to stay at the Hotel Giulietta e Romeo with a balcony outside her window? In spare moments I lean out just in case. "Hist! Romeo, hist!"

Montaigne, who found in Verona "nothing singular," never knew Shakespeare. Nor did Shakespeare know Verona, though tourists clamor to be shown where the star-crossed lovers lived and died. The Veronese are happy to oblige. Juliet's house, the Casa di Giulietta, is a thirteenth-century dwelling in the Via Cappello, with a cramped balcony too tiny for love duets. For a fee you can walk in the garden (for a fee they would produce the two Gentlemen of Verona, one of whom in the play set sail on the sea from Verona to Milan) and ponder the words: "Here stands the house of the Cappello family, whence came that Juliet for whom gentle hearts wept so sorely, and for whom the poets sang." (Dickens in 1844: "I was quite satisfied with it as the veritable mansion of Old Capulet.") Juliet's tomb, where lovers go to kiss, is in the crypt of the Church of San Francesco. I heard I could buy snippets of Juliet's nightgown, though Shakespeare never said she wore one.

Our hotel is across from a Roman amphitheater, once bloody with combats between men and beasts, men and gladiators. We walked to the main square opposite the statue of Victor Emmanuel—who thrives like Lenin as a national hero—to witness a live battle, a present-day mortal combat. It was Sunday. While crowds strolled by, a group of long-haired protesters crouched in a circle, as in an arena waiting their turn at deadly struggle. According to handmade placards, they were making a last-ditch fight against everything and everybody. Large posters denounced the enemies of freedom. One placard explained apartheid in South Africa by drawings of the white man's toilet, "WC francha" for him, "WC non francha" for the black man. Persistently damned were the Americans, guiltiest of nations in destroying freedom, equality, peace, and love. The bearded young men and pretty girls taking part in the silent protest whispered, laughed, kissed, and made newspaper hats to keep out the sun.

My mind went back to Catullus, who also hated as he loved, born in Verona before Christ was born. And to Dante, given refuge when Florence condemned him for his protests to be burned alive. We walked to the piazza where Dante lived, where beneath his brooding statue babies played, up to their knees in pigeons. "Pi-pi," the children yelled, till a frisky dog jumped in scattering birds and babies.

Vicenza. In the sixteenth century a young man fled to Vicenza from Padua where he had worked as a stonecutter. Sensibly changing his name from Gondola to Palladio—for Pallas Athene—he became the father of the Palladian style of architecture, which has affected the entire Western world, the style of Inigo Jones, Adam, Thomas Jefferson of Monticello, and the Capitol at Washington. For better or worse he's known as the most influential architect who ever lived, though not by Ruskin who dismissed him.

It's too elegant for my taste. Had I lived in Vicenza in Palladio's time I might have yearned to own a villa resembling a palace, with Corinthian columns and colonnades, pediments, pilasters, arcades, allegorical scenes, classical figures, and formal urns (that Horace Walpole thought looked absurd "when crowded into a closet"). Palladio must have been a nice man. His villas resemble stately palaces, but because of the modest means of their owners he built them not of marble but of rough bricks with a coating of stucco. The stucco, painted white, slowly deteriorated, peeled and turned shabby. Yet I kept thinking what an obliging man he was to pepper the town with the Palladian style—he who married a servant girl and for most of his life was poor. I hope he had many grateful friends who loved the monotony.

Palladio's last creation, in 1580, was the Olympic Theater, still used for Greek tragedy. It appears too small and dainty for Sophocles' *Oedipus Rex*, performed at the grand opening four centuries ago. With heroic statuary, seats arranged like a fan, it stands ready for ancient tragedians to stalk on for an oration. When Napoleon entered this theater he said, "Madame, we are in Greece."

Padua. Ted wears a bright green jacket, the color of the Fiat, which makes them both easy to locate in Padua, though Ted is larger and easier. In these Lombardy towns we park the car and walk in single file down narrow lanes while Ted leads the way looking, over six feet tall, like a green traffic light. For lunch we stop for pizza, which I had hoped was unknown in Italy, an American invention like Liederkranz or chop suey. But no, pizza parlors abound.

"Zuppa, grazie?" I ask eagerly from time to time. "Insalata, per favore?"

"Pizza," is the stern reply, just pizza.

This is Saint Anthony of Padua's town, whose bones are buried in the Basilica di San Antonio, and his tongue is preserved as well. When they opened his grave in 1263, thirty years after his death at thirty-six, they found the flesh gone to dust but the tongue healthy and ruddy. It is said to do what only a tongue can do—speak. Saint Anthony's speaks with God. Near the chapel where he rests is the evidence: crutches left behind, votive tablets to mark those whom by his eloquence Saint Anthony saved. A young couple came to press their wedding rings against his marble pillar, while in whispers they pledged their love or else asked him to restore it, since he was a saint who found lost things—except one's faith perhaps. A Franciscan monk, *Il Santo*, named at birth Ferdinand, he had a tongue that fishes leaped from the water to hear. When he preached a Latin sermon, "My dearly beloved fishes," they came and bowed their heads (as in nearby Assisi Saint Francis was preaching to the birds in the field, "My little sisters," and they flapped their wings and sang to praise the Lord).

But Padua really belongs to Giotto. Giotto was his given name. He came from Tuscany like his close friend Dante, who said in the "Purgatorio,"

> O empty glory of human powers . . .
> Cimabue thought to hold
> The field of painting, and now the cry is Giotto's

He had eight children as homely as he. When Dante asked how a man who produced such art could have such uncomely children, Giotto answered, "I make my pictures by day and my babies by night."

In Padua Giotto's Chapel of the Arena is a slender pink church whose interior is every inch covered with Giotto's paintings. Three tiers of frescoes tell the life of Mary, of Christ, his death and Mary's death. At the door is the Last Judgment, where among the blessed ascending to heaven Giotto painted himself, while the damned spill and tumble headlong to hell. It is all so understandable, the faces alive, the painter's wit making one laugh—at the smiling donkey in the *Flight into Egypt*, the astonished camel in *The Adoration of the Magi*. Here Dante stood marveling as he watched the master.

Venice. Betty and I sat outside Florian's in the Piazza San Marco, drinking a Cinzano and listening to the orchestra play sentimental waltzes. I wore my blue Venetian glass beads from the Murano Glass Works. The gold angel above the Campanile fluttered in the sun. Saint Mark's winged lion sat atop a column reading the Bible. From the clock tower two figures hammered the hour of five.

We sat among the living and the dead, the living unidentified and feeding the pigeons, the illustrious dead silent among us—Sir Philip Sidney who met Tintoretto and was painted by Veronese, Ruskin, Goethe, Wagner, Byron, Jean Jacques Rousseau—what traveler in his day had not visited Venice? Only the author of the *Merchant of Venice* and *Othello, the Moor of Venice* (though Chekhov liked to point out the very house where Desdemona lived). Of the cities of the world, Henry James said, it is the easiest to visit without going there. Except to wonder why the Piazza itself wasn't under water and full of gondolas, I was daydreaming, merely joining the scene: the golden presences, the tourists, the greedy birds. Nietzsche mentioned the pigeons. Gibbon saw them with disgust. Horace Walpole objected to the stink.

A newsboy passed in front of us holding up a copy of the *Paris Herald Tribune,* and we read the headline, "Governor Wallace Shot." Another assassination? He too it seemed was a victim of hate and violence, like the two Kennedys, like Martin Luther King.

The afternoon grew suddenly dark. We got up shivering from our easy chairs and hurried through the pigeons out of the Piazza.

"Our crazy country," I said to Betty.

"Our crazy world," she said with more accuracy.

The Dalmatian Coast. On the wide autostrada we began a new journey by driving from Venice to Trieste. Marcus Aurelius and Hemingway came this route but branched off here. For us Trieste was the start down the Dalmatian coast beside the Adriatic to the border of Albania, which shuts us out as intractable enemies of Communism.

I used to love reading in the papers when the Duke of Windsor was king about his romantic cruise down the Dalmatian coast in the summer of 1936 with the still-married Mrs. Simpson. He took her and a few friends including the Duff Coopers aboard a chartered yacht, the *Nahlin,* escorted by two British destroyers. Thinking it over thirty-six years later, I had to admit that the quality of pleasure being equal, a yacht is as good as a Fiat.

When I told my students this spring I was going down the Dalmatian coast, "Why?" they asked. "Is it in California?" "I had a Dalmatian dog once."

Dalmatia, formerly a kingdom of the Austro-Hungarian empire, is today a thin coastal strip within the federation of the six states: Slovenia, Croatia, Bosnia-Herzegovina, Serbia, Montenegro, and Macedonia. A new country, Yugoslavia, came out of World War I with the Treaty of Versailles when these kingdoms with their four languages, three religions, two alphabets, were gathered up to make one nation, the common language Serbo-Croatian, the name Southern Slavs.

This was nothing new in the history of Dalmatia. By 1918 she had lived through several thousand years of occupation. The Illyrians came five centuries before Christ, the Greeks founded shore cities followed by the Romans. Often a battleground, it was ravaged by a progression of Goths, Ostrogoths, Huns, Magyars, Avars, Tatars, Byzantines, taken by the Normans, Franks, Turks, Venetians, recently held by the Austro-Hungarians till the Germans came, then the Russians. Hitler occupied all of Yugoslavia in 1941 after which—the old story—it was liberated by the Russians under Tito. Since 1948, when Tito quarreled with the Kremlin to a threat of war, the air is freer. Yet one can't help feeling uneasy in Dalmatia with its mixture of Serb, Slav, Croat, Slovene. After Tito, what?

Split. I can't describe grandeur. Its color, I'd say, is blue. For days we've followed a winding, deeply indented shoreline next a sea backed by towering mountains. We've climbed impossible heights, made steep descents, and always the radiant blue of the Adriatic accompanied us. We've passed through towns with queer names—Rijeka, formerly the Italian Fiume; Poreč, Slavic for Parenzo. Split, now in Croatia though on the Dalmatian coast, was Spalatro, where Diocletian built his palace in a.d. 307. Diocletian was born of humble origin in Dalmatia. Exhausted at fifty-nine from persecuting the Christians and building Diocletian baths, he abdicated as Roman emperor and retired to this palace to plant cabbages seventeen centuries ago. Here he spent his last eight years, and when he died perhaps by suicide the palace was so mammoth that the populace moved in. Some three thousand people, they say, are living inside it.

We entered like pilgrims on foot through the Brass Gate. Before us stood the temple of Jupiter, converted in the eighth century to a cathedral of the Virgin, to the hated Christianity Diocletian tried single-mindedly to destroy. His body rested in the center of the cathedral for three centuries before it disappeared. An Englishman coming up beside us scoffed to his companion, "Good heavens, Elsie, it's Roman *and* Romanesque!" So it is, from Roman pillars to the irony of a Christian cross.

While we lingered under the portico, five Croatian schoolgirls greeted us in English, then turned their backs and lighted cigarettes. A Catholic priest on his way into the church stopped in horror and, while they bent their heads to the blast, delivered a powerful rebuke in Serbo-Croatian that obviously went like this, "For shame, foolish children. Why do you behave in this unbecoming manner, before strangers too? Why aren't you obedient to God?" As if caught in the act we listened penitently. I knew he would wink at us in the end. He bowed and did.

I preen to remember the night we spent twelve miles from Split in the district of seven old castles on the Castel Riviera. At the Hotel Palace, English was not only not spoken but not recognized. After trying a little German on us, they settled for nods and shrugs.

A tall, dark, and handsome porter brought my luggage to my room with such courtesy and lingering attention that I gave him ten dinars and a warm smile in gratitude. He thanked me with rapture and left with reluctance. A moment later he burst in without knocking, tremulously beckoning me to the telephone by my bed to indicate I should call 111 (*ein, ein, ein*) which I could plainly see was not the number of the front desk. What number was it? He pointed to himself—his own. At that he pulled me to him and kissed me hot on the mouth. I laughed and broke away, shaking my head at such extraordinary service.

"Ein, ein, ein," he said.

"Nein, nein, nein," I said.

Giving up gracefully, he left laughing. This must be what they mean by the people's republic.

Dubrovnik. The few signs along the road were for Kent cigarettes and *Mimi crake zoo* (animal crackers). Asphodel, harebells, yellow broom lined the roadside. By afternoon we reached Dubrovnik, and so far as I was concerned I meant never to depart. G. B. Shaw wrote, "Those who seek Earthly Paradise should come and see Dubrovnik." Why make the mistake of going away?

It is the rarest jewel, set on an island in the Adriatic, encircled by extremely thick walls. It was built in the thirteenth century, its name Ragusa changed in 1918. By the west gate—once guarded by Franciscans, the east gate by Dominicans—you enter the Plaka, the main street, which is the length of two city blocks ending at the clock tower and harbor. At evening the populace strolls serenely up and down. The guidebook to Yugoslavia says the people of Dubrovnik are "amiable, harmonious, and urbane."

We viewed it from the ramparts, though it takes piety and endurance to struggle up the steep, narrow steps, past houses built along either side. Dubrovnik is a fortress, with towers and bastions, that has never been taken, never conquered, the claim is. An inscription says, "Liberty is not for sale, for all the gold in the world."

Next day we cruised the Adriatic, inspired by the Duke of Windsor and his royal love affair. At Dubrovnik they had been greeted by a jubilant crowd chanting, "Zivila ljubav" (Long live love). We went aboard the *Artas* with fifty-two clamorous tourists, mostly Germans starting their holidays full of din. The sea was tranquil as the Germans were not, while we sailed down the Dalmatian coast and I tried to feel adored like Mrs. Simpson. Once we stopped among palms and cypresses on Lokrum, the Island of Love, not named in honor of the Duke of Windsor. Archduke Maximilian had occupied a palace there before going to Mexico to become emperor, be condemned to death, and die. His nephew, the Austrian crown prince Rudolf, lived on Lokrum before love destroyed him and the lady in the mysterious tragedy at Mayerling in 1889.

It was Saturday night in a delightful restaurant in the Plaka—the

Jadran—with a loud pop group for the dancing. The music was good, irresistible in fact, as was the slivovitz, the national drink made of plums that tastes fine in Dubrovnik. When a man at the next table asked me to dance—a Czech, it turned out, on a business trip—I hopped to my feet without ado and soon we were flinging about the crowded floor in a Czech variation of rock and roll, or maybe the dipsidoodle. Betty and Ted, already dancing, glared at us, hurriedly left the floor, and raced to our table where they sat stunned. I felt guilty but of what?—of a disgraceful performance as I soon learned. In the joy of being asked I had pranced off and abandoned Betty's huge tote bag left in my care, Ted's precious camera, and my own handbag containing my worldly wealth. They told me I had lost my wits. Luckily nothing else was missing.

I still believe that in Dubrovnik, that other Eden, there are no thieves.

Titograd. Montenegro begins thirty miles below Dubrovnik. Some declare this fringe of coast to the border of Albania the loveliest in all Yugoslavia. When Albania like a dragon barred the way, our only choice was to turn north from the Adriatic for that part of the journey Ted worried about, with the rumor of hazardous roads, cutthroat gypsies, precipices, primitive inns, the Cyrillic alphabet, and regret for our folly. We were warned. The guidebook promised "spine-tingling" travel, which sounded more sinister than picturesque.

Yet ever since, if someone asks me, "Where have you been lately?" I say with pardonable pride, "To the mountains of Montenegro."

In midafternoon we reached Titograd, the capital, and found rooms in the Cerna Gora ("black mountain" or "Montenegro"), a "luxury" hotel verandahed and ornate on the outside, drab within, with an elevator so full of shakes one automatically praised God for deliverance to one's floor. When I opened the door of my room the handle fell off in my hands. But dinner on the candlelit terrace was a feast of roast lamb and wine; we were treated with high courtesy and regard. Rebecca West, in *Black Lamb and Grey Falcon*, found the Montenegrins brave, beautiful, and vainglorious. She was told, "They are nothing but heroes. If they eat or sleep it is so that they shall wake up heroes. If they marry it is so that they should beget little heroes, who would not trouble to come out of their mothers' wombs were they not certain that they would grow up in heroism." I found them handsome and sober except for yells of laughter at our struggle to make ourselves understood. Oddly, the language they too sought to communicate in was German—the language of the destroyers, since Titograd was leveled by Hitler and has been entirely rebuilt.

Now it is Tito's town, his picture meets you like Lenin's in Russia. The Montenegrins, a proud people who for six centuries kept their independence of the Turks, convey the idea they are pleased with life in their new city. It is ugly as sin, raw and functional, with depressing shops of shoddy clothes for women whose native costumes used to glow with magnificent embroideries.

A local proverb says, "Tomorrow is wiser than today," and another, "God had so many extra rocks he made Montenegro." We proved both sayings true this morning as we left Titograd, where at the tourist office they had no information, nothing but frowns and headshaking at the lunacy of setting forth. We took the road to Kolašin, on vertical mountain-sides next to gorges and sheer cliff walls. All day we wound through rock canyons, plunged into black tunnels (I counted forty before giving up). It was worse than spine tingling, it was like the thousand natural shocks that flesh is heir to. And the road sign we watched for, quick to obey, was a large exclamation point placed at frequent intervals beside the road to tell us to expect trouble, a dire crisis ahead or impending catastrophe. In mountains where the Cyrillic alphabet made *Stop* a word slow to decipher, an exclamation point was eloquent and enough. Ted drove with tremendous care, exclaiming as he went, till now and then we would pass a gypsy camp or some beautiful dark-eyed children leading water buffaloes, and even the buffaloes were glad to see us and ready to throw kisses.

Priština. It used to be the capital of Serbian kings. To the west of Priština is the plain of Kossovo, the Field of Blackbirds, where on a frightful day six hundred years ago, June 28, 1389, the Serbians were mowed down and vanquished by the Turks. The defeat at Kossovo brought Turkish occupation that lasted until 1912, when after centuries of waiting the Serbs conquered the Turks and destroyed the Turkish Balkan Empire. Each spring these six hundred years, blood-red peonies have sprung up from the blood shed by the Serbs, covering the plain like the poppies of Flanders. As we passed by today, the fields were red with them, a scarlet peony with a gold center that grows nowhere else. And the blackbirds were flying.

Now Priština is a kind of flop, still part Turkish but bright with gypsies roaming the streets. The single hotel, the Kosovski Bozür, had a flashy exterior with a mosaic of a mounted warrior, inside grubby, dirty rooms. My tiny bathroom was awash under two inches of water. Orange peels and cigarette butts strewed the table and floor. My telephone rang, and somebody swore at me in Serbo-Croatian.

Skopje. Were I to spend my life in Skopje, capital of Macedonia, if young and poor I'd live on the left bank of the Vardar among the gypsies. Beside the Turkish quarter, their vivid shantytown is one of music in the air and considerable squalor. In Skopje I learned that on Hitler's instructions the gypsies were exterminated wholesale like the Jews, for the same reason—non-Aryan undesirables, a danger to the purity of the master race. In May 1941 when Hitler invaded, General Bohme issued orders, "Gypsies are to be treated as Jews." Entire families were taken to be murdered at Auschwitz, sterilized, tortured, eliminated by the Nazis.

Macedonia remained under Turkish rule till 1913, the last of the Balkans to be liberated. Now the Turks stay on, clinging to their mosques and bazaar, their cheap wares and mud alleys. We crossed the arched bridge to the new town, recently rebuilt of concrete with a Grand Street, a Grand Square. A road sign, Respect the Limitations, reminded me of the one in Newmarket, Beware Racehorses, and London's Walk Warily. God knows I try to, ready and willing to obey any admonition or exclamation point to take heed and live.

Stobi. Always travel with an historian to see the world, especially lost worlds. On our last day in Macedonia we stopped at a dig, the site of ancient ruins of Stobi, which may be Greek as well as Roman, depending on which archeologist you talk to. In part excavated are the ruins of a Roman city containing a Roman theater, a few colonnades, a few inscriptions, the disturbed dirt of centuries. The place grew stark and forsaken as night came on.

An ardent group of diggers from the University of Texas was spending the summer at Stobi, and we stayed in a little motel at the campsite. They told us they hope to prove what so far is speculation—that Philip of Macedon built a city and lived here as he progressed through Macedonia, king and conqueror. Though slight evidence exists, Alexander may have lived at Stobi as a child, since he was born in 356 b.c. at nearby Pella, where Aristotle came to educate him. The diggers ache to find the hidden story if it is there.

Mount Olympus. I don't know a soul who has slept at the foot of Olympus except the nine Muses, daughters of Zeus by Mnemosyne, with whom, says Hesiod, he spent nine consecutive nights. I didn't sleep.

I spent the night on my moonlit balcony at the Hotel Xenia, after dining not on nectar and ambrosia but mushroom omelet, gazing at the lofty mountain over my head. The ancients believed it touched heaven at the top, but I should think it was heaven itself, home of the gods. Apparently not one foolhardy mortal climbed up to see.

On the border of Greek Macedonia and Thessaly, Olympus rises like a rock, covered with forests and precipices. It looks, I'd say, as Olympus should, lifting through shreds of cloud, the gate of cloud that permitted the gods to descend to earth on mortal business. Like Eden, it was said to be a place of eternal spring, though tonight I could plainly see snow at the peak, sorry to contradict Homer who wrote of the weather of Olympus,

> Eternal of the gods, which never storms
> Disturb, rains drench, or snow invades.

Ted complained he was kept awake all night by braying donkeys, which in our world reside at the foot of Olympus, the only Muses left. But at breakfast a large bee swooped over the Greek honey, and who is to say it wasn't Zeus looking for a pretty girl?

By now, of course, Olympus has been scaled and conquered a number of times. That recklessly romantic traveler Richard Halliburton told in *The Glorious Adventure* how in 1927 he climbed the sacred mountain to the top. Accompanied by a college friend and a shepherd boy named Lazarus, he reached a spire of rock ten thousand feet high, where the fog closed in and forced them to spend a harrowing night clinging to a slender ledge. For presuming to "violate the sanctuary of the immortals," Halliburton wrote, Zeus hurled Olympian thunderbolts at them followed by Olympian winds and drenching rain. They held on till dawn, astonished to be alive. Halliburton postponed his death till twelve years later when he tried to cross the Pacific in a Chinese junk painted red and gold.

The Meteora. Today, as was only fair, we visited the Christian God's heaven, as near as we could get. The Meteora is close enough for me, an unearthly group of rock monasteries in Thessaly. They were erected in a forest of gigantic rock pillars, weird in shape, soaring to heights of 1,800 feet, some thin as needles, some like loaves, some stalagmites—once believed to have been hurled by an angry god but, in fact, formed by the erosive power of the sea. Each rock held a monastery perched at the peak, a refuge for pious hermits who were drawn up in rope baskets, later by means of hinged ladders worked by ropes and windlass.

In the fourteenth century the Meteora ("rocks in midair") were built as hiding places in time of war when the Serbians invaded Thessaly and conquered the Byzantines. They were all but impenetrable. The monk Athanasios with nine brothers founded the highest, the Great Meteoron (Monastery of the Transfiguration). Others followed till, by the sixteenth century, twenty-four monasteries existed, austere retreats for the contemplation of a male heaven. They were completely forbidden to women. If such a creature got herself up that far and dared to beg sanctuary, she was exposed on a ledge to die. The word *woman* was forbidden. The horror of the female sex extended inexorably to female animals—cats, dogs, hens—excluded as unclean.

Remote as the monasteries were, they grew fabulously rich from the world they had renounced and eventually corrupt, falling to decay. Only six survive; of these four are inhabited though they stand nearly empty, and as superstitious relics of the past are very poor. The German occupation of Greece brought them to further desuetude; snow and wind swept the others away. The hermits of the past are gone.

In the 1920s steps were hacked into the rock face so that one no longer clings to a ladder or rides up in a basket. We climbed to St. Barlaam's, perched like an eagle's nest just below the Meteoron. Or, to be accurate, I climbed the 762 stone steps alone to investigate the meaning of a vaguely worded sign at the foot. My fears were quickly confirmed at the door—no, no, no—in pants I could not enter the portal. By that time Betty had walked the quarter mile to the parked Fiat and changed her clothes. With the door slammed in my face, I climbed down in the eighty-degree heat, raced to the Fiat, got a skirt out of my suitcase, wrestled to put it on in the car, and sweating profusely ran back to where Ted and Betty waited halfway up the long ascent. "Where's your veil?" Ted called.

It was worth the struggle for a woman to gain admission, since flesh is still offensive on Meteora; we were suffered to visit by showing as little of it as possible. Two monks were visible, one at prayer in the ornate chapel where olive twigs burned instead of holy candles, and one who passed us with lowered eyes to avoid the painful sight of a female. At the door somebody was selling postcards and souvenirs.

Thermopylae. The pass at Thermopylae once seemed to me no more than a fantasy, a myth, along with such legendary wonders as Olympus, Fujiyama, Queen Nefertiti, and the waterlilies of Monet. It is reassuring to discover they all exist or existed. However, what was once a small mountain pass 4.5 miles long and 8 to 14 yards wide is now a broad public highway. The general location is marked by an inept monument, erected in 1955, of a naked Greek warrior in a helmet poised to hurl a lance so long it could never have cleared the pass or pierced a single Persian. But the real shock, on rereading Herodotus, was to find the staggering figures the great historian used to prove the courage of a few brave Greeks against an army of millions. If his numbers were accurate, the Persians crammed into the pass must have tumbled over, squeezed each other to death without help from the three hundred Spartans. Xerxes brought a mighty host, says Herodotus—who was a boy when the invasion of Greece began—with 1,700,000 fighting men, 80,000 cavalry, 1,207 ships, 20,000 men in charge of camels and chariots, though as Herodotus gets carried away these figures increase alarmingly. Sir Thomas Browne noted that he "besprinkled his work with many fabulosities."

Well, the cavalry, camels, ships, and chariots can be eliminated from the battle. But the Persian foot soldiers, who supposedly shot so many arrows they obscured the sun and a Spartan said, "Then we can fight in the shade," were called by Herodotus uncountable, "multitudes without number" slain in the pass. You can't trust anything you read, even by the father of history, who did say, "I am bound to repeat what is currently said; I am not bound to believe it."

Edward Lear visited Thermopylae during his wanderings in Greece. A limerick came of it, which differs from Herodotus' account but may be the way Lear visualized the battle:

> There was an old man of Thermopylae
> Who never did anything properly.
> But they said, "If you choose
> To boil eggs in your shoes
> You shall never remain in Thermopylae."

Athens. Ted says Athens is becoming another Miami Beach. And I say, never go back. B. and I were here nine years ago—a time not to be lived twice. When we stopped at Delphi yesterday, I asked again, as one does, help from the Delphic Oracle. Since the answer is always a riddle, it hardly matters how often one asks. At the Castalian spring, where again I lay flat on my belly to drink the water of inspiration, an excited Frenchman tried to stop me, shouting I would poison myself. "Defense de boire!" he cried. He was probably right. Such water is drunk nowadays at your own risk, though eighteen centuries ago Pausanias called it delicious.

Athens is crowded, screeching with traffic. Is it a sign of the times that the worry beads sold everywhere are enormous, the size of hen's eggs? The shops, full of tourist tawdry, feature this year a bronze statue of the naked foot soldier of Thermopylae. Nine years ago it was the mask of Agamemnon. At the Acropolis the final destroyer will be ourselves, the tourists, crumbling the stones under millions of trampling feet.

So the circle comes full round. As Betty and I sat in Constitution Square late this afternoon drinking tea, another newsboy passed waving a paper to tell the tragic news of the world. We stopped him and read the headline: "Duke of Windsor Dead." This was the last day of our journey together, for tomorrow we must part—Betty and Ted to fly to Crete, I to fly on to Zurich alone.

The king is dead. We had followed him, Edward VIII, Defender of the Faith, and Mrs. Simpson down the Dalmatian coast to Greece, and now the story of his thirty-five-year exile with her was faded and fabulous. The long day's journey had ended for him. For us it was the end of May, and it was time to go.

June

Olympic Airlines took me over the Alps this morning after a frisking at the Athens airport by a silent muscular woman wearing plastic gloves, who ran her hands down my body in search of hidden bombs. As I emerged from customs at Zurich, six Bevingtons appeared, Sarah at past two wearing one of Kate's dresses that reached her toes and turned her into a Medici princess besmeared with Swiss chocolate; Stephen ten and Philip nine with hair to their shoulders like boy angels; Kate at seven whispering, "Love you, love you," to be sure I knew. David on leave from the University of Chicago has brought his family to the land of the Bodensee, the lower Rhine, where, far from willing to spend a holiday merely enjoying himself, he enrolled in the Goethe Institute at Radolfzell, working ten hours a day on his German. Today was Corpus Christi, when everybody takes a holiday and goes around saying, "Grüss Gott."

In the new Mercedes we drove the forty miles from Zurich, while all six talked at once to describe our super living quarters. They sounded formidable. As we reached the frontier between Switzerland and Germany, stopping for customs, the German guards rushed out to greet us wreathed in smiles. We were home. The house David had rented sat so squarely on the frontier that once we reached the front door we were inside Germany. In the garden we were back in Switzerland, the sheep in the meadow were Swiss sheep, the guards opposite the house were Swiss guards. By crossing the road we changed countries, with a white horizontal line to say so.

Herr Wenz, a retired German dentist, lives with a Swiss wife on the first floor of the stucco house straddling two nations, posted with an official sign in German ordering anyone entering or leaving the premises to report to customs. David and Peggy have the second floor, I have the third with a balcony looking over the treetops to the Rhine. The three rooms, a featherbed, and a bookcase of *Das Beste aus Reader's Digest*, cost me ten dollars a day, and I want to stay forever, this time I mean forever.

It's not a journey but a sauntering. The thing to remember is which country I'm in and carry my passport for a stroll in the fields. Each morning the family emerges, except David off at school, and by turning left to Switzerland walks down the country road a kilometer to the village of Stein am Rhein. We're allowed the equivalent of three dollars a person to bring food and drink into Germany free of customs, though the guards are too polite to examine our purchases, much as they love to hear Peggy explain her possession of six boxes of cornflakes. Or by turning right on alternate mornings, where the sign says *Bundesrepublik Deutschland*, we cover the same distance in Germany to reach the still smaller town of Öhningen, where the meat is better.

Like any good hausfrau, Peggy and I shop every day in sunshine and downpour. We come home to eat enormous meals of good lentil soup, good German bread bought in Switzerland, good Swiss cheese bought in Germany, good sparkling Rhine wine from either country. We come home through fields of barley, stopping to listen to a cuckoo and the distant churchbells, lingering a last moment in Switzerland to look in on Herr Zimmermann, our nearest neighbor, who is an entrepreneur of prodigious zeal—the owner of the seventeen bleating sheep, of a hotel that by various signs he calls *Gasthof Fremdenzimmer, Gasthof zum Grenzstein, Lebensmitteln,* and Hotel, of a general store, a souvenir shop full of cuckoo clocks, a Gulf gas station, a camping ground, and a pay swing that we use free by simply pushing it around. Herr Zimmermann is a stout waddling man whom nobody loves because he is cross and greedy and his sheep get into Frau Wenz's garden. When I report to the *Zoll* our intention of crossing the road and leaving the country, "Wir gehen nach Herrn Zimmermann," the German guards laugh so loud I fear I am saying we are going *after* old Zimmermann, as anyone would be justified in doing with a shotgun.

It's uncertain what Frau Wenz thinks of me. She is fond of Peggy, who speaks German with endearing courage and manages our communications. To me Frau Wenz says nothing. She is a shy woman, plain and angular, a meticulous housekeeper, younger than her gorgeous husband whose manners are impeccable, who wears a hairnet to keep his coiffeur smooth. Soon after I arrived, the Wenzes climbed the stairs to pay a courtesy call. I greeted them in French, which Frau Wenz is said to speak, but when she paused at the door embarrassed, I shifted to German. "Setzen Sie!" I commanded, as if to a dog. At that they looked startled and shook their heads, declining to sit. Frau Wenz gave the signal, they bowed and left with polite murmurs from Herr Wenz, a nervous glance round at my housekeeping from the Frau.

Stein am Rhein is a medieval storybook town, its balconied houses adorned with mottoes, the owner's coat of arms, painted frescoes of goddesses, battle scenes, a cow, a sunbeam. The motto on one house goes like this—I think from Gottfried Keller—"Whatever the eyelashes will take in, hold on to that much from the golden overflow of the world." On the hilltop above the village rises the Schloss Hohenklingen of the eleventh century, with a cannon aimed at the countryside. At night when the castle of Hohenklingen is floodlit like the Parthenon and I get out of bed to gaze at it against the sky, I look down at the border police to be sure they're there—the Swiss in their capes, who glance up and call softly, "Gute nacht," the Germans a few yards away watching over us with no threat of gunfire. I go back to bed and try to think of a plot for a spy story involving this house, where *die Mutter* is never questioned but is allowed to come and go, carrying secret messages to both sides.

Radolfzell is a large German town, to which David drives the fifteen miles to the Goethe Institute. He is the only college professor in his German class, the only American among Turks, Frenchmen, Orientals, and opera singers. The teaching is stereotyped, with homework and scoldings by Frau Schultz, but David revels in learning grammar. On Wednesdays, market day, we drive him to school while we explore the flower and vegetable carts, greeted by nodding farmers and their beamy wives. After that we seek out the public garden with a German lion boldly outlined in petunias, a tall live stork walking about in lordly indifference. We sit in the grandstand and watch David, the top of whose head we can see in his classroom, waiting for him to emerge at noon. The students are fascinated by David's raggletaggle family that rushes to embrace him. One student broke the strict rule of the school by addressing me in English: "Good day, madam. How goes it?" "Fine, danke sehr," I said, avoiding Frau Schultz's cold eye.

One night the Goethe Institute sponsored a program of Mozart at the Gymnasium. David sang Mozart canons with a Turkish soprano, a Chinese mezzo, and a French operatic baritone. He had to strain his bass voice because the arrogant Turk pitched the songs too high. David said, "I have never met a Turkish soprano I could love," though his encounters admittedly have been few. We six sat down in front, where Sarah promptly squalled and had to be carried out. She missed hearing Herr Reimann, the little music teacher, fat and short of breath, who played a Mozart solo for the bassoon that was hysterical. His wife, Frau Reimann, a stately woman with a head cold, played a Mozart solo for the flute and fluffed all the high notes. It was so funny I wept into my handkerchief, while the audience went mad, deafening with huzzas and bravos.

On these days of summer we hunted for rhinestones on the beach or took boat rides up and down the Rhine on the river steamer *Stein am Rhein*, which flies a Swiss flag, plying back and forth between Switzerland and Germany, zigzagging from shore to shore. Downstream to Lake Constance (the Bodensee), the prettiest town we passed was Gottlieben, which once proved its love of God by imprisoning John Huss in the Dominican monastery. Each waterfront had a clock tower, swans, flowers, a thin church spire, and tranquility. About noon we reached Constance—in Germany with a Swiss suburb Kreuzlingen—a pleasant city of towers where we ate bratwurst in buns beside the lake, then dutifully visited the cathedral, in which John Huss was condemned to death in 1415. The children, unaccustomed to churches, whispered in awe and respect. Sarah whispered like a steam kettle.

But Sarah's patience with churches had its limits. On another Rhine trip to the island of Reichenau, which is one great garden three miles long (imagine *acres* of green parsley) where the Benedictine monks of Charlemagne's time became such expert gardeners that ever since the populace has followed suit—here at Reichenau we made the tactical error of visiting two churches out of a possible three. At the abbey church of the Mittelzell we ran into mutiny.

In the nave before the glittering baroque altar, Sarah burst into fury and started pummeling Kate, shouting "You dammit it, Katie!" till we dragged her down the aisle shrieking and kicking, to the older children's joy. The more they smothered their laughter to hear her raising the roof at Reichenau, the louder she howled. Once outside the door they said, "Now Sarah will be damned by God." But Sarah was in fine fettle. She had got us out of there, my pussycat, *meine Schnuckiputz*.

"Sometimes people feel sad," said Peggy.

"Why?" asked Sarah.

Twice a Rhine boat took us in the opposite direction to Schaffhausen, past trim Swiss villages and woods of jackdaws, till—would you believe it?—just below Schaffhausen we reached the Rhinefall, the roaring Niagara of Europe, one of the great waterfalls of the world. We had disembarked first. Thousands of years ago the Rhine was blocked by a reef and ever since has seethed and plunged in torrents and giant roars. To show David its magnitude, on Sunday we badgered him into going and went again. I am proud to say he behaved better than Wordsworth, who on a walking tour in Europe in 1790 came to Schaffhausen to view the Rhinefall and wrote, "I must confess I was disappointed in it. I had raised my ideas too high." This was the poet who in "The Thorn" carefully measured a mud puddle: "'Tis three feet long, and two feet wide." On reaching home David announced he had lost his passport down the waterfall. Life stops here without a passport. His cries alerted the border guards of both nations, the Wenzes, Herr Zimmermann, the whole Swiss canton. Then he found it in his coat sleeve and we lived again.

Our last journey was to the country of Liechtenstein. To prepare for it, Peggy and I consulted the travel agent in Öhningen, though why a hamlet with a public well needed one I don't know, except that the Germans are a thorough people. His office was open an hour a day, to which nobody came but us, whom he greeted with a brisk determination to send somewhere. Ach no! he exclaimed in annoyance, he had no information about Liechtenstein. Nobody went there. Where would we care to be directed? Spain? Costa Rica? the States? I murmured I had already been to America, in fact lived there.

"Ja?" he inquired, then corrected my pronunciation, mocking my accent. "Nein, nicht North Carolina. Das ist North Caroleena."

It's a miracle we got to Liechtenstein, since David chose to drive first to Säntis, a Swiss Alp dear to professional skiers. While the three older children climbed with David to the snowline and skied down the slope on the seat of their pants, Peggy and I walked with Sarah high in the Alpine meadows covered with cinquefoil and strawberry blossoms. We had been to Säntis before and went again because, David says, he doesn't like to travel, he likes to *return*. I, on the contrary, want to go to the world's end; that's why I read atlases whereas David avoids at any cost attending a travelogue, mine in particular.

Where was Liechtenstein? After hours of dawdling we drove from Säntis in search of a picnic place, which eventually we found in a farmer's field far above what might or might not be Liechtenstein. From the map you couldn't tell. We ate our lunch listening to cowbells, then lay back in the tall grass where David seemed not only content but determined to spend the rest of the afternoon. At least we had come close.

Liechtenstein, the smallest independent state in Europe, was purchased 250 years ago by a wealthy Austrian prince for his own principality. On the right bank of the Rhine nestled between Switzerland and Austria, it is microscopic, a mere twelve miles long. With no frontier to stop us, we were in the middle of the realm before realizing we had arrived. On the one main street rose the single landmark, the spectacular seven-hundred-year-old Castle of Vaduz, occupied by His Serene Highness Franz Joseph II, the constitutional monarch of some 20,000 people. As we slowed down to look, Sarah started to bawl, convinced we were about to visit another church. With her remarkable instinct for self-preservation, she howled louder each time we paused to admire the castle perched like a fortress against the Alpine sky, never stopping for breath till we reached the frontier of Austria. I'm not sure I saw one Liechtensteiner, but I envy him his luck in claiming a country of no poverty, crime, unemployment, race problems, taxes, nightclubs, or a standing army. On the other hand, the women have no vote, and its main industry is the sale of postage stamps.

David agreed it was a splendid excursion, well worth the frustrations of travel. He made clearer to me Steinbeck's puzzling remark: "People do not take trips. Trips take people."

That was the happy life it was, till one day I had to leave them and go home. When they asked which pleasure I put first during the month of wandering about the Bodensee, I said, "Living in this house with you." No doubt about it. *Alles gute.*

So I lost the dear ones where I had found them in the Zurich airport and crossed the Atlantic by Swissair. At home my house had taken care of itself, intact after being abandoned, no emptier than usual. I love my house, it is not to be blamed. I am with myself again, aware that the longest journey is from room to room, from night to morning.

July

I endorse entries. After two months of travel, entries about what? Travel:

1. "Let us not forget that the world makes no sense."—Jules Renard
2. Pike never climbed his Peak.
3. "When in Rome, do as the Greeks."—Kenneth Burke
   "When in Rome, do as you done in Milledgeville."—Flannery O'Connor of Milledgeville, Georgia

4. "I have no antipathy, or rather idiosyncrasie, in dyet, humour, ayre, any thing; I wonder not at the French, for their dishes of frogges, snailes, and toadstooles, nor at the Jewes for locusts and grasshoppers . . . I feel not in my self those common antipathies that I can discover in others."—Sir Thomas Browne, *Religio Medici*
5. "The influence of the moon was believed to produce wandering of two kinds: travel and lunacy."—C. S. Lewis

Travel hints: Learn alphabets, at least Greek and Cyrillic.
     Try at all times to be punctual, good-tempered, healthy.
     If possible, cultivate a sense of direction.
     Don't struggle or trample people.

August

I've rented a white farmhouse on Stumpville Road near Jefferson, Ohio, where of all the world I want to be. Peggy and David are back from Germany, living with their children in a yellow house for the rest of the summer, and I'm in the white house beyond the pond. David works tirelessly on the text of Shakespeare he is editing.

The events are small but dramatic. Sarah peed in my tennis shoe this morning, and when I put it in the sun to dry a yellow butterfly settled inside. I'm trying to write a *Grosstochterlied*, a song in praise of grand-daughters. There are three tamarack trees at the farm. Frau Wenz had them in the Öhningen garden.

Sister Kate

She has two brothers, slightly older,
And a sister Sarah, nearly three.
With boys she's brave as nails to climb trees,
Make tigers tame, or bait a fishhook
To catch leviathans for supper.
She rides with centaurs, runs with lemmings,
And walks with unicorns, her weapon
Against alarm or armadillos
(Or her two brothers, slightly older)
Being a piercing scream the like of
Which not this side of hell's own gate
Is screamed except by Sister Kate.

And yet with Sarah, nearly three,
Kate's putty in her hands. Together
They play Rapunzel or Godiva,
Two Hecates, two hobbyhorses,
Two Princes in the Tower, whatever,
Till Sarah starts to scream—from boredom,
For mastery, for the joy of screaming—
And pummeling, scratching, howling, brawling,
"Damn you!" she falls upon her sister,
Who laughs out loud and hugs the roarer.
"I love you," Kate says, kissing Sarah.
"O.K.?" And Sarah answers, "Yeah."

September

Phyllis McGinley and I began a correspondence a dozen years ago when she wrote about a book of mine and, with each book, kept on doing so. She telephoned my editors and hectored them into thinking well of me. Through the years she sent words of love, encouragement, faith, and I sent them to her in praise of her lightness of heart and deftness of verse—though we have never met.

Now in September comes a terrified cry. Her husband died in the spring, and like me she is alone. As I did, she asks how to go on living. "Can it be done? Does time really lessen grief? Tell me how to get back to writing." In her panic she signs herself, "Despartely yours, Phyllis."

I dash off a four-page letter of false report, as if I were an authority on solitude. Yes, time conquers grief. Yes, you write to save the pieces. You sit down and make a new start each day. Yes, it is a way of life. Yes, it is a solution.

October

The Colosseum in Rome is falling down, falling down. The Acropolis is corroding from air pollution. The Sphinx at Giza is crumbling, losing stones from her left rear leg. Venice is slipping into the sea. The Tower of Pisa is in the news again, sinking fast these days, inclining toward its destruction.

In 1950, when B. and I climbed the spiral staircase to the top of Pisa, reeling about inside the bell tower, it was sixteen feet off center. Now they say it tips at seventeen feet, leaning a little more each year in the Square of Miracles. Chaucer was a small boy when the lovely marble campanile was completed in 1350, though in the relaxed manner of the Middle Ages it took so long abuilding, 178 years, that it leaned four feet, four inches at the grand opening. Travelers believed the tilt was intentional. Galileo climbed up to lean from the leaning tower, absorbed in the meaning of gravity.

One day it will collapse and crash and become a legend. I am ready to topple myself, keeping a precarious balance. So was Mark Twain, who climbed the tower in 1867—only thirteen feet off center then—and confessed how scared he was. It made his flesh creep.

The Leaning Lady

To climb the Leaning Tower like Galileo,
I left the perpendicular at Pisa
And, veering to diagonal, barely made it
Up to the turret of the seven bells—
Where at the top leaned one Italian woman
Alone in splendor, beaming at Tuscany
Below and the far distant Apennines.
Her face was drowned in sweat. She panted hard
After the struggle up the *torre pendente*,
For, being pregnant as she plainly was,
Her own small center of gravity askew,
She leaned obliquely, very like the tower
(Now seventeen feet off center and still slipping)
But backward, in the opposite direction.
The way they slanted really staggered me,
Yet I felt proud of her and that triumphant
Climb in the golden steps of Galileo.
She would get down all right. And so would I.

November

V. S. Pritchett, in his autobiography *Midnight Oil*, says he is not a natural diarist because he lacks "the secretive, snaillike temperament." I used to know Mr. Pritchett in London, a hearty downright Britisher with a booming voice who spoke his mind, and wrote his memoirs, expecting to be heard. He didn't remind me of a snail, but I can't think of a diarist who does either.

[October, 1973. Günter Grass has just published *From the Diary of a Snail*.]

Diarists may be secret but they're far from secretive, their habit being to show and tell, keep tabs on life. Jules Renard said of his diary it must serve to mold his character and straighten it out. "Ah, the way life steps on one's toes!"

John Manningham kept a diary on 6" × 4" pages for only two years when he was a young law student in London, 1602 and 1603. But as he jotted down the day's small events, Raleigh and Bacon passed by on the street. He knew Ben Jonson who, Manningham said, "scornes the world." He had time to record John Donne's scandalous elopement with Anne More ("Donne is undonne") and the death of Queen Elizabeth: "hir Majesty departed this lyfe mildly like a lambe, easily like a ripe apple from the tree."

December

In the last meeting for the term before Christmas, my poetry seminar turned into a session as joyous as it was educational.

The group arrived in festive humor, hiding behind their backs not books but bottles—four bottles of sherry. We didn't drink four, since one proved sufficient, but they meant to be hospitable, unsure of our capacity. We had forthwith a sherry party and read a poem of Robert Lowell's, whose confessions became as the hour progressed less and less sobering.

"My mind's not right," he said in "Skunk Hour." With that the students laughed, not at Lowell whom they like as a splendid poet, not at all, but at the reeling of their own minds. When I sang for them "Love, oh love, oh careless love," they nearly fell out of their seats. And so did I. In a choked soprano I gave them the old sweet song Lowell was listening to on the car radios one summer night in Castine, Maine, when he peeked into cars to spy on lovers by moonlight.

By the time he got to the skunks marching past the Trinitarian Church, reminding him how the world reeks of skunk, we were red in the face, wiping our eyes at that ceremonial parade. "I've never enjoyed a poem so much in my life," a student said, completely swept away.

I suppose a poet might consider, no matter how satanic his mood, the chance that his readers are in the midst of light refreshments, and accept them as celebrants.

E. B. White, who lives within spitting distance of Lowell's Castine, Maine, near Penobscot Bay, reports differently the available attractions and has nothing against skunks. Says he had one that lived under the garage. Marianne Moore goes further, calling skunks noble little warriors, sweet-faced little wood-weasels, nicer than people. "Only / Wood-weasels shall associate with me."

1973

January

I began the new year with a resolution to give up teaching, a warmed-over resolve served each year and put back in the icebox. This morning I came into my office where the students who are risking a poetry course for the spring term were gathered around the big table. What did I find for an opener? "Hello, girls," I said. They looked at me in blank astonishment.

"No way, ma'am," spoke up the one with long curls and a round face. "I'm Robert."

"Fred here," said the one at the far end, whose hair was lank and lengthy.

How could I tell? After these years I'm still unable to distinguish prose from verse, him from her. (Colette: "What can be more normal than to quake in the presence of the young?")

January 27, 7:00 p.m. The cease-fire exists. Our "military intervention" in Vietnam that lasted eight years is over. If it's peace, it's an uncertain peace, bringing a dull feeling of relief, a fear of rejoicing too soon. The words on the evening news were guarded: "It now appears the war may have ended." We used every weapon on them but a nuclear bomb, and we lost. The slough of Despond is very cold this time of year.

February

A review I'm writing of Louis Simpson's autobiography, *North of Jamaica*, is giving me a bad time, much as I like people who write about themselves.

Louis Simpson is a poet who smolders a lot. As poet he tells the story of his life, saying, "People who have no poetry in them never manage to see life as it is." He speaks in many voices, as Eliot claims poets do, each voice separate but clear. Except for the voice of love, which is missing.

His voices express strong opinions, measuring experience from child to man: his parents' divorce, the discovery he was a Jew, the mental breakdown after the Second World War, the years of teaching at the University of California, his decision to be a poet. He sounds sure of his answers. "The secret of living well," he says, "is to treat other people decently, that's all. It was a secret my father never learned, and all my life I have been trying to learn it." He doesn't say the secret of living well is also to love other people. I think it is. I think the theme of poetry is love.

In passing, Louis Simpson mentions a wife and child without giving either one a name or the child a sex. He drops them altogether, and there is no reading between the lines. So far as women are concerned, he explains why: "As Tolstoy said, I will tell what I think about women when my coffin is open and I can jump in and slam it shut." If one stops to consider how intimately we know what Tolstoy thought of his wife—how revealing it is to know—the quotation sounds comical. Anyway, Tolstoy wasn't a poet.

I'm not asking much, just proof of the existence of love.

A week before Tolstoy married Sophia in 1862, he brought his voluminous diaries for her to read—as his character Levin does in *Anna Karenina*—that she might learn the details of his dissolute life: his love affairs with married women, habitual lechery, drunkenness, infatuation with tarts, resort to his own serf girls, his bastard child, his venereal disease. Sophia was not yet eighteen, innocent and horrified. "They upset me very much. He shouldn't have done it; it made me cry as I looked into his past."

In resentment and revenge, she adopted his habit and let him read her diary, into which during their long married life she poured her hysterical rages, suspicions, bitter jealousy. Sometimes a note of protest on the margin would be in his handwriting. Each read every word the other wrote, though for thirteen years Tolstoy discontinued his diary to avoid the punishing entries, the scenes of endless discord. At one time each kept two diaries.

She would write in tears, "It is terrible to live with him." "His diaries only deepen my despair." "At his wish I have been pregnant sixteen times."

March

Robert Graves, still at it, has published *Poems* 1970–72, written between his seventy-fifth and seventy-seventh year. He is a great-grandfather, confident of his role, perfectly sure that love is his theme and his due. He expects to be adored. Stephen Spender says in a review, "There is still no doubt in his own mind that he is loved, fallen for."

Regrettably, in Graves' cocky opinion women don't hold up as well. You don't find sexy Picassos among them at ninety. They don't grow into lovable, ageless poets like him. In "Age Gap," he writes: "Boys never fall in love with great-grandmothers."

It must be nice to be irresistibly male. William Carlos Williams felt younger every year, more sex-appealing, as he told Robert Lowell:

> I am sixty-seven, and more attractive
> To girls than when I was seventeen.

Do you want to bet?

April

Friday, April 13. This morning a special-delivery truck drew up to the door. The entire truckload was for me, from the *Times Book Review,* thirty-eight garden books. I lined them up on the floor of my study. If they were sex books I could open a bookstore out here on Guess Road. Nobody in this countryside wants to read garden books; they know how to already.

These were How-To books (how to enjoy your weeds, how to grow waterlilies—first you dig a pond), books on organic gardening, bugs of distinction, trees with character, compost with a difference, 25,000 types of orchids, perspectives and retrospectives on pruning, herbs, hanging plants, lawns and landscapes—everything I know nothing about. The *Times* went to all this trouble to uncover my ignorance as a common garden variety of reader. I counted them over and walked away. You can't scare me on Friday the thirteenth.

Saturday, April 14. A letter from Charles Simmons, one of the editors, tells me not to worry. Ignore these books at your pleasure, he says, "Talk about other books, in or out of print, classic or unknown. Talk about anything you like, so long as it concerns gardening. What we want really is an essay on the activity itself. Looseness is all." Looseness is what he will get.

Apparently one book got tucked inside another, raising the total to thirty-nine books. I must start to dig and delve. Let's see, what is mulching?

Monday, April 16. The *Times* grows uneasy over this business. Now Raymond Walters writes, referring to my gardening "hobby" (which I have not got). His message is don't worry. What they want is an essay, not a review clogged with book titles. I have decided not to worry. Ignorance is all.

Tuesday, April 17. Book #40 arrived today, *Talk to Your Plants.* I have two houseplants, an aged philodendron and a begonia that has had it. We have a good deal in common; talking to them about Medicare might discourage us even further. My spring garden is full of chickweed. The six pots of herbs I received for my birthday molded and died.

May

The only gardeners I know are Virgil, Thoreau with his nine bean rows, and Mr. White of Selborne. Having read these forty gardening books, living the horticultural life till mayflies flew out of my head, I've turned to Erasmus' *The Praise of Folly.* Folly is a female like me ("I am she—the only she, I may say—whose divine influence makes gods and men rejoice"). She sounds unrepentant. Come to think of it, Sin is a woman, unless you mean Original Sin, and Nature is a woman. Erasmus calls her Stepmother Nature. She is responsible for breeding gardeners, who write garden books instead of books on How-To save the human race.

And I'm reading for respite the *Analects* of Confucius, who so far as I know ignored gardening and sat indoors all day on a mat to talk about humanity. He was a Man of Virtue 2,500 years ago but no rousing conversationalist.

Confucius was a fussy man who wouldn't sit on his mat unless it was straight, required ginger with every meal, and didn't converse while eating or talk in bed. On a sudden clap of thunder his countenance changed. He sang to the lute and was capable of tears.

Withal he taught the simple things, sincerity and modesty, scorning pretense. "When you see an admirable person, try to emulate him. When you see one who is not, turn and examine yourself." Asked what virtue is, Confucius said, "It is to love men." He added, "Wisdom is to understand them."

June

We are over our heads in the Watergate hearings, the melodrama of the century. The Senate Committee headed by rotund old Sam Ervin, senator from North Carolina, listens bemused as the revelations unfold, while the rest of us sit at the television screen absorbing the scandal. I saw a slogan today pasted on a mailbox, Impeach Nixon. It was like Mail Early, a directive to the people.

John Dean in five days of testimony implicates Nixon in the Watergate break-in, which occurred a year ago, June 17, 1972, and the subsequent frenzied attempts at cover-up. Dean says the truth always comes out in the end; we may have to wait but truth prevails. I don't believe that.

[Dean was right: twenty-five of the Watergate figures went to prison, all but Nixon, who was pardoned.]

The language of the hearings is as appalling as the testimony. These are lawyers, who use jargon as if taught it in school. Nobody would be caught saying "before"; it has to be "prior to." They say "at this point in time" (meaning now), "time frame," "in this context," "in this area." They speak of a political posture or dialogue or episode, the thrust of the problem, the frame of reference. Everything is structured, indicated, inoperative, or finalized. Words are used for hedging, blurring, blunting, avoiding direct statement, less by John Dean than by others like Jeb Stuart Magruder with his proud name.

July

Never go back: if landscapes do not change
Then the familiar will but seem more strange.
—Robert Hillyer

But I always return to Paris, taking my selves along—past self, customary self, the self I never had. B. and I stayed at no fancy hotel like the Hotel Lutétia on the Boulevard Raspail, yet here we are, Betty, Ted, and I. By presenting myself to the desk clerk according to plan as one tottering on the verge of claustrophobia, I was courteously moved from a boxed-in closet to a sunny room in pink Regency style with a view of the

Au Bon Marché department store. This formula, so far infallible, I learned from a hairdresser in London, who said as I sat perched on the edge of my chair, "Only a fool is uncomfortable."

One can't call Paris unchanged or, perhaps, be dismayed at the changes. Charlemagne still sits his horse at Notre Dame, there are the chestnut trees. But as we walked about Montparnasse and the Boulevard St. Germain, past the Deux Magots, the Café Flore, now tourist traps, I stopped short before an enormous poster covering a brick wall, *Les Temps Sont Difficiles*. And I thought, keep this straight in your head: you may return many times but you can never go *back*. In Montmartre the old Moulin Rouge was gone. Incredibly, the roofs of Paris were no longer Renoir blue from the heights of Sacré Coeur. Place Pigalle swarmed with sex shops, voyeur palaces, total nudity (*nues integrals*), pictures of copulating couples—all of which appeared to bore the passing crowd, shabbily dressed and uninflamed. Montmartre has long supported vice, but this was ridiculous. We sat for a while at an outdoor café, without being mistaken for habitués or deviants.

And I dreamed of Paris as B. and I saw it for the first time, of the Folies Bergère with its daring nudity, where a fully dressed showgirl would trip across the stage, pause, and slyly opening her blouse reveal one bare breast. In a moment she would return from the wings, hastening along in the opposite direction, and again she would stop and expose one bare breast, causing the bug-eyed comedian in a state of shock to hold up two fingers and exclaim, "Elle a deux!"

Yet I love Paris—who doesn't? It takes talent to find peace, but there are ways. Ted's way is to visit Sainte-Chapelle, built by Saint Louis in the thirteenth century, with a lower chapel for servants (less worthy in God's eye) and the upper chapel fit for royalty where the sun on walls of stained glass blazes straight from heaven.

My way is to look at Monet's waterlilies. On the first floor of the Orangerie in the garden of the Tuileries was a temporary exhibition of Soutine, whose convulsive pictures scream the message that the world of cruelty and terror is not only awry but about to explode. Red is his color like a burning. Red dominates the distorted landscapes, the twisted, hurt faces. A scene of tilted houses and uprooted trees on a hilltop appears half blown away. A dog with entrails gaping is held open by two forks. (Wright Morris: "Soutine has painted a strung-up plucked rooster as if it had been lynched.") A bloody putrid side of beef that hangs dripping resembles the fearful carnage of war. He used to install a carcass of beef in his studio and pour buckets of blood on it, till the stench brought the police. I wouldn't live with a Soutine in the house. He is unforgiving. He makes one cry, "Stop it! Let go!"

Down the steps where we went reeling from the turbulence, Monet's *Nymphéas* told us all was well, to be still and comforted. André Masson called it the Sistine Chapel of Impressionism. In the two large oval rooms are the blues of serenity. And such stillness. Eight panels set in the wall make a band of water with no beginning or end, a blue mirror reflecting sky through patches of waterlilies. Monet painted them in old age in his garden at Giverny, over and over some two hundred times—the changing light and the waterlilies. They gave him no peace. They were a torment, an obsession that maddened him with a sense of failure. In a black mood he would drive his foot through a canvas or slash it with a penknife (Soutine too stabbed his paintings). Monet wrote of burning six canvases along with the dead autumn leaves. "Life is a silly affair," he said. He hated his moods and the black night of death that hurried him on.

Clemenceau, his friend for many years, obtained the waterlilies for France lest he destroy them all. Before his death in 1926 Monet said, "What do you think of them? Moi, je ne sais pas. I no longer sleep because of them. It is enough to make one give up hope. . . . Tomorrow, perhaps."

It's hard to believe Monet and Rodin exhibited together in 1889. Rodin is the puzzle of Paris to me. When I first saw the Musée Rodin he appeared vulgar and absurd, swayed as I was by the reputation he had as an inferior sculptor, a sentimentalist who made marble pant and shriek. Edmond de Goncourt said the amorous embraces of his figures (*The Kiss*) were like the writhings of earthworms. His merit is clearer to the experts now. Kenneth Clark calls Rodin's Balzac the greatest piece of sculpture since Michelangelo. Balzac died in 1850 when Rodin was ten years old, yet he made seven models of the writer naked, after getting the exact measurements of his fat, squat body from his tailor. Rodin delivered the finished statue wearing a friar's robe to the Société des Hommes de Lettres—which had commissioned it six years before—only to be told he had insulted France, that no actual body could be conceived under such draperies. Rodin politely withdrew the statue. My choice among the working models is the comic potbellied Balzac, standing naked with widespread legs in the museum.

Another charmer is the bust of Mrs. Potter Palmer (the Mrs. Astor of Chicago society) partly emerging with bare shoulders and a pompadour from a slab of rough marble. She looks stuck, as if her plump bosom held her fast and Rodin had backed off with a shrug and walked away. Most appealing is *The Centauress*, a lady centaur with her beautiful breasts and lovely lifted face, all horse beneath. I never think of centaurs as being female, but why not? when Lear said of them

> Down from the waist they are Centaurs
> Though women all above:
> But to the girdle do the gods inherit,
> Beneath is all the fiends'.

Centaurs supposedly dwelt, lustful and savage, in Thessaly among the Greeks, yet the Roman poet Lucretius doubted they ever existed. The horse would be in its prime, full-grown, by the time the child was three. The horse would wither and die fifty years before the man.

Pliny says he saw one embalmed in honey.

August

Last summer as a Rhine maiden I saw enough of the river to want to follow the 820-mile length of it. After that I'd like to spend the rest of my life riding up and down the rivers of the world: the Nile, longest at 4,132 miles, the Amazon 4,000 miles of anacondas and piranhas, the Congo, the Limpopo River all set about with fever trees. I was born on the Susquehanna, a modest stream half the length of the Rhine, B. was born on the Ohio, my sons on the Hudson at 168th Street, Manhattan. Most people are river-minded. "The river is within us, the sea is all about us," said Eliot. Like our bloodstream, its rhythm is our own, a river flowing in our veins till it reaches the sea of time and eternity.

With this more or less in mind, Betty, Ted, and I drove from Paris across France to Basel, where this evening we went aboard the Rhine boat the *Nederland* for a cruise down the Rhine. I wanted to start at Schaffhausen where I left off last year, but the roaring Rhinefall isn't very navigable. The *Nederland* is a luxury liner, narrow since the river is narrow. You can nearly touch either bank, where placid folk are fishing, swans dive, dark woods lead to the Black Forest. Our cabins on the main deck have, instead of a porthole, a picture window.

I soon found out why we are going down the Rhine though headed straight toward the North Sea: the Rhine flows north but downhill. This morning I woke to find a man squatting on the dock gazing with flattering lust into my face as we disappeared from sight thirty feet down a lock. It's clear too why the ship pokes along, stopping to allow us to go ashore, tying up at a dock for the night. It will take some clever dawdling to keep us afloat for five days rather than dump us into the North Sea. At Strasbourg we went by coach to admire the pink cathedral and buy pâté de foie gras, then docked for the night at Speyer that the English stubbornly call Spires. In fair weather we stepped into a coach for Heidelberg, the old university town about which the myths are true: it has a Philosophers' Walk of one mile (how many miles to make a philosopher?), and the Sigmund Romberg operetta *The Student Prince* was written by a real student prince, who loved the landlady's daughter but left Heidelberg to marry a princess. Twenty miles away our boat waited at Worms, where in the *Nibelungenlied* Siegfried is conveniently buried in the Worms Cathedral and Siegfried's gold treasure in the Rhine. Liebfraumilch is made from the vineyards of the Gothic church of Liebfrauen. Our Lady's Milk comes from Worms.

One night we spent dancing at Rüdesheim, in the wine district of the Rheingau, where the best Rhine wine is the Rüdesheimer. Straight as a thrush flies, we flew to the Drosselgasse (Thrush Lane), a single path lined on both sides with several dozen taverns, scrubbed and identical. The one we fancied was open to the sky with red tablecloths. The musicians were a Dutch go-go group obligingly blaring out what the patrons wanted, "The Beer Barrel Polka." Whole families crowded in, dancing, hollering, drinking the cold white wine. Nobody was allowed to sit still and watch—why were you there unless to have a fling? As their ancestors had, the Germans flocked to Rüdesheim for a rowdy night of it. And I was as German as anybody.

Heinrich Böll in 1960 wrote a book *The Rhine*, calling the river dirty and majestic. But for the poets, he said, it starts near Rüdesheim —the Middle Rhine, with ruined castles, looming mountains, and ninety miles of a winding gorge.

At breakfast a Mrs. Skidmore at the next table cried out, "Oh oh, I'm going to miss the Lorelei! I've an appointment with the hairdresser."

The Lorelei is an echoing rock four hundred feet high, massive and towering, with a German flag on top. As we passed slowly, the ship's orchestra played

> Ich weiss nicht, was soll es bedeuten,
> Dass ich so traurig bin,

and I sang along, the only Heine song I know.

She was a maiden who threw herself into the Rhine in grief for a faithless lover, then changed into a siren to lure fishermen to their death. She sits on the rock combing her golden hair, singing her wild sweet song. And the spellbound fishermen are seized with longing as they look up from swirling waters to the mountain that will split their boat and drown them. We got safely past this time.

One man on board didn't give a damn for the Lorelei, or for Byron's "castled crag of Drachenfels" and his wailing tears,

> But one thing want these banks of Rhine, —
> Thy gentle hand to clasp in mine!

From early morning Andy, fifty-one, had stood motionless at the rail like a man on starboard watch, waiting for the sight that brought him on this cruise—Remagen. He was there once before, and now he had returned to relive the awful episode of twenty-eight years ago.

Remagen is on the left bank between Coblenz and Bonn. On March 7, 1945, when the U.S. 9th Armored Division had nearly reached the town, a German prisoner gave warning that in forty-five minutes, at 4:00 p.m., the last remaining bridge over the Rhine—the Remagen railway bridge—would be blown up. The Americans raced to reach it, young Andy among them. While two charges were exploded in the Nazis' frantic attempt to destroy the span, they crossed under heavy fire barely in time. This advance into Germany spelled the end of the war with Hitler. Today nothing remained to mark the place but the stone piles at either end, since the collapsed bridge was never rebuilt, nothing of Remagen but the scene in Andy's eyes. And he stood at the rail and wept.

On the tip of my mind was Saint Ursula and the 11,000 virgins. In the fourth century a cargo or multiplicity of English maidens of singular beauty sailed the Rhine with Ursula, a king's daughter, in eleven ships from Basel to Cologne, where they were promptly leaped upon and murdered by the Huns for loving the Lord and choosing to die as virgins. Wallace Stevens wrote a witty poem "Madame Ste Ursule, et Les Unze Mille Vierges." Carpaccio, Memling, Tintoretto, and, more recently, Claude painted her and the famous martyrdom.

Once the boat docked in Cologne, Betty, Ted, and I took off for the Basilica of Saint Ursula on the site where the 11,001 damsels supposedly died defending their chastity. An inscription of the fourth or fifth century claims this as the burial place. In 1794 when Mrs. Radcliffe was in Cologne (as she wrote in A Journey), the inexhaustible numbers of heads and bones of Saint Ursula and company were on view "handed to you from shelves like books in a library." Henry Adams' wife, Clover, on their honeymoon in 1872 wrote from Cologne of "an old church where 11,000 virgins were killed and their bones are stuck all over the walls, their skulls decorating every nook and corner."

According to the account in *Lives of the Saints*, the names of 1,079 have been recovered, such as Languida and Inez, possibly Undecimilla. I regret that the Catholic Church has summarily dropped Ursula from the saints' calendar because her authenticity is in doubt (what about Saint Leonorus of Brittany who hung his coat on a sunbeam?). Not Saint Jerome nor the Venerable Bede mentions her, though Geoffrey of Monmouth includes her in his history. However the church fathers regard her, it seems unfair to the Ursuline nuns, whose order was formed in the sixteenth century when the ghost of Ursula appeared and so commanded. Unfair also to Christopher Columbus, who on his second voyage, 1493, discovered the Virgin Islands and named them himself in honor of Ursula and her traveling companions. To me it is unchristian to unmake her, when one miracle is like another in being miraculous. *The Golden Legend*, thirteenth century, tells how a religious man was asked in a dream by one of Saint Ursula's murdered virgins to recite the Lord's Prayer 11,000 times. This he did and fell over dead.

Cologne is full of miracles. In the cathedral, the Three Kings—Kaspar, Melchior, Balthazar—lie buried, their skeletons in gold crowns brought from Milan by Barbarossa in 1162. On the high altar are the gifts of the Magi. Heinrich Böll says that in this drafty Gothic cathedral one can confess to greater crimes than in the confession booths of smaller churches.

I had an errand in town before returning to the ship. When B. and I were here just after World War II (with 90 percent of the city destroyed), I had a strong desire to buy a bottle of eau de Cologne to sweeten the foul air of death. Coleridge wrote about the smells of Cologne:

> I counted two and seventy stenches
> All well defined, and several stinks!

What fussy travelers the English were, forever objecting to reeks and stinks as if they had none at home. Dr. Johnson complained to Boswell in Edinburgh, "I smell you in the dark," Horace Walpole held his nose in Venice, Trollope in Bath at "a compound of villainous smells," Oscar Wilde in the U.S.A.

B. and I were too poor to afford the Kölnishes Wasser, invented by an Italian, Farina, in the eighteenth century. Today, with money jingling, I went into a shop in the Plaza, where the clerk recommended her most expensive bottle of eau de Cologne, made by Revlon in America.

"But you see I'm American," I protested. She thought that a coincidence but no deterrent. I wanted and got #4711, for as J. Pierpont Morgan wrote from Cologne, "Buy the *genuine* brand." I presume, though, they all smell alike.

After Cologne the industrial landscape spread on both sides, a skyline of factories and loading docks. The river branched out into a vast delta, and the passengers lined up to change their money into Dutch guilders. The Rhein became the Rijn of windmills and dikes, of Rembrandt van Rijn who was born on it.

We left the *Nederland* at the port of Rotterdam, downcast to end the river journey except that a few miles ahead by motor coach was that sweet town Delft. It looks like Vermeer, who lived there all his life, the way he saw its composure and placid blue sky, the way Delft's light is Vermeer's light.

Tonight in Amsterdam at the Pulitzer Hotel, which blooms with two rose gardens beside a canal, I sat on a bench stool at the bar before dinner waiting for Betty and Ted. Henry Somebody from Queens (a passenger on the *Nederland*) sat down beside me.

"I like you," he said, "and I'm going to buy you a drink because you are a widow. My mother is a widow. My sister is a widow. Someday my wife will be a widow." So he bought me a Scotch, and I hastily bought him one in return, and that took care of a couple of widows.

Is Amsterdam as beautiful as Venice? I guess not. Built though it is in the sea, its streets tree-shaded canals that at night glimmer with leaf-hidden lamps in midair, still the Dutch are a neat, orderly, plain people. Rembrandt's solid burghers would never feel at home in Venice.

And yet they are a flower people and Amsterdam is the hippie capital of the world, where thousands are welcome to stay, make protest speeches, and camp like derelicts in Vondel Park. The famed red-lit Zeedijk district flourishes, where in its "streets of pleasure, streets of vice" we were advised that a woman will not be molested in broad daylight provided she walks with a man and behaves herself circumspectly. Ted managed it with a woman on each arm.

And there is the movie, *Wie is bang voor Virginia Woolf?*

September

W. H. Auden has died in a Vienna hotel at sixty-six. He found America too perilous to live in, fearful of dying one day in a New York apartment and being discovered a week later by the mailman. He moved back to Christ Church, Oxford, in his carpet slippers, to a mother college's protection.

I despair of my poetry course. It used to deal with the living dead, as Eliot called them. They kept on writing books and thumping tubs.

Surprisingly, according to the OED the word *homosexual* appeared as late in the language as 1897. It wasn't in common use in Virginia Woolf's youth; in her essay "Old Bloomsbury" she called them buggers: "I knew that there were buggers in Plato's Greece, but it never occurred to me that there were buggers even now in the Stephens' sitting room at Gordon Square." In a letter she described Logan Pearsall Smith as "buggeristical."

He was also a humbugger.

October

Sarah worked up enough breath to whisper Hello over the telephone from Chicago. "This is Helen," I said.

"What kind of Helen?" asked Sarah.

I wondered what kind tonight. Governor Jim Holshouser rose to speak at the banquet at the Hotel Sir Walter in Raleigh, saying, "This is the greatest honor that the state of North Carolina can bestow." In the past the awards have been given to Carolinians like Paul Green, Jonathan Daniels, Frank Graham, Frances Gray Patton, each a true Tar Heel. Tonight one of them was Senator Sam Ervin. Oh dear, I'm from New York State.

My citation was read in her legal voice by Judge Susie Sharp, Chief Justice of the Supreme Court of North Carolina, a prim, spectacled lady elegantly dressed in pink glitter. Governor Holshouser put a heavy gold medal around my neck that jerked me so close to his mouth we nearly kissed. Though I'd had nothing to drink, I felt full of consequence. (Jane Austen: "One's consequence, you know, varies so much at times without any particular reason.")

At the governor's reception, Senator Ervin and I stood side by side for two hours while he beamed and the weight of the gold medal pulled me forward as if I were bowing to everybody. A lady stopped the receiving line to ask, "Do you belong to him?"

"Tell her yes, ma'am," he said. "Yes, ma'am, she surely does."

"I was afraid she was a northerner," the lady said sharply. "Anyway, I'm relieved a *working* woman got it."

November

The talk of impeachment of Nixon grows thunderous, with a call to him to resign and let Gerald Ford become president—not a likely event. Nixon is determined to bluff it out. "I'm not a crook," says Nixon.

At Duke we are suddenly back in the jangling 1960s, with new excuse for clamor. The students are whipping up the mob, making speeches in the Quadrangle demanding immediate impeachment. The Law School leads the attack, since Nixon earned his degree here. "Oust him!" they yell, shaking their fists.

At Chicago, where I've gone for Thanksgiving, they hold "Impeach-in" meetings at the university and, for variety, "Sexual Identity" sessions for straights, bisexuals, gays, and undecideds. They hammer away at life harder than we do. We stay more undecided.

I watch for the sign along the Lakeshore Drive when we go downtown: Turn Left to Trauma Center. That is where we are, in a state of trance.

It's the wonderful *noise* in David's house that eases the mind. I reproach David for never having heard of Thomas Bastard, a minor Elizabethan poet who wrote seven books of epigrams. "What, you don't know that old Bastard?"

"A terrible poet," says David, without reading him.

At least he wrote one good line that fits this household: "Methinks 'tis pretty sport to hear a child."

December

Yeats's *Journal*, the secret one he sealed up in 1921 with the notation, "Private, not for publication now, if ever," is newly published. At twenty-seven Yeats had not yet kissed a woman on the mouth. Tempted by a prostitute, he told himself, "No, I love the most beautiful woman in the world." But he hadn't kissed Maud Gonne either in what he called a "perplexed wooing."

He tried to know himself, led astray by ego, unhappy love, Tarot cards, crystal balls, seances, astrology, magic, mysticism, and the Spiritus Mundi.

He said, "I do not listen enough." There was the perpetual waiting for something to happen that never happens, a bell that never rings (like Beckett waiting for Godot who will not come, since whatever or whoever one waits for does not exist). He said, "I cry out continuously against my life." His friend Gogarty thought Yeats was tired of being irretrievably Irish.

Yeats told a story of an old woman who was walking in a country lane and met Synge, the playwright. "God bless you," she said.

"And may God bless you."

"Do you believe in God?"

"No."

Peggy gave me the *Larousse Encyclopedia of Mythology*, though the sad thing about myths is they ought to be true and aren't. For the gods the real myth was immortality, which even for them didn't last. Zeus in his wisdom showed a proper sense of mortality by pursuing so many mortal women—Niobe, Io, Semele, Danae, Europa, Leda, Alcmene . . . But why did he adopt those fanciful disguises? Who would want to go to bed with a cloud, a shower of gold, a swan, a bull, a horse, a pigeon? Alcmene had all the luck: she thought Zeus was her own husband.

1974

January

I can't understand why people resist making resolutions, such a pleasure they are, such a chance to say, "Myself I will remake." And "I do resolve to live a better life." And "Forgive me my trespasses."

My resolution this year is painted in black letters on a silver plate affixed to a red wooden block twelve inches long, manufactured by IBM. My friend Winfred (a thoughtful man who boasts he has never eaten a marshmallow) owns a collection of them in various languages, of which he offered me a choice — *Think* (for IBM junior executives), *Denke* (but I can't think in German), or a beauty in Arabic, Winfred's favorite because he can't read Arabic and so doesn't feel ordered about. Mine says *Réfléchissez*. It might have said *Pensez* in six letters, but what I need is to reflect, think twice, consider, *mediter en soi-même*. I placed it in my study beside the TV, where it looks humiliated when I turn the set on.

Too busy building a wheelbarrow that took his attention, E. B. White was late with his recommendations for 1974. He knows our sickness and says so in an essay "Downhill All the Way." We need trains, now that gas is short. We need to begin proceedings for the impeachment of President Nixon. We need to harness the tides, capture the sun for heat, free the mail from invasion of privacy. "Meantime, along comes 1974, with the country headed downhill all the way," picking up speed, next stop Rock Bottom unless by then the bottom has dropped out.

Meantime, I build my own wheelbarrows, awaiting the decline and fall.

January 30, 1852: "I doubt if Emerson could trundle a wheelbarrow through the streets because it would be out of character. One needs to have a comprehensive character." — Thoreau, *Journal*

The *Atlantic Monthly* has printed three essays from my new book *Beautiful Lofty People*. They call the piece "Three Nice People," Sir Thomas More, Ben Jonson, Sydney Smith—beautiful, lofty, and not damned.

A colleague stopped me in the hall to say he had read the *Atlantic* essay. "Is this Sydney Smith a relative of yours?" he asked. "Your maiden name was Smith, wasn't it? Was he your grandfather or something?"

Another asked me to explain the book's title. "Is it about the faculty at Duke?" A third asked what I meant by *lofty.* "Is it about your ancestors?"

I should call it *All My Wares Bee Trash* ("Though all my wares bee trash, the hart is true"). Or *No More Than Fritters.* Or *What Larks.*

At 3:30 p.m. Saturday, a telephone call came from the Raleigh-Durham Airport. "This is Jill Krementz," the voice said. "I'm a photographer. The *Times* wants your picture, so I hopped on a plane at La-Guardia and here I am."

I didn't waste time changing my clothes from pants and an old ski jacket or stop to measure the gas tank. I made it in half an hour, driving fast. Jill was standing in the rain on the platform, her long brown hair flying in the wind, looking as casual as a photographer's model and as unmistakably chic. Her only luggage, her camera, might have been a tote bag slung from the shoulder.

"Do you know Kurt Vonnegut?" she asked as she climbed into my car.

"No," I said.

"Have you heard of him?"

"No."

It was an odd admission that startled her. By now it seems an odd admission to me. "Anyway, I live with him," she said. "He likes your book."

On the way home we passed an A&P. "Excuse me while I pick up a couple of steaks for dinner," I said. "I won't be a minute."

"No, no, the *light!*" she cried. "Besides, I can't stay for dinner. There isn't much daylight left. Look at the sky." It was threatening a downpour.

I asked if I should change into an evening gown or something tailored, if I might put on some lipstick and brush my hair, if we could please have a drink. Shaking her head decidedly no, she jumped out of the car, surveyed the premises and took me by the hand, leading me up and down the dooryard, the garden, the gravel driveway. In a fast dwindling light, storm cloud and mist, she clicked the shutter several hundred times, talking constantly, laughing, trying for the candid poses for which she is famous, catch as catch can. She found a sharp rock and set me down on it. "Don't wince, smile."

Personally I think outdoor candid shots are strictly for the young, like Jill herself. She disagrees. "I've seen the studio portraits Bachrach did of you," she said. "They're so old-fashioned they kill me."

"Old-fashioned like Gainsborough," I said.

But we were instant friends, and I enjoyed the zany performance as I hope the neighbors did. Then I took her to the airport for an 8:00 p.m. flight back to New York, bought her some vegetable soup and myself a paperback of *Slaughterhouse-Five*, kissed her good-bye.

On the trip home, I suddenly thought, "My God, no gas!" Every filling station in North Carolina was closed.

February

To hurry January out of town, I gave a university lecture yesterday, fifty minutes to the dot, on the idea of walking naked. Today I'm thinking over my folly. When asked last July to speak six months later to several hundred persons on any subject I chose, I hastily picked the confessional poets, for no reason except that confessions are likely to interest people and poetry isn't.

Sixty years ago Yeats told how "I made myself a coat / Covered with embroideries / From heel to throat"—a fancy dress that by 1914 he had discarded because "there's more enterprise in walking naked." Sound though the plan, Yeats found it harder to go bare than it looked. Like the rest of us, he liked playing the hero, wearing masks, assuming identities (Michael Robartes, Owen Aherne, Red Hanrahan). From poem to poem he was a triple-self, double-self, anti-self, momentary self. In the end he kept some secrets (where does a naked person hide them?), advising Lady Gregory to do the same: "Be secret and take defeat,"

> Be secret and exult
> Because of all things known
> That is most difficult.

Yet to walk naked has become a popular performance if not epidemic, with our fantasies on parade along with the undressed skeletons hauled from the closet. Theodore Roethke cried, "My secrets cry aloud. I'm naked to the bone." An anthology of younger poets is *Naked Poetry*, of the Beats is *Naked Angels*, of American women poets, *Naked and Fiery*

Forms. Then there's *Naked Hollywood*. Confession is not new, though confessional poets in the past, says Alfred Kazin, paraded their personal soul in epic form. King Lear tore off his clothes to become the thing itself, unaccommodated man, "a poor, bare, forked animal."

The advantage of stripping to one's pelt is obvious—to make flesh visible, truth apparent. There *is* more enterprise in walking naked. It takes courage to reveal oneself even to a psychiatrist. It takes daring to expose body and mind before strangers. The benefits may be lasting: to discover who one is, who the other strippers are.

But the dangers of walking naked are also great. The primary one is that nobody can do it: it's self-defeating. Truth becomes half-truth. Instead of showing all, one exposes the worst, the scars and disfigurements, failures of relationship to parents, lovers, friends, the humiliations, guilts, betrayals. The subject of confession is suffering—to be human is to suffer. The danger is that it sounds like self-pity, intimate, embarrassing, before long tiresome. The listener shrugs, "Everyone has problems."

Robert Lowell was leader and inspirer of the group, though he dislikes the label, his book *Life Studies*, 1959, the masterwork. Two of his students, Anne Sexton and Sylvia Plath, took Lowell's method further than he did. The poetry of Sylvia Plath is "the longest suicide note ever written."

He said he couldn't breathe without these confessions; the reader is his confessor. The first thirty-five pages in prose give a dejected account of "91 Revere Street," Boston, where Robert lived an only child with his parents. From boyhood memories he shows his father a weak failure, a washed-out ex-naval officer whom Robert and his mother despised. The mother is an aggressive snob, "hysterical even in her calm," who bullied his father, ruled and browbeat him. Quarrels and bickerings in that house brought on unbearable tensions, "I felt drenched in my parents' passions." He reveals himself as a horrid child, maladjusted, dominated by his mother, dishonest, disloyal, churlish. And lonely. "I bored my parents they bored me." Beyond dubiety this is true. One can't doubt his sincerity, except that he recites the part that went wrong. In a recent interview Lowell said, "You leave out a lot. You emphasize this and not that." He writes as an angry child whose hurts are deep, though he was in his forties when he wrote the book. There is the one speaker, Lowell, who accuses and condemns, belittles those who can't defend themselves, pays them back, inflicts wounds because he feels wounded.

Missing from so much honesty is compassion, love neither given nor received. He hasn't taken the step from a child's resentment to a man's forgiveness. In a poem "Night Sweat" he says, "Always inside me is the child who died, / Always inside me is the will to die." He recalls less the pain he gave others than the pain they gave him. And that is a child's view.

The poems in *Life Studies* echo the prose. A friend said, "I don't know how you survived that family." He shows that he didn't survive, not very well. His life became a series of predicaments, repeated mental breakdowns, unhappy marriages. Yet I ask myself what scenes he didn't recall —the time, say, when he first fell in love, when his daughter was born, when he discovered he was a good poet. Why isn't happiness worth confessing to? Coleridge said, "When a man is unhappy, he writes damned bad poetry, I find." What would Coleridge, given to dejection himself, think of the confessional poets?

This, I believe, is not walking naked. It isn't confessional in the sense it lays bare the human soul, which is capable of joy as well as grief. It is an outcry at the moment of drowning. Or one might explain it as therapy, clinical diagnosis, a case history. But the therapy doesn't work. Confession has not been good for the soul and the soul is not healed. The patient is not cured.

In the past year Lowell published on the same day three books of poetry, still confessional. Again he recounts defeats and failures, though he says, "I'm tired. Everyone's tired of my turmoil."

> I have plotted perhaps too freely with my life,
> not avoiding injury to others,
> not avoiding injury to myself.

One line says, "I come like someone naked in my raincoat." He isn't naked, nor is he indecently exposed, but in disarray, dressed in a raincoat that is too much covering for a man walking naked. For decorum it's not covering enough.

Sylvia Plath intentionally repeated the pattern of confession. She was sure Lowell's method was right if one had the courage to tell it true. Here is the same narration in prose (*The Bell Jar*), same hatred of her father, same analysis of her mental breakdown, broken marriage, resentment, despair. Only Sylvia Plath died of it.

She was fifteen years younger than Lowell, born in Boston like him, a lesser poet narrower in her life studies. *The Bell Jar*, published one month before she committed suicide in 1963, shows her a student at Smith who loses her virginity in a spectacular fiasco, falls into depression, makes her first attempt at suicide by swallowing a bottle of sleeping pills and hiding in a cellar behind a wall of bricks. Two days later she is found miraculously alive and is put for five months in McLean's, the mental hospital where Lowell went. She is under a bell jar, suffocated, like Lowell unable to breathe.

Though the novel doesn't blame her father (except to show her weeping at his grave before trying to die), the poetry violently does. Otto Plath of German birth, a professor at Boston University, died when Sylvia was eight. For this she blamed him, accused him of abandoning her by a death that was an act of betrayal, swore to get even if she had to die to do so. In "Daddy" the hatred erupts and explodes. If Lowell's father is less than a man, hers is a monster. She calls him a Nazi, herself his victim identified with those tortured and murdered. He is a vampire like her husband, who drank her blood. She addresses him in childlike fury, in singsong rhyme:

> There's a stake in your fat black heart
> And the villagers never liked you.
> They are dancing and stamping on you.
> They always knew it was you.
> Daddy, daddy, you bastard, I'm through.

She used to read the poem aloud in a rage, implacable, her voice hoarse. For twenty years she built up the anger and now has killed him off. She is both victim and destroyer.

Hers too is not really confessional writing. It is a child's attack. Sylvia Plath like Lowell stays at the center of the nightmare, the accusing voice, one that sounds deceptive. What did she know of torture in a concentration camp? She had suffered no atrocities. She was a woman, with supposedly a woman's understanding. She wrote "Daddy" after the birth of her second child.

Her marriage to the British poet Ted Hughes had ended. Following their separation she lived alone with her infants, Frieda and Nicholas, on the two upper floors of a shabby house in London. There, aged thirty, she wrote the poems published after her death in *Ariel*. She too saw herself naked: "I am nude as a chicken's neck, does nobody love me?" The poems are suicidal, poured out as many as three a day, seven days a week: "Somebody's done for," trapped, doomed. In "Lady Lazarus" she counts her attempts to die: "I have done it again. / One year in every ten I manage it." On a February morning, Sylvia Plath prepared and left food for her children, one and three years old, went downstairs to the kitchen and put her head in the gas oven like a Jew dying at Belsen. The poem "Edge," written in the last week, says, "Her dead body wears the smile of accomplishment. / She is used to this sort of thing."

Robert Lowell said, "Her death is part of the risk, the imaginative risk." He meant the price she paid as a poet. It seems a terrible price to pay.

Four years older than Sylvia, her friend Anne Sexton, also from Massachusetts, also Lowell's student, also in mental hospitals after breakdowns and two attempts at suicide, also the mother of two children and divorced from her husband, wrote "Sylvia's Death," in her volume *Live or Die.*

O Sylvia, Sylvia . . . with two children wandering loose in the tiny
playroom . . . how did you crawl into, crawl down alone into the death
I wanted so badly and for so long?

[In October 1974, Anne Sexton killed herself by leaving the motor running in her car. She was forty-five. She too joined the poets of our time—John Berryman, Randall Jarrell, Hart Crane, Vachel Lindsay, Sara Teasdale—who demanded death as the only choice.]

Horace said long ago in the *Ars Poetica*, "You must allow poets to have the right and ability to destroy themselves."

We are the onlookers. But when they tell us life is not worth living, are we to agree? They provide no pattern to follow and no solution. Both Lowell and Sylvia Plath resented their parents for failing them, yet were capable of failing their own children—Sylvia by dying, Lowell by simply going away. I wish they might have walked naked in a clearer light, might have put more love into it.

March

I was invited by Case Western Reserve University in Cleveland to spend the spring term as "Visiting Scholar" at so swollen a fee I was tempted to accept and retire a rich woman in June. Other "Visiting Scholars" have been Erich Fromm and the New York Pro Musica Antiqua. But they overlooked the fact I was committed to teaching at Duke, so we settled for a week in March during my spring recess that doesn't coincide with theirs.

I prefer "Visiting Fireman," putting out more fires than I set. I gain the impression that creativity is ablaze at Western Reserve, if not out of control. By day and by night I visited classes in Creative Writing, Advanced Creative Writing, Graduate Creative Writing, read manuscripts in snatched moments, conferred, confronted, opined, and sat in on the Finley Foster Open Workshop. The students asked if they might mail me their works for the rest of their lives.

One night the group that edits the literary magazine *Fresh Winds* took me to a health-food restaurant, where the food tasted like seaweed and we drank herb tea, but our talk was suitably gusty, full of fresh winds. Next night a poet-professor asked me to his house, where a graduate group of poets meets each week. The professor is a bearded man of opinions he is careful not to express, which appears to be the critical method favored by the faculty, to remain neutral. However, inspired by red wine, we questioned what the poems were seeking to say. I don't see what is wrong with that. I've never been neutral in my life.

On Wednesday came the hour I wanted to avoid, described in the brochure as "an open lecture on a woman writer to a course in Images of Women in Literature." Since I regard women not as a separate and distinct breed fighting for recognition but as part of humanity, I was allowed to talk about Marianne Moore. With poems on the jellyfish, mongoose, snail, and wood-weasel, we weathered the crisis. Nobody asked the obvious question, what Miss Moore's interest in exotic animals like the musk ox had contributed to the liberation of women. She pictures the ox as an admirable male and invites you to "Bury your nose in one when wet." Nobody inquired, "When *who* is wet?" They were a submissive group.

It was followed by a writing class that attracted the interplanetary science fiction crowd, whose horrendous plots floored us all, followed by a reception in Baker Lounge, where the banquet table was littered with Seven-Up and potato chips.

"What's your racket?" asked a passing professor. "Home economics?"

"Social hygiene," I said.

With more Open Workshops, Open Discussions, an Open University Lecture given by me to wind up the tuckered-out proceedings, we closed down the school for the holiday. Writing as a student movement seems a healthy substitute for riots, protest meetings, drugs, or (perhaps) sex. If I could have stayed the whole term, I might have learned from them what good it does.

April

The *New York Times Book Review* sent me five volumes of fairy tales. I've no objection to fairy tales, or gardening books, though for review they might be put into professional hands. A lady asked me once,

"Do you like forget-me-nots?" a question that stunned me, for who would damn a forget-me-not? This applies to fairy tales, a universal pleasure. While they appeal naturally to children, a tale of enchantment is not in itself childish—unless, as I hate to believe, one grows up to enter the opposite world of disenchantment, no fairies in it, no Rapunzels with golden hair, no happy endings.

Dylan Thomas wrote a poem "We Have the Fairy Tales by Heart," to say they protect us from fear of thunder, the retribution of the gods, and bishops. In them is a simple faith that good conquers evil, love conquers all.

Two small boys I know will listen to anything—to Chaucer's interminable Tale of Constance—and quiver through to the end. They can figure out and kindly explain Tolkien's plots, beyond my grasp. They keep straight in their heads those entangled ethnic stories with Finnish or Eskimo names, those sagas of Norse heroes, as well as the 99 characters of *Bleak House*. They have a tolerance for storytelling, whether a tale of dragons, bogies, goblins, broomed witches, or ordinary mortals engaged in slaughter and bloodshed. They listen. And I envy them. "Marvellous is the mind of a child," wrote Laurence Housman in his autobiography *The Unexpected Years*, where he tells why he wrote fairy tales. To a child enchantment is an orderly process, no good if it isn't believable. Charles Kingsley would have you believe in *Water Babies* that the likeliest fairy in the world is Mrs. Doasyouwouldbedoneby, but Housman permitted no moral nonsense like that. His fairies are a cheeky lot who bestow favors like rubies, changing a white peahen into a maiden and marrying her off to whoever claims her—considered a happy solution ever after.

The traditional tales by the masters stir in me the same emotion I felt as a child of eight. Rapunzel, for example, is the limit. The loveliest damsel ever shut by a wicked witch in a tower, with twenty yards of hair of no use except as a ladder for a prince to climb, what did the girl do? She said to the witch, "Why are you so much heavier to pull up than the young king's son?" For that piece of blabbing she got her hair cut off while the prince leaped into a bramble bush and blinded himself. When he stumbled upon her in the desert, the mother of twins, she shed two repentant tears, that's all.

"The Princess on the Pea" begins as it should, not a word wasted, nothing unclear: "There was once a prince. He wanted a princess, but it had to be a true princess." At age eight, I soon saw the basic problem —bad manners. For all his breeding, the prince displayed the manners of a goatherd, and the princess was worse. It is impolite to put a pea into anybody's bed. It is rude to complain to one's hostess next morning of the sleeping accommodations, and my mother would have spanked me for that. "I've hardly closed my eyes all night!" wailed the sulky princess. By this royal tantrum she was recognized at once as the real thing.

The marvel is that, if the stories are unchanging, so is oneself the same person, who wants a story to unfold properly without tricks—the witch outwitted, the harmony restored. I'm tired these days of grown-up fantasies of death and disenchantment.

May

I will go home and write a book, *My Three Days in Fiji*. It will be as full of happy recollection as James Morris's account, in which he said he wouldn't mind being eaten in Fiji, because they would cook him gently and be extremely merry at the feast.

I went with Betty and Ted once more in search of paradise, which may still be on the map. The trip had an eeriness about it from the start. Soon after takeoff from Raleigh-Durham Airport, the pilot announced, "Welcome aboard. Our next stop is Raleigh-Durham." Though he corrected himself, it was clear we had left solid ground. At Los Angeles, where we stopped briefly, a huge sign above the rest rooms said, Maximum Occupancy 1,470 Persons. In San Francisco we spent the time between planes in Gump's, pricing precious jades and rubies that nobody wears in the South Seas, before boarding a 747 of the Qantas Australian Airlines to Fiji.

Fiji is barely on the other side of the international date line, but all we lost was Mother's Day. I had supposed the international date line, like the equator, the continental divide, and the Mason-Dixon line, was created by God in one of the six days. It turns out to be man-made, a crooked, bulging, imaginary line, allowing Fiji to claim that each day on earth starts here and the *Fiji Times* to brag it's the first newspaper to print the news of the world. If so, I don't want to hear a word of impeachment proceedings or Nixon quoted saying, "Confidentiality in this point of time."

Lewis Carroll asked the question "Where does the day begin?" in a lecture before the Ashmolean Society. He wrote to a number of government officials, but no one could answer him. In 1883 a world conference met in Washington to establish the international date line from North to South Pole that jogs west in the Pacific to include Fiji and east to include

Alaska. Lewis Carroll, who died in 1898, lived to receive his answer—the day begins in Fiji. I doubt that it convinced him.

We landed at 4:00 a.m. in the world's first sunrise that came up like thunder, flaming the sky and our faces crimson. The International Airport at Nadi stood aglow with tropical flowers and Fijian maidens, one of whom had come to meet us. She ran about in distracted fashion looking for the rest of our tour party, but to her amazement and ours there were no others. We *were* the tour. By some trick of the gods who never explain, we were the sole members of Tour #2 organized by the Australian Travel Service.

A smiling driver took us the forty-eight miles from Nadi to the Coral Coast and the Hotel Fijian on Yanuca Island, connected to the mainland by a causeway. We are now in paradise, which I will define as (unlike the saints and innocents) I understand it to be—a luxury hotel of great ease, civilized but sensibly remote from civilization, a suite to oneself at ground level, flowers in the grass, a blue lagoon, and beyond it the pounding coral reef of white breakers. If the myth of Eden is in the mind, then to my mind there is a lot of Eden to be found in Fiji.

The Fijians, one of the fiercest people in the Pacific, were till the middle of the last century given to tribal warfare, strangling of widows, burying alive of the aged, child murder, and cannibalism as an everyday treat—they having developed a taste for human flesh, even the roasted flesh of friends and relatives. A respectful way of performing the burial of next of kin was to eat him. Or a man might devour his wife because he found her flesh appealing.

Now that they've stopped eating tourists, they greet you without show of appetite, a hospitable, handsome people. The men are tall, well built, erect with pride of bearing, and adorned (besides the shirt they wear) with one rose-colored hibiscus behind the left ear, which means "I want a sweetheart." Over the right ear means "I have one," but so far I have noticed only left ears. "Bula," they say, "hello, welcome." The beautiful island women with their swayback walk and flowered shifts pass my door beside the crimson bougainvillea. "Bula," they say.

This afternoon a rattling carriage of the Paradise Coach Co. took us to Yadua, a tiny group of dwellings twelve miles away. Yadua couldn't be mistaken for anybody's paradise. A rough, grassy field was encircled by a few palm-thatched bamboo huts, a meeting house for tribal affairs, and a sagging Methodist church with broken windowpanes, an unframed, flyspecked picture of Jesus, and so many wasps we were urged not to venture inside. Two years ago a hurricane followed by a tidal wave destroyed the village except for the church, where the people fled and threw themselves in terror on floors soon flooded. The survivors began again, helping each other. They have no plumbing, no water except what can be piped in, no taxes, no stores, no school, no possessions but seashells. There are a few cocoanut palms and breadfruit trees. They eat fish from the sea beside them, the killer and preserver. And everybody smiles and smiles.

The men in Fijian grass skirts and leis gave ceremonial welcome, beckoning us to squat on the ground and clap hands before receiving the communal cup of mud-colored kava dipped from a wooden bowl. They showed us how to drink the soapy liquid in one gulp, clap hands again, and cry "Bula!" Kava is made from crushed pepper root, tastes like clay, causes a numbing of the tongue. It can produce a dreamy state, can stupefy.

After that hospitality the men lined up for tribal dances, baring their teeth and brandishing sticks, joined by several beflowered women chanting as they danced. Soon we were dancing together, Fijians and tourists, performing the taralala in a weird conga line, reversing, swinging to center. "Vinaka!" they cried, "bravo, good." When the party was over, we couldn't thank them with money, a discourtesy in Fiji where one who receives a gift must present a finer one in return.

Tonight the Hotel Fijian had its version of a tribal ceremony, a native barbecue attended by guests in formal evening dress, the sumptuous banquet tables sinking under roast pig, steaks, enormous fish, curries, passion fruit, English trifle and pound cake. It was lavish and dull, with an orchestra for dancing. A Fijian soul singer in a white jacket with kinky hair to his shoulders looked depressed and sounded so. I liked it better in Yadua.

No, I don't want to live here. Paradise is worth investigating, and on the surface the Fijians appear indifferent to colder worlds and to all the ways there are to be unhappy. For them ignorance may provide true philosophy. But I have one benefit they haven't—I do not fear my ancestors' ghosts.

We left unwilling, driven through frightful roads to Nadi, where the streets are lined with sleazy Indian shops, since there are more East Indians in Fiji than Fijians and they are the shopkeepers. At 3:15 a.m. we departed in a downpour on a Qantas flight to Sydney, after being not frisked for bombs but fumigated. Across the aisle a Fijian couple in red-flowered garments kissed and snapped their gum, having seen, I guess, too many American movies.

John Gunther said of Australia, "There are those who love it, and no wonder." This doesn't include Charles Darwin, who while visiting there thanked his good fortune to be born an Englishman. Gunther called Sydney less a city than an experience. It was a chilling experience to arrive in November, when yesterday was May in Fiji, with the frost of autumn in the air and women on the street in winter coats, astonishing affairs of kangaroo or sheepskin. I saw one hardy soul at the beach swimming the Australian crawl.

What about Sydney? Parts of the city have names like Bullaburra, Warrimoo, Woolloomooloo; others are called Hyde Park, Kensington, Paddington, Waterloo, though Sydney is anything but English or aborigine. It's a brash, bold carnival city, built in every architectural style known to man, with a leaning toward fretted ironwork in clashing colors. A peculiar apartment complex called the Gazebo looms like a celestial beehive. People say "yis" and "Austrylia" but with civility. "A tasty male," said the waiter at lunch, as we ate to "Waltzing Matilda." "Better than hame-cooked." You can go to a Boomerang School to learn how to throw a boomerang. You can buy an opal anywhere in town if opalminded ("For thy mind is a very opal"). But the safe way is to take a course first in recognizing purity in gems, or buy your opal at Prouds and pay a fortune, or think of it as an amorphous mineral of hydrated silica and do without.

Betty and Ted's middle son, Frederick, has lived in Sydney for the past three years in an apartment on Bondi Road with one wall of glass overlooking the harbor. We are staying at the Macleay Street TraveLodge, a block from Kings Cross, the Soho of Sydney, full of sex shops and strip shows flourishing among chrysanthemum gardens, a neighborhood lending library, and a pinwheel fountain of rainbow mists. In the parks the seagulls and pigeons mingle companionably without producing any seapigeons.

While Frederick teaches at his school, we three wander about like newly arrived convicts, touring the harbor that Captain Cook called Botany Bay, staring at Sydney's new Opera House that juts into the water with a soaring roof meant to resemble billowing sails, resembling instead a child's toy of toppling blocks.

In a bookstore Ted picked up a volume of poems by an Australian poet and, leafing through, was stopped by an opening line, "One last fuck and on to other planets." What a way to travel! We left the shop laughing, though I wish I had bought the book. I'll never know how the second line went.

Tonight Fred gave a champagne party that glowed with Beautiful People, the costly bored kind, whose talk was of yachts and sailing one's own around the world. Fred told me that everyone is lonely and restless, longing to be elsewhere on a yacht, in Cannes, say, or Singapore.

"Are you a poetess?" somebody inquired of me, silencing the others who lifted astonished eyebrows.

"No indeed," I said. Nobody asked me if I owned a yacht.

It was an all-day trip to see the koala bears, by way of the Hawkesbury River—where the kookaburra bird laughs in woods along the shore—to their sanctuary in the Pennant Hills. We rode through bush country and miles of eucalyptus trees, frightening trees, Ted thought. Norman Douglas, who hated them, said, "A single eucalyptus will ruin the fairest landscape" with its withered branches and metallic rustle like a chattering of ghosts. Yet the trees give off an oil that floats in the air and colors the mountains an unearthly cobalt blue. Koala bears (not bears at all but marsupials) will eat nothing but eucalyptus, feeding on the buds and young shoots that make them tipsy.

The bears were on view at the sanctuary, each sound asleep hugging a eucalyptus tree. Three or four were persuaded to wake up and lumber about, as sprightly as sloths, far less attractive than teddy bears, too big for a child to hug. They were two feet long, mouse-colored, tailless, with large ears, balloon cheeks, and mean little eyes. The Australians love them dearly and yearn to cuddle them. I hear they will snuggle in your neck and cry like a baby.

I was happy to see a wombat, also a marsupial, also asleep, because it reminded me of Christina Rossetti ("One like a wombat prowled obtuse and furry"). A wide-awake emu stalked about looking for potato chips, which are sold at the gate to feed the kangaroos, wallaroos, and wallabies that roam freely in the park. Actually there are more kangaroos than people in Australia, a nation of marsupials including the bandicoot, and in my opinion they are sick of potato chips. When D. H. Lawrence was in Sydney in 1922, he was so attracted to them that he wrote a novel *Kangaroo* and a poem "Kangaroo." The poem, about a "Delicate mother Kangaroo," says she is very fond of white peppermint drops.

After a week in Sydney, we flew over the Tasman Sea to New Zealand, to Wellington the capital, about which ignorance proved a blessing. It was better to know nothing of Wellington and the wind, a harbor city so habitually turbulent that often planes can't land. We landed, doubting the pilot's sanity. As we stepped from the plane, the racketing wind stood our hair on end, tried to sweep us out of the country. Only once before was I roughed up like that, in Iceland.

You wouldn't expect gentle Wellington to be stirred by a breeze. Houses painted pastel shades of pink and blue clung daintily to cliffs or climbed the staircase of vertical streets above the harbor. This didn't look like the bottom end of the planet. It looked like a posh English seaside resort in Victoria's reign named for the Duke of Wellington.

Katherine Mansfield, born in Wellington, said she wanted to make her beloved "undiscovered" country known. Yet on her bitter departure from that prison world in 1908 she cried, "How people ever wish to live here I cannot think." We heard its paradisal nature lauded tonight at dinner with two friends of Ted's, Diana and Ian Wards. To reach their house we rode straight up the mountain beside the harbor in a tempest of wind and rain. As New Zealanders they love mother England with uncommon zeal, a homeland they have never seen. Ian is a civil servant, Conservative, conformist, loyal to the queen, British in speech, at present engaged in making an atlas of his country. He doesn't feel remote—remote from what?—untempted to abandon his surveys to visit the U.S.A. I was sorry he felt so little drawn to the topography of North Carolina. Next day he made sure we inspected the New Zealand sheep, for, just as Australia is full of kangaroos, New Zealand has far more sheep than human beings. He drove us thirty miles to a merino sheep farm owned by Robin and Barbara Ray, who fed us mutton for lunch with a hospitality possible only to those able to endure so many sheep.

I wet my finger to test the wind, not knowing the dire prophecy it made. A tremendous storm was on its way, bringing a week of torrential gales and catastrophic floods, disaster and death as far as Sydney. In innocence we left Wellington a moment before too late, flying north to Rotorua, resort town and spa, known as an earthly paradise. It looked like hell tonight, or Yellowstone National Park, with steam rising in the darkness, eerie shapes issuing from thermal springs and fumaroles. The stench of sulphur was overpowering, but our accommodations were sweetsmelling at the DB Rotorua Hotel (DB for Dominion Breweries). Had we chosen to bathe outdoors in late November, we could have plunged into their pool, where mists heavy as smoke emerged from invisible chimneys.

Some consider Rotorua a wonderland, the most spectacular thermal spa in the world. Others quail and run away. Katherine Mansfield was outraged by "that little Hell," to her a loathesome place. G. B. Shaw said, "I would willingly have paid ten pounds not to see it," a queer remark from one who cordially praised hell in *Man and Superman*, more congenial than heaven and the true paradise of man.

This morning we walked to the Maori village of Whakarewarewa, Whaka for short, two miles from the post office. Here the Maoris live in a ghostly world of thermal springs, shooting geysers, boiling pools, and bubbling, hissing mud. Hundreds of them settled here in 1886, when their village in the Te Wairoa valley was buried by a volcanic eruption, though only fifty or so remain while the young ones leave. Our guide, a Maori woman with a sure command of English, took us around accompanied by a throng of small nephews and nieces. Clearly proud of her people, she has moved to Rotorua to live in greater comfort.

The wives do their cooking at the many steam holes, where a ham suspended in a pool will be done in three hours. No one ventures too near the Pohutu Geyser that shoots a roaring sixty-foot stream of scalding water into the sky. The Maoris bathe in these mineral waters, breathe the sulphurous mist, stay healthy, and when they die are buried in a stone box aboveground, since just below the shallow surface is water. There are frequent cave-ins. In front of each crude dwelling stands a totem pole dyed a vivid red, carved into menacing figures with the tongue hanging out denoting fierceness to terrify the enemy, joy to procreate, or love to win the lady, either or all.

The Maoris are beautiful, their faces no longer tattooed, not negroid in feature like the Fijians but true Polynesians—dark brown, with straight noses, great dark eyes (the soul is thought to dwell in the left eye). They discovered New Zealand and, like the American Indian, were driven back from their lands till a series of bloody Maori wars resulted. Now they live at peace with the white man, the *pakeha*, and are said by New Zealanders, who are fond of them, to be indolent, warmhearted, pleasure loving, happy. A Maori still courts his girl by sticking out his tongue at her, but whether they rub noses I don't know. Darwin watched two Maoris rub noses and so strongly disapproved he disliked them thereafter. Formerly they were cannibals, with appetite only a little less lusty than the Fijians'. They ate shipwrecked sailors and missionaries as well as those defeated in battle but feasted generally on the heart of the enemy, his brain or tongue, and made his bones into flutes.

The word *cannibal*, however, came from our side of the water, used by Christopher Columbus for the tribe of red-painted Caribs of the Caribbean, small and potbellied, cruel and bloodthirsty man-eaters.

Once, according to Samuel Morison, they were made violently sick by eating a friar. Some cannibals believed white people to be unripe. Or too salty.

Cannibalism presents an interesting problem for those who believe in a physical life after death—the Mormons, for example. A book of Emily Hahn's, *Breath of God*, mostly about angels and demons, considers the peculiar riddle created by centuries of cannibals steadily eating people, as their parents did and their ancestors before them. If then the body is eventually reunited with the soul on the day of Resurrection, what happens to flesh that has been hopelessly scattered about by having been consumed at a cannibal banquet? And what happens to the cannibals themselves whose own bodies are made up of a variety of other human bodies? One eighteenth-century Fiji chief was credited with having eaten 900 people in his lifetime. As for you and me, Loren Eiseley says, "The grain you eat was, to some extent, grown in (and in a sense, is) the remains of mingled ancestors." The problem will be God's to get everybody disentangled.

Each night in Rotorua the Maoris give a performance of their native dances in one or another of the hotels. Since none was scheduled tonight at our hotel, after dinner we set out to find the place. As we hunted about, a man stopped his car beside us. "My dears," he said, "you look terribly lost." We appreciated his concern. Getting lost in Rotorua with its one main street and flat landscape would take talent. "We always look that way," we told him. The Maori concert turned up at the TraveLodge, where we settled in the lounge with the other tourists, among them a couple of boisterous Americans.

The troupe bounded in, led by a warrior's whoop—four men, four women, three young girls, in grass skirts, beads, flowers in the hair. They were members of the same family, mothers, daughters, nieces, nephews, and an elderly, unsteady aunt. Their chants and dances were inexpert, appealing because they tried so hard to please, though Ted and Betty were soon bored.

The leader, a fierce Maori woman whose face had the look of a warrior chief, barked out directions in Maori, attempting to keep the troupe from falling apart. While the girls fluttered their hands in love and welcome, the men lunged and stuck out their tongues, her misery grew. Somebody was forever stumbling or dropping his poi balls. Her stout sister at the other end of the chorus line laughed outright at their mistakes. "We're amateurs," she shouted.

As the performance tapered off to mild applause and people rose to go, the leader turned and came straight to me, seated in the second row. She looked down with, I think, her soul shining in her left eye and held out both hands. "I watched your face tonight," she said. "I couldn't take my thoughts from you. I like you." We looked deep into each other's eyes and touched hands. "I like you too," I said. I was very happy.

To reach Auckland, New Zealand's biggest city and biggest Polynesian city in the world, we took a five-hour ride by coach from Rotorua through a countryside of sheep and falling autumn leaves, through bush country of towering ferns sixty feet tall. And we rejoiced to be on the right road, Tour #2 on the driver's list for Auckland. Somebody out there kept an eye on us.

This city of gardens is in Eden County, with Mount Eden rising up among gun emplacements and no visible sign it was intended as the original garden. Traffic signs, No Standing At All Times, would disabuse you of that hope. Auckland shares our every problem except Nixon: inflation, litter, the fuel crisis, and television reruns of "I Love Lucy."

But I had come to see the kiwi bird. This morning our search took us to the University of Auckland, where enrolled in the fall session now under way are kiwis, the Maori word commonly used for New Zealanders. Ted sees no reason for sightseeing at universities, which look alike to him and remind him of home, but I feel secure there. In the afternoon, by driving through subtropical bush dense with giant ponga ferns, we reached the Auckland Zoo.

The kiwi is found only in New Zealand and, like the koala bear, sleeps a lot. As a national emblem it's a remarkably torpid bird, unable to fly, nearly extinct, resembling a large brown hen except for its feathers (that Marianne Moore called "the kiwi's rain-shawl"), its big feet, and long curved beak with two nostrils at the end of the bill. Because its habits are decidedly nocturnal, the zoo keepers have devised a clever plan to fool the kiwi. By keeping its quarters pitch-dark, they confuse the bird into waking up in the daytime and feeding in a junglelike area, where it sniffs in the leaves for worms and insects. At night the lights are turned on so it can get a little sleep.

We filed in blinded, trying to focus our eyes on the absurd fowl, as beloved and unworthy of love as the koala bear. Though taking pictures was forbidden because of the danger of sending the bird back to sleep, a Japanese ahead of me took a flashlight photo that gave us a good front-row view. For any seeking further acquaintance, the kiwi appears in every souvenir shop in the land, comic in bronze as in life.

The Auckland Museum, which has the world's finest Maori collection, was full of gods. Tiki is the god who made mankind. Anything in the shape of a man is a tiki—a statue in wood or stone, a green jade figure crouching grotesque in the fetal posture, or a red carving with glittering eyes of abalone shells—since man is the embodiment of the god who created him. I brought away two carved tikis, undeterred by their well-known power as fertility symbols.

Tahiti may be what we were looking for, the lady of the Society Islands, the paradise of the Pacific, incomparable in its beauty—I say as one who has never been to Bora Bora or Pago Pago. Again we arrived with the sun coming up crimson in the South Seas, and a pretty Tahitian girl tossed hibiscus leis around our necks and drove us, Tour #2 intact, through dust and traffic to the Hotel Tahiti, a sprawling place with a thatched roof. Our rooms are at the end of the verandah next the sea. Behind us rises a jungle grove of lush tropical plants and cocoanut palms. By opening a small gate I step over to the Ropps' porch and, when a ripe cocoanut misses my head and falls with a crash nearby, join them in a cocoanut party with beer.

Papeete (pronounced with four syllables) is still French but no longer the arid little shantytown you read about in Gauguin's time, a dirty hole that filled him with horror. Along the waterfront Papeete is a resort shaded by acacia trees, its cafés filled with hippies and other exotic customers decked in shell necklaces, its narrow streets bearing names like Rue Maréchal Foch, Rue Paul Gauguin. The Tahitian women wear a short flowered shift or *pareu* tightly drawn under the armpits to make a sheath, flowers in their black hair falling to the waist. They should stay forever young and slender, but they say, "Onatu"—"what does it matter?"

The idea is to leave Papeete and travel around the island, a journey of 120 miles, taking as long about it as possible, preferably years. We went in a car driven by a laughing Tahitian, who had learned English in high school and knew the names of things. If he forgot the word for a flower, he struck his head and groaned, "I am lazy. You see how I learn my lessons."

Tahiti is far lovelier than Fiji, more lush, breathtaking. The land rises steeply to impenetrable, fissured mountains, neither accessible nor in-habited. The whole population lives at the base in a thin coastal strip a half-mile wide beside the sea, with one road to take along the jagged shore line. They live in windowless bamboo huts with roofs of cocoanut-palm leaves where the lizards make their nests. They live in tropical profusion, able like Adam and Eve to reach out and pluck their supper. They were never cannibals. They live without money, in plenty and in peace. There are fourteen kinds of banana trees; thirty-two kinds of mangoes; limes, grapefruit, oranges, pineapples, papaws—everything but apples in this Garden of Eden, everything but snakes. Without them, how can it have sin in it or temptation? There are ferns, waterfalls, lagoons, grottoes, flamboyant flowers—frangipani, yellow jasmine, crystal white gardenia, hibiscus, bougainvillea—everywhere the plenitude, the haze of green. Unbelievable. Bougainville said when he was here in 1768, "I thought I was transported into the Garden of Eden." Darwin in 1835 found it a fallen paradise. Melville cried, "God help thee! Push not off from that isle, thou canst never return." Matisse, who visited Tahiti in 1930, thought it superb but boring. "Such immutable happiness is tiring," he found and departed. Some say Tahiti is tarnished, ravaged, spoiled by tourism. I think this is a lie: nature has won out.

Gauguin came to Tahiti in 1891 when he was forty-three (without his wife and five children), searching for paradise. He soon moved out thirty-five miles from Papeete to Mataiea, to live like a native in a bamboo hut with a thirteen-year-old *vahine* named Tehura. Tahiti was Gauguin's Eden, where he wasn't innocent enough to belong. "I am beginning to think simply," he wrote in his journal. "I am no longer conscious of good and evil." Yet after two years, tormented by exile, he went back to France where he found so-called civilized life unbearable and, in 1895, returned to Tahiti. "For it is true: I am a savage." Eventually he moved to greater isolation or hiding in the Marquesas, built a hut and died in it of syphilis in 1903. "I remember having lived," Gauguin wrote. "I also remember not having lived."

The Gauguin Museum, partway round the island, is exquisite, oddly so since few of his pictures are there, most of them still in private hands. I saw Gauguin for the first time in this fit setting. He loved the Tahitians and painted them as true Polynesians with a stone god tiki in the background, no missionaries or priests in evidence though they were plentifully on hand, claiming, "We are beginning to civilize them." There is peace, candor, love in his pictures, untouched by what Melville called "the horrors of the half-known life," and there is stillness. Gauguin said, "The silence of the night in Tahiti is the strangest thing of all."

Tonight at our hotel, furious entertainment burst forth with the appearance of a group of Tahitian dancers, six men and six girls accompanied by their drummers. They were highly professional, each girl outdoing the other in her variation of the hula. Since the hula originated in Tahiti, no other people perform it so expertly with lightning rapidity and grace, faster than the eye can see. It was an orgy of native dances—the otea, aparima, paoa, tamura (frenzied), upaupa (indecent)—and they did them all, barefoot, in grass skirts, flowers circling the neck and in the hair, pride shining in their eyes. After a while they came to beckon us sitting in a rapt circle to jump up and dance with them. The handsomest Tahitian, his teeth gleaming with laughter, pulled me by the hand to the center of the floor, where we moved to the beat of the drum. (Why didn't my mother teach me to gyrate my hips?) At the end he crowned me with a carnation lei, indicating I had won the prize. Once more, as it was among the Fijians and Maoris, I was happy. Maybe I belong in paradise after all.

The writer Laurie Lee calls the game of choosing one's paradise rarely a rewarding pastime. We tend to create a heaven, he says, which is perfection overdone and monotonous. As a piece of Christian propaganda it never got off the ground. Then he steps forward to define his own version of paradise. It is holding on to the familiar, a perpetually green landscape between mountains shelving to the sea, with tactful weather and silence except for music in the head inaudible to others unless they wish to share it. With no longing for past or future, any thought of eternity is erased from the mind. There would be a few mortals around to recognize but not remember. Each love would be first and only.

The one *Christian* paradise I've heard rumors of worthy of the name, unlike the Eden we so dismally lost, was Prester John's. He seems to have deserved it, and for all I know dwells there still.

Prester John, no more mythological than Adam, was a Christian king and priest descended from the Magi, who ruled over a vast Asian empire in the twelfth century. Marco Polo searched for it, and Vasco da Gama. Pope Alexander III wrote Prester John in 1177 to ask his help in the Crusades. In this domain was a fountain of eternal youth that changed its flavor hour by hour. In the sand magic pebbles restored sight or made one invisible. The main marvel was peace. With everything available and free, there were no beggars, murderers, thieves, flatterers, no greed, lies, sins, snakes, or "querulous" frogs. Possibly no women. Sir John Mandeville in his travels said, "And some men call it the land of faith."

Since the salamander lived in the fires of his realm, Prester John wore robes of the salamander's skin and was inextinguishable, washed in flame. He occupied a palace where at an emerald table 7 kings served him, 62 dukes, 256 counts, while 12 archbishops sat at his right hand. The apostle Thomas in a red beard preached annually before him, though Thomas had been dead for centuries. When Prester John went to war to regain the Holy Sepulchre, 13 gold crosses were carried on wagons, each cross followed by 10,000 mounted knights and 100,000 footmen. Yet in spite of this supercelestial magnificence, the greatest monarch under heaven was known as Prester John, Priest John. Thus he dwelt in paradise, in God's grace, without pride and in humility.

One of Marianne Moore's best poems, "His Shield," praises him whom she sought to emulate: "I'll wrap / Myself in salamander-skin like Presbyter John." It isn't necessary to go that far, when his manner of saving himself from man's tendency to fall was simply by avoiding pride. His shield was his humility.

The Traveler Who Went

I was a traveler who went,
Looking for Eden on a holiday,
For paradise presumably I meant,
Though I asked nothing but the usual thing—
The coral beaches, the hibiscus flowers,
And love and innocence and eternal spring.

Authentic heaven, mythic in my mind,
If still available to passersby,
In Fiji or Tahiti I might find
It. Sightseers do, in Samarkand,
Tourists in Bali on a guided tour
Bring back their boastful tales. Why shouldn't I?

Was there an Eden left on earth? Not one
But countless Edens, of hibiscus flowers
And coral reefs and paradisal song,
Where I, a traveler, found everything
Except the love you have to take along,
And innocence of course, and eternal spring.

June

"This is a fan letter," it began, postmarked Wales, a letter that left me plumed and grateful—but for the tone of apology, the fear I wouldn't like hearing from the sender. Why wouldn't I? Who am I to reject praise? From reading his many books, I knew the writer well as James Morris, former foreign correspondent of the London *Times* (who covered the climb of Mount Everest by Hillary) and the *Manchester Guardian*. I was a fan of his for the travel books on Oxford, Venice, the U.S.A., with their wit, visibility, depth of understanding. I thought him the best travel writer of our time.

In the letter he signed himself Jan Morris, husband and father of five, who recently underwent a sex change. I answered quickly to thank her for holding out her hand. As I wrote, the pronouns were awkward in my mind. The farthest of her travels had taken her from gender to gender.

Jan Morris then sent me her new book *Conundrum*, a confession that ends in a solution. It's a Tiresias story, the Greek legend of a man who for seven years was changed by the gods into a woman, though Jan Morris has no desire to return, as Tiresias did, to being male. Wise Tiresias, said Ovid, "to whom love was known from either point of view."

T. S. Eliot assumed the character of Tiresias in the *Waste Land*, an inspired device for his poem ("I Tiresias . . . throbbing between two lives"). How else could he write with knowledge of the sexes unless he partook of both? Milton's angels changed their sex at will, but human beings seldom have the choice. Lately I've reread *Madame Bovary* and *Anna Karenina* to see if Flaubert and Tolstoy in their genius could look inside a woman's mind. I was relieved to conclude they couldn't. As men they confidently told how Emma, how Anna, behaved, with insight into the consequences of her destructive acts rather than her motives. Flaubert claimed "Madame Bovary, c'est moi," not "Je suis elle." Emma is stupid, Anna acts by caprice. Each woman learns from love how to give pain and to die. Each is shown willful and selfish in her passion, her shifting moods, more so than perhaps she was. Neither Emma's nor Anna's death is to me inevitable or wholly understandable. Certainly Jane Austen, with her canny knowledge of Emma Woodhouse, failed to create a believable man. Only Shakespeare knew both sexes—and so destroys my argument.

The parts I copied out from Jan Morris's book have to do with the double knowledge of male and female she may have gained:

> We are told that the social gap between the sexes is narrowing, but I can only report that having experienced life in both roles, there seems to me no aspect of existence, no moment of the day, no contact, no arrangement, no response, which is not different for men and for women. . . .

> The more preposterous handicaps of the female state are clearly doomed: nobody of sense can support them. . . . The lesser social bigotries and condescensions, and the female responses they evoke, will doubtless survive us all.

That I can believe.

July

At Chicago's O'Hare Airport, Philip waited at the gate to meet me. Together we hurried down a mile of corridors to TWA for a flight to Albuquerque. My son didn't say, "You're welcome to come." He said, "I want you to come, just you and me, babe."

Phil the nuclear physicist, professor at Case Western Reserve, conducts experiments in the immense Los Alamos Scientific Laboratory in New Mexico, which was begun in secrecy thirty years ago for the sole purpose of building a nuclear bomb to bring an end to World War II. Unlikely as it was that the laboratory would survive the war and the exodus of the scientists, instead it grew till it is one of the world's greatest laboratories, a center of research, no longer a bomb factory.

Phil's connection is with the Los Alamos Meson Facility, two years old, where a giant accelerator one-half mile long, of unprecedented intensity, speeds up atoms to form a beam. This beam of nuclear particles, flying at 84% the speed of light, is made to strike a target such as liquid hydrogen, and from the interaction billions of new particles are studied from data taken by computers to provide a picture of the activity *within* the nucleus of the atom.

Like anyone not a nuclear physicist, I scarcely grasp even the vocabulary, though I know that like all mankind I'm a collection of atoms. So are the stars. (Robert Frost addressed a star: "Talk Fahrenheit, talk Centigrade. Use language we can comprehend.") I wonder at myself living in the nuclear age, able to read Anglo-Saxon but not the words for the forces around me. Seeking a place to begin, I say like a kindergarten child, "The atom has a nucleus," and Phil nods with a grin. Yet ignorance is not surprising when an ordinary proton weighs less than one hundred millionth-billionth-billionth of an ounce; when the atom itself is 99,999,999,999,999.9% nothing —*nothing* within it but electrons whirling in a cyclical pattern and the nucleus. To work with that kind of material takes imagination. In the Middle Ages the Schoolmen debated the quodlibet "How many angels can dance on the end of a needle?" The number, they agreed, was infinite. Now the scientists estimate how many atoms can sit on the head of a pin: 36 billion, so I've read.

Phil's experiments deal with particles that are the basic building blocks of matter—protons and neutrons held together by pions or pi-mesons, which keep us all from coming unglued. The pion, not discovered till 1947, has a short life of one hundredth of a millionth of a second before it splits into a muon and a wisp called a neutrino. I ask Phil if I am to take this on faith, and he laughs. "Suit yourself."

Since hoards of new particles have lately been discovered (as late as 1958 at a meeting when Pauli spoke on the theory of particles, Niels Bohr rose up and said, "We are all agreed that your theory is crazy"), by now the "particle" physicists have done what nuclear physicists struggled half a century to do. They have split the particles themselves into partons—or *parts* of particles—known as quarks, from a line of whimsy in Joyce's *Finnegans Wake*: "Three quarks for Muster Mark." The nonsense word was adopted by the physicist Murray Gell-Mann in 1962, who says the taunting cry of gulls was in Joyce's words (whatever gulls have to do with it). Quarks, therefore, may be the building blocks *out of which everything else is formed*.

Thus far no such thing as a quark has been isolated. It's still a hypothesis, a convenient description of the *behavior* of particles within the nucleus. The actual discovery of the quark may provide the key to the universe. If creation began with the quark, is the quark to be called God?

I wish I could visualize as Phil does an unseen nuclear world, the patterns of birth, life, death within the atom that are the patterns within an infinite universe. When I ask if he minds being so little understood and people not listening, he says, "I like working on the frontiers of science." In a sense one doesn't know what one seeks, only that it must be there.

Los Alamos, a hundred miles north of Albuquerque, is on a sunlit mesa high in the mountains of New Mexico. Renting a car, we drove beside the Rio Grande to Santa Fe under the blue of the Sangre de Cristo Mountains that some call the loveliest on earth, a heavy dose of splendor. From there we climbed rocky heights beside mesas like tabletops in a row, slashed by steep canyons, where J. Robert Oppenheimer in 1942 found a spot remote enough for the secret work at hand, the creation of a weapon that would change the history of the world.

The official marker outside the little town says: Los Alamos—the Atomic City—Birthplace of the Atomic Age and the A-Bomb.

For thirty years I've wanted to go to Los Alamos. My close friend Donald Flanders was one of the makers of the bomb, a mathematician invited by Oppenheimer to join the group. On his way there in the summer of 1943, he stopped overnight in North Carolina, careful to tell us nothing. We didn't ask if he was headed for the moon but he acted like it. Whatever was in the wind, it was urgent and frightening.

"Whatever it is, write it down," I said. "Be sure to write it down."

"I'll be far too busy."

"Then make Sally do it."

His wife Sally would follow shortly with their children. Any experiment of living in a hiding place would need recording. She must keep notes as her duty to God and man. He agreed this was true: the story, however it turned out, would have to be told.

Sally set none of it down. The letters she wrote were strictly censored, containing not even a description of the scenery that might reveal the location. Without Laura Fermi's partial account, limited to fifty pages of her autobiography, *Atoms in the Family*, we would have no picture of the women's side of life in Los Alamos. So far not a single diary has come to light. To keep one was strictly forbidden.

In November 1942, the Los Alamos Ranch School for Boys, on a high plateau in the Jemez Mountains, was bought as a site for the Manhattan Project, so-called to conceal its purpose. There was no town of Los Alamos. The school had fifty-four buildings, the nearest town was sixteen miles away, the nearest neighbor the deer, bear, elk, coyote, rattlesnake in the mountains. Oppenheimer promptly took the place off the map. All approaches were sealed off. It simply disappeared.

For nearly three years, Los Alamos had no name or identity except P.O. Box 1663 in Santa Fe. Among trailers and hutments, the hastily built barracks for families looked alike, painted green to match the piñons and junipers. Whether the worst problem was lack of water with the constant danger of fire, the overcrowding, or lack of morale is a ponderable question. The two gates, East and West, were guarded by MPs in battle helmets; the project was operated under contract with the U.S. Army in the charge of General Leslie R. Groves, who ran it like an army operation and in his *Recollections* takes credit for the whole show: "Before long I was involved in every activity which I deemed essential for the success of the entire undertaking." The scientists hated his guts. He found them "the greatest collection of crackpots the world has ever known."

Most wives didn't know of the creation of the bomb, which might have increased their restlessness at being threatened with extinction. Husbands worked night and day under tremendous pressure pledged to silence. For amusement people had to invent their own. My friend Sally was expected to use her talents to organize social groups for square dancing, chamber music, choral singing, but she didn't get far. Laura Fermi says the women became high-strung, driven to "unreasonable and pointless rebellion."

They raged at being kept in the dark, confined like prisoners till the end of the war. It seemed less a military installation than a concentration camp with barbed-wire fences. The place itself they called The Hill (and still do), ramshackle, chaotic, unsightly in the midst of mountains of aspen and ponderosa pine. Nothing that would identify this lost world was tolerated. In a nowhere children were registered at school with no last names. Babies were born with no birthplace. Uneasy wives felt a sense of injustice at what they called snobbery and discrimination (the privileged had bathtubs and lived on "Bathtub Row"). They were bewildered, frustrated without supplies beyond a commissary and trading post. And, with reason, they were afraid. Women don't thrive under military command. It took a lot of character.

On rare occasions the wives were dashed by army bus to Sante Fe for a few hours of frenzied shopping, while army intelligence trailed them to see they spoke to no one on the street and mailed no letters. This created further alarm among the suspicious citizens of Santa Fe, who could only speculate as to what was going on up there on the mountain. They surmised the worst, that the scientists were working on death rays, making a spaceship or, some said, developing windshield wipers for submarines. The rumor spread it was a hospital for pregnant WAVEs and WACs.

In the desert of Alamogordo, called for security reasons "Trinity," the bomb was exploded July 16, 1945, though July 4 had been set for the test—a tactful way of shooting off fireworks. Oppenheimer named it Trinity from John Donne's holy sonnet, "Batter my heart, three person'd God"—a patch of blistering desert two hundred miles south of Los Alamos, without water, alive with rattlesnakes, scorpions, tarantulas, already known as the Jornada del Muerto. The Conquistadors found it a place of death.

In the short twenty-eight-month span the scientists built two kinds of bomb, one using uranium-235 as its nuclear explosive, the other using the man-made element plutonium, the deadliest substance known to man. It was the plutonium bomb they tested at Alamogordo, the one finished first.

When Donald Flanders described the night at Alamogordo on his return from New Mexico, he was a haunted man. From a shelter miles away, equipped with smoked glasses, they lay face down while first came the burst of searing light that lit all of central New Mexico. A ball of flame became a mushroom cloud, with it they felt a shock wave, heard the thunder of a doomsday blast. Oppenheimer was reminded of the Hindu words, "I am become Death, the shatterer of worlds."

Before the moment of zero, while a thunderstorm postponed the explosion till 5:30 a.m., in their minds were the dread possibilities ("What if lightning hits!"). It might be a failure, a dud, a fizzle, which would mean trying again too late. Or it might set the atmosphere on fire, extinguish life on earth, start a chain reaction that was unstoppable, circle the planet with flame, tilt the earth off its axis, blast them into nothingness sending death far and wide in radiation and fallout. It could be the end of the world for all they knew. As we know, it can be.

The other bomb, the uranium-235, was exploded three weeks later over Hiroshima, the one they called "Little Boy." The already tested plutonium bomb, "Fat Man," watermelon-shaped and sixteen feet in circumference, fell on Nagasaki August 9. Those two, plus the one set off at Alamogordo, were the *only* bombs in existence. Together they killed some 100,000 people. As the copilot over Hiroshima said, "My God, what have we done?"

For a keepsake, in August 1945 Donald Flanders brought me in a matchbox a piece of fused desert sand, glazed like green glass. He never knew how ungladly I received the gift, in revulsion threw it away. You can buy these relics in souvenir shops of Los Alamos. Yet, I now realize, this is the third piece of historic rock I've seen, each a tiny fragment bearing witness to man's conquests in my lifetime. At Cape Canaveral I studied a piece of the moon plucked from the Sea of Tranquility in 1969. It looked like a hunk of dusty coal. At the Alpine Club in London, I saw a sliver of rock that Hillary brought down in his pocket in 1953 from Mount Everest. Three simple rocks. I make little sense of them—the conquered peak, the conquered moon, the conquering destroyer.

For twelve more years Los Alamos remained a closed town, its gates locked and guarded. Incredibly, two spies had flourished there. Klaus Fuchs, the effective one, was a German scientist who stole plans for the Russians, a self-effacing, mild little fellow with a giggle, in demand as a babysitter. It took the Soviets four years to explode their first nuclear bomb, in 1949, which hastened the making in the Los Alamos Laboratory of the thermonuclear H-bomb. After the war the laboratory had nearly perished. With Oppenheimer's resignation there was no plan to keep an expensive white elephant on a remote mesa in New Mexico. Its mission as a war plant had ended. Its second mission, as fate decreed when President Truman ordered another crash program, was to produce a hydrogen bomb infinitely more powerful that would derive its energy from the fusion of nuclei, not the splitting of them. By 1952 the superbomb proved through tests it could wipe out *three* cities the size of Hiroshima. But Russia had that secret as well. With the hydrogen bomb, Einstein said, the elimination of life on earth was a technical possibility. In the midst of the Korean War that brought us to the brink of a third world war, the one way left for man's survival was peace.

Today Los Alamos ("the cottonwood trees") still puts a strain on wives—a town heavily policed, with forty-seven fallout shelters and a hospital prepared for radiation emergencies. Its population consists mostly of Ph.D.'s who, if they invite you to dinner, may absentmindedly forget to remove from their collar the dosimeter badge to record radiation doses. Husbands disappear each morning into the laboratory. It is the only industry.

I love the town for its lack of bustle or crime, its Ashley Pond named for Ashley Pond, founder of the Ranch School, which makes it Ashley Pond Pond. It has no railroad, bus, or taxi service, though a small aircraft makes round trips daily over the mountains to Albuquerque. Who would believe, without the boastful marker to say so, this is the spot that gave us the Atomic Age?

Philip and I live in White Rock, on the next mesa above the gorge of the Rio Grande. It came into overnight being in 1949 when the laboratory was moved from cramped quarters behind chicken wire to occupy a thirty-mile shelf on the mountain beyond town. White Rock sprang up to house construction workers who promptly moved on when the job was completed, leaving a ghost town that died and returned to life. The new White Rock, begun in 1962, is unequipped with fallout shelters or history of a heroic past. We keep house in the White Rock Motor Lodge. Walk a hundred yards and you're downtown, in reach of the supermarket, White Rock Pub, White Roxy movie, and a chiropractor named Dr. Wisehart. I ask what is missing for the good life and I can't think of a thing.

James (now Jan) Morris was in Wyoming a while ago gathering material for his book *Places*. After staring with glazed eyes at the exhibits of native crafts and attending nonstop festivals of tribal dances, he said to his guide, "I am tired of Indians." He might say so in New Mexico, as no doubt the Indians are tired of us. Two thousand years ago the Pueblos, most of whom live in this state, built the cliff villages in Frijoles Canyon. Before the Spaniards came and the rest of us, the land and sky belonged to them, turquoise sky and brown earth where turquoises were hidden. To wear a turquoise meant being protected by the sky people. Then in the nineteenth century the Navajos created a thriving turquoise-and-silver industry with their squash blossom necklaces, concho belts, bolos, rings, medallions.

This afternoon Phil and I drove to the Pueblo of San Ildefonso, where some three hundred Indians live and the temperature was 100 degrees, so dry the little cemetery of the mud-brown adobe Catholic church looked too parched for the dead to endure. The San Ildefonso Indians and their world-famed Maria make black pottery without a pottery wheel, firing it with dried cakes of manure in a dung kiln. This was a festival of Zunis, Hopis, Apaches, Navajos, Pueblos, gathered to exhibit their wares, and the place was in uproar, jammed with visitors. At each small stand sat an unsmiling Indian family. When a glossy-haired boy whispered "Two-fifty" as I held to the light a string of unevenly cut blue beads, I wondered if I wanted it at the price. The workmanship was crude, the azure color lovely.

"Two dollars and a half?" I asked Phil. "Too steep?"

"That depends," Phil said. "The price is $250."

I laid it down. We wandered over to the tribal dancing, continuous and free in the plaza under the only shade of a cottonwood. Each dance resembled the next—eagle dance, turtle dance, horsetail dance—a thumping up and down performed by the elderly with stony faces. Where were the young braves and Indian maidens? I laughed to remember the savage Fijians, rhythmic Maoris, tempestuous whirling Tahitians. What would they say to this folk art? And these prices?

I didn't like Taos at first sight, on a hot Sunday in July during the tourist season. It looked exploited and artificial, with shops of dreadful pictures. The town was overwhelmingly adobe (by mandate?)—the Piggly Wiggly, J. C. Penney's, the filling stations, the abounding motels. I'd hate to try to build a colonial mansion there. Instead of a simple mountain village, it might have been an amusement park. Dung-colored houses were by intention out of plumb, with tiny crooked windows shutting out a view of the Sangre de Cristo Mountains—named Blood of Christ by the Spanish explorers, either because the snow peaks turn bloodred at sunset, or some say because in early legends Christ's blood was white. The town seemed stuck with itself, isolated in the highest mountains of New Mexico, supporting more than eighty art galleries, a hippie colony of would-be artists, and a practicing witch doctor.

I was hasty to damn it on the spot. Taos must be real behind its facade to those who find it another Eden. For a while it meant that to D. H. Lawrence, who wrote, "For a greatness of beauty, I have never experienced anything like New Mexico. So beautiful, God! so beautiful." In fact Lawrence lived there a total of less than two years. Restlessly he came and went; without him the town would have little claim to fame. Georgia O'Keeffe spent a summer in 1929 living in the house Lawrence and Frieda had occupied, but she moved seventy miles east to Abiquiu and a wilderness of cow skulls and poppies. New Mexico was her chosen country: "There's something in the air. The sky, everything, is different."

Mabel Dodge, who was living with her lover the Pueblo Tony Luhan, had summoned the Lawrences (strangers to her save through his book *Sea and Sardinia*) to settle there, study and interpret the Pueblo Indians. They arrived reluctantly in September 1922. He was thirty-seven, Mabel forty-two. Though Lawrence believed in what he took to be the Indian mystique, a primitive response to life, he didn't like them as a people, refusing to identify himself with them ("All this poking and prying into the Indians is a form of indecency"). They were savages. It gave him a sick feeling "to get into the Indian vibration. Like breathing chlorine." He avoided their battered seven-hundred-year-old dwellings on the outskirts of Taos, which form the most spectacular of the nineteen Pueblo villages in New Mexico—two terraced beehive structures of adobe mud four or five storeys high separated by a mountain stream, together containing some one thousand Indians.

Lawrence was content nowhere. Mabel furnished her guests with a house near her own, but with quarrels and scarifying scenes that began soon after their arrival ("I hate her and the whole atmosphere") Lawrence and Frieda moved in December seventeen miles up to the Del Monte Ranch, spent a severe winter in a log cabin at nine thousand feet, left for Mexico, returned to England, and a year later in March 1924 were back in Taos. This time he and Frieda brought along their artist friend the Hon. Dorothy Brett, and Mabel, always generous, gave them her guest house. Lawrence now had three possessive women on his hands—hostile, jealous, full of tears, angry confrontations, and a notable lack of humor, all in love with Lorenzo. Brett, a great trial to Frieda, was deaf and forty, carried a brass ear trumpet, and adored Lawrence openly, his handmaiden. Frieda she thought unworthy of him. Mabel, even more troublesome with her cosmic emotions, told Frieda she wasn't the right woman for Lawrence. In *Lorenzo in Taos*, Mabel says, "I wanted to seduce his spirit. I persuaded my flesh and my nerves that I wanted him. . . . The womb in me roused to reach out and take him." He had written her, "One day I will come and take your submission. When you are ready."

Frieda would have none of that. The rows and spats, the tensions grew. Again Lawrence and Frieda moved out, to a place on Lobo Mountain two miles above the Del Monte Ranch, which Mabel impulsively gave them and they accepted, changing its name to the Kiowa Ranch. Lawrence bought a cow named Susan, the only female who failed to excite his fury.

Once more they left for Mexico intending to grow bananas, where he learned he had tuberculosis, and in April 1925 returned to Taos for five months before departing for good. By now Lawrence and Mabel were so estranged after venomous battles they refused to meet. She never saw him again. It had been his idea to write the story of her life in Taos, but he had taken fright through Frieda's tantrums and Mabel's attempt to bully him. Each thought the other evil, even murderous. "We do not take this snake to our bosom," Lawrence wrote, and Walter Lippmann advised Mabel, "Don't you know that you can't make a pet out of a snake?" In 1927 Lawrence was raging from Italy, "I'd rather go and live in a hyena house than go live in America," a place neither brave nor free. Yet a month before he died in southern France, he sent word to Mabel from Vence, "If we can manage it, and I can come to New Mexico, then we can begin a new life, with real tenderness in it."

The last time Lawrence returned to Taos was five years after his death, when in 1934 Frieda's third husband, Angelo Ravagli, built on the Kiowa Ranch a shrine of concrete bricks like a garage with a phoenix on top. Frieda had Lawrence's body exhumed and cremated, the ashes brought from France by Angelo for burial. Mabel, however, declared they must be scattered to the winds and planned to steal them. Frieda settled the matter her way by mixing them with sand and cement, forming a block weighing a ton to become the altar of the chapel. Like his emblem the phoenix, Lawrence rose up, or his ashes did, and went back to New Mexico.

After he died at forty-five, some mysterious urge held the three women in Taos for the rest of their lives, where they saw, resented, slandered each other, wrote books each to tell her own version of wrestling with Lorenzo. Frieda lived on for twenty-six years, marrying Angelo after his wife in Italy consented to a divorce. When she died on her seventy-seventh birthday, Angelo returned to wife and children.

Mabel died six years later in 1962—the wealthy socialite who had gone from her fashionable home on Fifth Avenue to Taos in 1916, purely as a whim to stay the weekend. Discovering she had found the meaning of life and love ("Here I belong, and here I want to stay"), she abandoned her newly wed third husband, the artist Maurice Sterne, for Tony Luhan. Tony, already married to Candelaria, was a strong massive Pueblo who wore the traditional blanket and his hair in two braids bound with ribbon, who could barely speak English, who, captured by Mabel, hated her turbulent scenes and greedy ways. Tony remained at Mabel's side as lover and husband for forty-six years, and with her death died soon after. He was buried among his own people.

Only Brett lives on in Taos, a local celebrity. [She died there in 1977.]

August

We were on our way to Sante Fe for dinner at the Palace (red plush velvet and French cuisine), but my mind was on roadrunners, the state bird, which I am forever hoping to see flash by, racing up and down highway and byway at 15 mph as it is supposed to do. A brown bird two feet long, half of it tail carried at a cocky angle, should be easy to recognize, since it poses in souvenir shops on ashtrays, greeting cards, cocktail napkins, T-shirts, and Hollywood cartoons. New Mexico is proudly called the land of enchantment and roadrunners. Enchantment, yes. The roadrunner—a furtive kind of cuckoo that prefers to run rather than fly—pointedly avoids me. I went all the way to New Zealand to see the kiwi bird. In New Mexico, no roadrunner.

At 7:00 p.m. on our car radio came the voice of Richard M. Nixon, delivering his speech of resignation as president. It was a grievous moment of history, not altogether a surprise. Twelve days ago, the House Judiciary Committee accused Nixon of obstructing justice in the Watergate cover-up and recommended he be impeached. The House was to debate the resolution late this month. Nixon would go on trial in the Senate.

Now he was removing himself from office, entirely in the wrong words, the wrong tone of voice full of nobility, like the sound of an elder statesman handing over the reins of government. He spoke without remorse, apology, or admission of wrongdoing and of being caught at it. He had betrayed us, a dishonest man. What Gerald Ford might be—but why speculate on him?

I turned sadly to look out the window for roadrunners.

September

Josephine Johnson, who reviewed my book *Beautiful Lofty People*, saw no excuse for my including verse along with the prose. "The poems that follow each prose section only cap and recap a story that does not need comment," she said in reproof. Robert Lowell was berated for the same fault in *Life Studies* by critics who recognize no difference between prose and verse. They may be right, now that verse has gone prosaic.

Yeats, for one, made a habit of testing a theme first in prose. Of "Words" he wrote, "Today the thought came to me that she never really understands my plans or notions or ideas." In verse he said it again but it sounded better:

> I had this thought a while ago,
> 'My darling cannot understand
> What I have done, or what would do
> In this blind bitter land.'

Of "A Woman Homer Sung" he wrote: "My emotions were exasperated by jealousy, for everyone that came near Maud Gonne made me jealous." Then he found the language for it:

> If any man drew near
> When I was young,
> I thought, 'He holds her dear,'
> And shook with hate and fear.
> But O! 'twas bitter wrong
> If he could pass her by
> With an indifferent eye.

October

John Leonard sent me sixteen books to review and by special delivery added a seventeenth. I picture his office in Times Square piled with books, the editor moaning, "Sweep them out!"

"Where to?"

"Try North Carolina. Mrs. Bevington likes to read."

They're about people, a queer assortment: Scott and Zelda Fitzgerald, Solzhenitsyn, Winston Churchill, Frost, Thoreau, Mark Twain, Gilbert and Sullivan, Galileo, Columbus, Marlborough, Pitt the Younger, Lord Nelson, J. Pierpont Morgan, Charles VII of France, Philip II of Spain, Nicholas II of Russia, and Jesus Christ.

Apparently the one thing their lives have in common is contradiction. Happiness and misery are their theme, the race to and from triumph and disaster. Solzhenitsyn in a stark autobiography reveals a man incapable of smiling. But Heinrich Böll said of him, "What surprises me most is the calm that he emanates."

Kathleen Morrison wrote of Frost's last tempestuous years. After his wife's death he was fractious and unmanageable, cutting ties with his children and stumbling about alone, by his own choosing bereft. It was then the Theodore Morrisons took him in, the guest who became a fixture. Someone had to look after him, put up with his formidable ego and fits of rage, know his worth and love him. He required not only praise but tribute. Shortly before he died, Frost observed, "One of the best things in the world is just to be goodnatured," a quaint remark from so irascible a poet.

Mark Twain adds up to the funniest and saddest (*Mark Twain and His World*, by Justin Kaplan). His seventy-five years, spent in wild contradiction, took him from poverty to riches, riches to bankruptcy, hilarity to despair, love of his fellow man ("sociable as a fly") to hatred of the human race. Born lucky, he cursed his luck. After his daughter Susy's death he lived in seclusion, only to emerge a diner-out and showman in his immaculate white suits. "In God We Trust is a glorious motto," he said. "I don't believe it would sound any better if it were true."

John Churchill who became Duke of Marlborough (*The First Churchill*, by Corelli Barnett) set eyes on Sarah Jennings when she was fifteen ("My Soull, I love you so trully well"), rose to be hero of Blenheim and Ramillies, husband of the divine and terrible Sarah, and descended to a tragic figure fallen from greatness. Before his full-length portrait by Kneller in 1712, he paused one day to study its heroic proportions, remarking sadly, "There was once a man."

He had a face, a man's face (*The Faces of Jesus*, by Frederick Buechner) that for twenty centuries has been portrayed by painters, sculptors, weavers, carvers, though the New Testament nowhere says what he looked like. The face is his face whether it appears on a silk screen, primitive carving, Renaissance mural, created in oils, frescoes, mosaics, in gold, wood, marble, ivory, china, glass; whether a Japanese Christ crucified, a surrealist *Christ over New York City*, a Russian Orthodox Christ wearing a halo like a ferris wheel, an El Greco cleaning the temple, a Salvador Dali at the Last Supper. Recorded on an embroidered altar cloth, a gold coin, or the Sacred Heart woven into a rug, he is a contradiction of grief and serenity. And it is always the same face.

November

The Mayflower Cup is an award given by descendants of the *Mayflower*. I never knew that. Tonight I received the cup at a banquet of roast beef and a chocolate eclair, where the speaker of the evening, Ivor Richard, Q.C., reassured us in good humor of England's tolerant attitude in 1776 toward the skirmishes of the American Revolution; the French Revolution excited her anxiety far more. Glancingly he referred to the War of 1812, a bad year for war if we wanted to attract England's attention; Napoleon took precedence in English minds. Mr. Richard didn't mention the Pilgrims at all, whose exodus probably escaped his and England's notice.

It's a loving cup with handles, too large for champagne, too small for a punch bowl. It should be filled with wine and passed from lip to lip, as the Pilgrim Fathers didn't do though the *Mayflower* was a ninety-foot cargo or wineship whose cargo had been wine. As the ship's log shows, on the *Mayflower* the Pilgrims drank beer. However, if the guests this evening were descendants of the 102 passengers, I say they came of gracious stock.

Grandma Moses was a *Mayflower* descendant.

December

Tonight in Chicago we had a dinner party for the Kolbs and McGanns, who brought with them a lovely snowfall. Jerry, a professor of English, delighted me by stoutly defending pedantry and pedants. Who would believe there was anything to argue in their favor—the pompous parading of book learning by a dusty scholar? Jerry claimed he was a pedant, proud of his calling. By biting my tongue I avoided the pedantry of quoting Bacon, who said they spin "cobwebs of learning," or Juvenal, who (according to Montaigne) said of pedants, "They copulate in learned style."

At year's end the *New York Times* finds the world "a horrendous mess." Sarah, a slender little girl with dark eyes and glowing face, skips about singing "Happy, happy, happy in the middle of the world."

1975

January

We went downtown in the bitter Chicago wind to see the Marc Chagall mosaic that stands in the cold at the Plaza. It was completed last year, and Chagall himself came at eighty-seven for the unveiling. He was unprepared for Chicago, which startled him, too immense a background for his work. His sculpture, *Four Seasons*, is cruelly dwarfed by the towering skyline—a little pink-and-gold sugarcake set down in the midst of giants. It is fourteen feet high, an oblong block with Chagall fantasies: floating angels, a blue horse, gold sunbursts, a fish, in light pastel colors on a white surface, very sweet, clean, and childlike.

I wish Chicago's recent acquisitions of modern sculpture might be placed in a row—Picasso's fifty-foot winged donkey, Chagall's sugarcake, and Henry Moore's bronze, *Nuclear Energy*, a great squat object that Jan Morris took for a bald head, meant to be a mushroom cloud shaped like a human skull. They remind me of Wallace Stevens' friendly measure of Chagall: "One whom reason would crush."

At the Friday luncheon of the English faculty, Ned Rosenheim and I talked about nostalgia. He teaches a course at the University of Chicago on life in the 1930s, wafting the students back to jitterbug, jam sessions, bobby-soxers, and boogie-woogie by playing old jazz records of Fats Waller and Benny Goodman, having them read Faulkner's *Sanctuary*, John O'Hara's *Appointment in Samarra*, Dorothy Baker's *Young Man with a Horn*.

Ned felt a nostalgia that at times choked him. The students felt none since they weren't born then and were glad to have missed the depression and the war in Spain. You can't evoke a past you never lost. They thought a running board was a skateboard or kiddie scooter. They hadn't heard of B.V.D.'s or spats. The innocent treatment of sex amused them without stirring their envy. They guessed that Lydia Pinkham was a Pilgrim housewife.

"Nostalgia," Ned said, "is something that overtakes me when I'm depressed." It means homesickness, the sunny side of the street. I feel it when I hear the 1934 song, "Blue skies smiling at me. Nothing but blue skies do I see."

February

In my poetry seminar I quoted the words I read last night in a memorial to W. H. Auden, "At any time there must be five or six supremely intelligent people on the earth." Auden, it claimed, was one of them. Not to me he wasn't.

I asked the class how many people in our century they could name who passed for supremely intelligent, and they were quick with answers, pleased with the guessing game—Freud, Gandhi, Einstein, Karl Marx, Proust, Joyce, Eliot, Yeats. But when it came to living persons, the room was silent. "Who are they today?" I asked, stumped myself. "Who are the immortals among us?" I honestly don't know.

The students sat in deep thought. Nobody wanted to give up without a single candidate. "Castro?" asked one girl timidly.

My student Jean is trying to convert me to Transcendental Meditation. She stayed after class to extol its powers. TM, primarily a student movement in America, is a science of creative intelligence that can lower the blood pressure, increase brain waves, decrease anxiety and sloth. It's good for gum inflammation, insomnia, and passing exams. Two meditations a day while chanting a *mantra* will bring a calm emptiness.

Because we talk in class about Yeats's fondness for magic, reincarnation, and communion with ghosts, Jean hopes I am ready for conversion to the mystic life. I tell her I'm satisfied with the Sanskrit syllable *om* that Allen Ginsberg says contains the soul and essence of the universe, though what we intoned in college twenty times twice daily, Coué's "Day by day in every way I'm getting better and better," worked just as well.

March

Philip Larkin is called, unaccountably, "One of the best of three or four poets now writing in our language." The other three must be

Robert Lowell. *High Windows* is Larkin's third volume, twenty-four poems. Every ten years he lets fall a small joyless collection as if tired of lugging them around. The poems have an air of defeat, of being celibate and sedentary, intimidated by love, uninvolved with sex or rejoicing ("Sex, yes, but what / Is sex?"). As a middle-aged bachelor, a librarian at the University of Hull, not much has happened to him, in childhood ("a forgotten boredom") or since. "Loneliness clarifies," he says, but it doesn't lead to lovesongs. So he admits to being taken by surprise by an event back in 1963, caught off guard aged forty-one. I read "Annus Mirabilis" with considerable relief:

> Sexual intercourse began
> In nineteen sixty-three
> (Which was rather late for me)—
> Between the end of the *Chatterley* ban
> And the Beatles' first LP.

Then in a bleak parenthesis he adds "(Though just too late for me)." At forty-one?

April

Before dining with Elizabeth Janeway, two of whose books are on the woman question—*Women, Their Changing Roles* and *Man's World, Woman's Place*—I read them both, trembling to think what potholes of discussion we could fall into, like primitive tribal customs of love and marriage, or the rise and fall of women's rights. Since Juanita Kreps was invited too, we might get to wrestling with their economic status. If called on, I was loaded for bear with a quotation from Adrienne Rich, the feminist poet who deals boldly with the problem of being a mere woman endangered by male society:

> It is
> A man's world.
> But finished.
> They themselves have sold it to the machines.

Of the thirty-eight states needed to ratify the Equal Rights Amendment, North Carolina is self-righteously not one. "For the first time since the War Between the States," said a state legislator, "North Carolina is a battleground—being invaded by those who would deny and destroy the sanctity of our homes." So the gallantry of the South rose up. "Stop ERA," they bellowed. "You can't fool Mother Nature."

May

The candor of *Half Remembered*, a personal history by Peter Davison, made me fear this was another walking-naked enterprise, revealing life in its appalling failures. I think not. Unlike the confessional poets he avoids self-pity.

But the irony exists: in the end the child must explain the man, though the child is too young for the part. Peter's father, Edward Davison, was an English poet who married the beautiful Natalie, a New York girl of prosperous family. The marriage grew increasingly discordant, while the children listened, the sound of rage "hanging over them like monsoons." "In a sense," Peter Davison reflects, "all unhappy families are alike." (Tolstoy says all *happy* families are alike; maybe they both are right.) Inevitably he rebelled and shut his parents out of his life. The tale is familiar as personal histories are: the impact lies in the telling, the recognition (for one thing) that you can't escape by running away. You can try to grow from the unforgiving child, accuser and rebuking judge, to the adult who judges himself. Peter names the hour when he began the search.

One answer came from Robert Frost, his father's close friend and Peter's own: "Two roads diverged in a wood, and I—,/ I took the one less traveled by." A matter of choice, Frost said, "And that has made all the difference." In a burst of independence, a flash of insight, Peter rejected this statement of dilemma as false. On the contrary, he told himself, the traveler may choose *both* roads if he likes. And in my opinion the world should be advised of this consoling fact: one is forever taking two roads, changing directions, avoiding if possible the straight and narrow. I laugh to think how long I've been fooled by that poem. As poet, editor, publisher, Peter has been happier than Frost ever was. Which proves there are fourteen ways to Sunday.

Did Frost ever read a story by O. Henry, "The Roads We Take"? In it Shark Dodson ran away from home at seventeen, heading for New York City to seek his fortune. He came to a fork in the road, studied it, and chose the left-hand fork. That night he met up with a Wild West show and traveled west with it, where he murdered a man. Sometimes he wondered how he would have turned out if he had taken the other road. "Oh, I reckon you'd have ended up about the same," said his friend Bob

Tidball. "It ain't the road we take; it's what's inside us that makes us turn out the way we do."

In the surprise ending, Shark Dodson only dreamed he chose the left-hand road. He took, in fact, the right-hand fork when he was young, arrived in New York as planned, and became a successful broker on Wall Street, where he betrayed and destroyed a man who was his friend. The road he took hadn't made any difference.

June

Our worst loss is in language. We don't hear it any more, what Swift called "proper words in proper order," Coleridge "the right words in the right order," Yeats "the natural words in the natural order," Eliot "the best words in the best arrangement." Verbs suffer the most: anything becomes a verb—to trivialize, to soapbox (Pauline Kael's invention in the *New Yorker*), optimize, showcase, urbanrenew, to ad hoc, to eyeball, to Martha Mitchell—such manglers of language we are, either supportive or self-actualizing. We maintain a high-profile posture, assume a lifestyle (homosexuality is "an alternate lifestyle"), engage in a dialogue to structure a scenario in terms of an area, achieving input or output of feedback, a ripoff or a putdown.

Hopefully (a word beyond hope of good riddance), we have less charisma now. The name of the game is ambiance and machismo. We talk weatherwise or otherwisewise, but the moment of truth and epiphany are becoming, God willing, inoperative as well as counterproductive.

Jules Renard: "What a saving in paper there will be when a law is passed that will force writers to use only the right word!"

July

A sound reason for staying alive is to avoid becoming one of the defenseless dead. It's Thurber's turn to be exposed in *Thurber*, as before him were Lytton Strachey, Virginia Woolf, the Bloomsbury group, the Harold Nicolsons, E. M. Forster, the Algonquin crowd. Frost is called monstrous, Evelyn Waugh an ogre, Cyril Connolly an unbearable snob. The method is to strip the subject of virtue and respect, deny him character, reduce his reputation as writer and citizen. (On the other hand, Carlyle called biography in his time "delicate decent, bless its mealy mouth.") Thurber was a wounder, we're told, hostile in his rages, a drunkard, a whoremaster, a mess. In the *Times Literary Supplement* he is damned as "about as big a mess as a man can be." Too bad he can't answer back.

August

Again Phil and I are in New Mexico while he confronts the nucleus of the atom. He lives in a world of computer figures like a man writing a formula of the universe, mystified by what it says.

At O'Hare, before our plane left for Albuquerque, I snatched up a paperback for the flight, bemused at an international airport by a bestseller called *Fear of Flying*. I was curious about Erica Jong, why a critic like John Updike praised the book as "the most uninhibited, delicious, erotic novel a woman ever wrote, a winner." (As a man, he presumably outdistances her.)

How can we survive our loss of language? The monotony in Erica Jong, more emetic than erotic, the suffocating repetition of words, numbs the mind. Why didn't she count the times she repeats the pornography that would shock Justinian's Theodora? (Paul Valéry: "When one no longer knows what to do in order to astonish and survive, one offers one's pudenda to the public gaze.")

Erica Jong says, "I want to inspire people." She admires Keats. She hitches her star to Colette, who wrote of sex with clarity and taste. Erica Jong's words offend the ear; she doesn't hear the sound of them. Colette did.

In my boredom I looked over at Phil's face, envying his composure and absorption.

We keep house as usual at the White Rock Motor Lodge. The magnitude of terra-cotta mountains reminds me I am back in love with New Mexico. The earth has the eerie quality of being created out of some sublime conception. Yet after the Civil War, General Sherman deemed New Mexico worthless and recommended we give it away. In 1906 Arizona turned down a proposal of statehood if it would mean union with New Mexico that tried to change its unhappy name to Montezuma.

I read a lot, take a walk, read Colette's diary written in her seventies called *The Evening Star*. "I don't always enjoy myself," she wrote, crippled and in pain. "I don't know when I shall succeed in not writing. . . .

If it is necessary to try, all right, I'll try." Colette wanted to leave behind no debts and tidy drawers. Neatness in everything, living and dying.

A *Rage for Order*

"Above all, no debts, no debts and tidy drawers"—
This was the way she planned it, this the order
Of her departure Colette had in mind,
Owing no one his due, leaving no clutter,
Outwitting chaos. So, accordingly,
One day she did depart. And so would I,
My own possessions folded, piled, arranged,
My words untangled, my life unperplexed
Save for the debts I owe, to whom and why.
God only knows what unpaid debts, what debts?

September

I remind my seminar that writing isn't the easy thing it looks and prove it by statistics:

Tolstoy wrote *War and Peace* seven times.
Hemingway wrote the ending to A *Farewell to Arms* thirty-nine times.
Dylan Thomas wrote a line 100 times, his quota two lines a day.
Yeats called one line a day's work, "stitching and unstitching."
Cummings developed "rosetree rosetree" through 175 pages of his notebook.
Henry James dined out between sentences 140 times in one London season.

Last night my student John spent two hours writing a poem and cut class to rest up. How can I persuade them writing isn't the whole problem? One needs something to write about. "Astonish me," I cry like Diaghilev. Kirti, my dreamy Indian girl, is good at titles: "The Tree in the Middle of the River," "My Self Lashing at My Self," but faced with the part that follows Kirti says, "How do I find my focus?" Philippa composes a celebratory poem, "Thoughts upon Turning 21," and her main thought is "Time may leave me with withered marks." Ray in a narrative "Growing Up" tells how you do it: you listen to rock and dream of chasing girls, you wake up on Sunday morning and say, "I am possibility." Bill, a dedicated scrivener, makes lists of future poems, notably of grandparents gasping on their deathbed. Why is dying poetic?

I love them for their pains. They stay after class to ask, "Is there hope?" Wallace Stevens said: "A poet, or any writer, must be held to what he *puts down on the page.*"

October

Like countless others before her, countless more to come, Kathleen Raine decided to take stock of her life and come to terms with it. If one is a professional writer, one confides in a reader and publishes the stocktaking as autobiography. If a poet, one creates a "lyrical" autobiography. Kathleen Raine is a poet. Her volume *The Land Unknown*, meaning the mystic land of self, shows the difference between prose and poetry: prose is not meant to be sung to a lyre; poetry (more often than not) allows the poet to place himself at the center of his concern, with the rest in shadow.

In 1973 Miss Raine published in England *Farewell Happy Fields*, starting as the custom is with infancy and childhood. She delayed releasing Part II because of the pain it would give others. Why only two years later her words will no longer give pain is unclear. In abject confession she is concerned to say where she went wrong "so often and so obviously." Her outcry of mea culpa is so contrite and prolonged that the reader—this reader—would be thankful to be told not so much where she went wrong as why.

She offers two reasons, many times rehearsed, for her plight: Kathleen Raine was beautiful, Kathleen Raine was a poet. She is hard to please; one can only sit in envy. In "Prayer for My Daughter," Yeats asked that his child be not too beautiful or "consider beauty a sufficient end"; certainly he didn't intend her to be a poet. Either condition may be miserable, while the combination of the two may be unholy, but I think most women would be glad to take the chance.

At Girton College, Cambridge, she knew herself talented and beautiful but with this knowledge "I was a monster indeed." She married Hugh, aware that her power to evoke erotic love had made her frigid, and from the brief encounter was rescued by Charles (the poet Charles Madge) who said, "Come with me, and I will give you a cause to live for." The cause was Communism, which failed in its mission. She eloped with Charles and lived as a somnambulist, in tears, guilt, despair. What Charles thought of the arrangement, or Hugh before him, is not revealed. Each is a cardboard figure, though Charles, whose poetry she ignores, became the father of her two children before she left him for the cardboard lover

Alastair. Her poems were grains of gold "calcinated from all that dross of life." Alastair went off to war.

The dirge of self-reproach is lightened by an occasional note of exultation that she was, after all, a poet on a legendary quest, a seer, a pythoness, granted off and on a glimpse of paradise. "Do only poets fail in the conduct of their lives?" she asks. For Kathleen Raine the question answers itself: people like her are set apart, dedicated, at odds with parents, husbands, lovers, children, dangerous to society. "Being what I was, I had to go my way," a way of wrong turnings. To save the woman at the expense of the poet didn't occur to her.

"Like a wounded animal" she retired with her small son and daughter to a rented vicarage in Westmorland, then left them with a woman friend to return to London to make a living. On impulse she took the insincere step of becoming a Catholic convert and found herself unable to remain in the Church. Her heart belonged to the occult, a higher vision of radiance. A line from "The Pythoness" says, "God in me is the fire wherein I burn."

The years that followed lacked radiance till a vision came to her, not through love or the solace of religion but in the British Museum through reading William Blake. There as an exile she took refuge, claiming him as one who walked beside her in hell, "my Virgil, my guide." (Surely Blake liked to walk in heaven too.) Quite simply she places poetry above human passion, worth the extraordinary sacrifice it demands, defining the role of poet as one by which unpardonable hurt is inevitably done to others.

I am far from being a good reader of Kathleen Raine, impatient as I am with the idea of the artist different *in kind*, who can't be expected to treat anyone well, intimate only with a muse. I wish with her sense of the power of love she had distinguished it from self-love.

November

For Blake the visions were real. When he was four years old, God put his head in at the window and made the child scream. Before he was ten he saw a tree full of angels in a hayfield, visions that increased as he grew older till "I am the companion of angels." A procession of monks appeared to him in Westminster Abbey, Christ and his apostles among the tombs. The archangel Gabriel on splendid wings paid him a visit before the roof of Blake's study opened and Gabriel ascended to heaven, where "he stood in the sun and, beckoning to me, moved the universe." The Virgin Mary communed with him. He saw Ezekiel sitting under a tree,

Homer, Moses, Socrates, Dante, Richard II, Milton ("I beheld Milton with astonishment descending down into my cottage garden"). When he began to draw, the spirits trooped in and sat for their portraits: Pindar, the courtesan Laïs—who in impudence hung around till Blake sketched her to get rid of her—Herod, Lot, Solomon, the majestic Job. He never used a living model but drew from the original.

Blake was constantly surrounded by guardian fairies, of whom he was fond. One poem tells how he captured a fairy in his hat like a butterfly.

"Did you ever see a fairy's funeral, Madam?" he asked a lady in a company.

"Never, sir."

"I have!"

It happened the night before as he walked in his garden. Under a flower petal he saw a cortege of green and gray grasshoppers bearing a tiny fairy on a rose leaf. With grasshopper songs they buried her.

Blake saw evil too. Having a sudden vision of a flea, he took up his pencil and drew the scaly demon holding a cup of blood, its long tongue flicking out of its mouth.

In 1787, when Blake's brother Robert died at twenty-four, Blake watched his soul rise through the ceiling, clapping its hands for joy. He made a watercolor of Robert with a star falling at his feet. Long afterward, Blake wrote to a friend, "Thirteen years ago I lost a brother, and with his spirit I converse daily and hourly in the spirit. . . . I hear his advice, and even now write from his dictate." The words would fly about the room.

Blake's faithful, loving wife, who believed in his visions, told a friend, "I have very little of Mr. Blake's company; he is always in Paradise." As he died he burst out singing hallelujahs, though these songs, he told his wife, were not his own. "My beloved, they are not mine—no—they are not mine." Angels, again. After his death he remembered to come back every day and sit with Mrs. Blake to talk on practical matters.

Robert Frost assumed that Blake had seen God in person: "It's God, / I'd know him from Blake's picture anywhere." As everyone agrees, Blake didn't always get a true likeness.

December

A critic once described a performance of Beatrice Lillie's as giving the impression she was playing the role of Nothing in *Much Ado about Nothing*. Tom Prideaux means no such thing in the title of his biography of Ellen Terry, *Love or Nothing*. He means what Shaw meant in a letter to her of 1897, "I am convinced that with you a human relation is love or nothing."

Every man who saw Ellen Terry fell instantly in love with her. Only Henry James had the fortitude to hold out against her and her free, familiar, "osculatory" style of acting; as he observed, "The amount of kissing and hugging that goes on in London in the interest of the drama is quite incalculable." The rest were, to a man, enchanted by a great actress and strikingly lovely woman with warm gray eyes, golden hair, husky voice, and laughing face. Oscar Wilde wrote two sonnets to her ("like some wan lily overdrenched with rain"). Buffalo Bill carried her picture wherever he went. Tennyson adored her. Gladstone was so stagestruck he had a special chair in the wings to watch Ellen and Irving together, once carelessly popping his head out in plain sight of the audience, who cheered. Lewis Carroll became her lifelong admirer, at a safe remove. Ellen wrote, "He was as fond of me as he could ever be of anyone over the age of ten." He wrote in his diary, "I can imagine no more delightful occupation than brushing Ellen Terry's hair!"

Shaw idolized her. The famous correspondence, begun in 1892 when he was thirty-six, Ellen forty-five, was a courtship on paper, kisses by mail, a lovemaking that stayed verbal yet was impassioned enough for Shaw to write, "I love you soulfully and bodyfully, properly and improperly, every way that a woman can be loved." Nine months later he married Charlotte Payne-Townshend, a union that left Ellen imperturbed. "What intrepidity," she wrote him. Not till 1900 did she finally meet Shaw in person, with his wife in tow, backstage after a performance of his *Captain Brassbound's Conversion* in which Ellen did not have a part. The immortal moment went awkwardly, a kind of disenchantment. They were right in agreeing, as Ellen had said, "I think I'd rather never meet you—in the flesh." But Shaw declared it without exaggeration the most enduring of all courtships, one that, in the ardor of its words, survived the death of the lovers.

Ellen Terry's story is not a fairy tale. She never went to school, the child of strolling players who grew up in the theater. With the innocence that always clung to her, she was married at sixteen to the portrait painter G. F. Watts, thirty years older, who called the stage an abomination and tried to remove his favorite model from it. He gave her her first kiss, which Ellen assumed had made her pregnant. After the wedding she broke into tears and Watts said, "Don't cry. It makes your nose swell." His attempt to tame and humble her lasted a bare ten months, till he dismissed her as incorrigible and sent her back home, banished. "I hated my life," she wrote in her memoirs, "hated everyone and everything."

A few years later again she deserted the stage and, legally married to Watts, ran away with a handsome architect, Edward Godwin, who taught her what love is. Her family believed her drowned, a suicide. With Godwin she had escaped to a hideaway cottage in Hertfordshire, where during the next six years she bore him two children—Edith and Teddy, who later called himself Gordon Craig—and asked for no other life, "the absolute devotion to another human being" that to her meant happiness. When the bailiff camped on the doorstep, she returned to the theater at twenty-seven to pay the bills. Godwin deserted her.

It was then Ellen Terry joined Henry Irving in a career that made them the most celebrated acting team in the history of the English stage. For twenty-four years they were partners at the Lyceum Theatre, where Ellen proved her amazing gift for playing Shakespeare. Max Beerbohm said she needed Shakespeare; he alone among dramatists could stand up to her. "My line is comedy," Ellen believed, and by nature she was lighthearted, witty, incapable of theatricality. Yet she endured a lifetime of fearful endings by drowning in *Hamlet*, suffocation in *Othello*, stabbing in *Romeo and Juliet*, hanging in *King Lear*, madness in *Macbeth*. She played them all except Cleopatra. When as Portia she said, "You see me, Lord Bassanio, where I stand, such as I am," the audience burst into applause. Her son swore that Ellen Terry could only act herself; what she was she taught herself to be through severe discipline, careful technique, infinite pains. "Even her eyelashes acted," wrote Virginia Woolf.

She made eight triumphant tours of the United States, where Henry Ward Beecher, who hadn't been inside a theater till he was seventy, found her irresistible. She was married three times, never permanently, never to the one man she loved (Godwin)—the last time in her late fifties to a young American actor, James Carew, from whom within two years she was unofficially separated. Shaw wrote to her, "This habit of getting married is the ruin of theatrical art. . . . Why could you not have been content with my adoration?"

Love was the one thing she ceaselessly gave and sought. She told her son, "The dwindling of love is the only thing to be feared in this world. I am sure of that." It was an elusive thing she offered freely and received in abundance. The greatest wickedness of all, Ellen Terry believed, is the grief we cause, the pain we give to others.

1976

January

Sarah has a book of children's stories written by Lafcadio Hearn. One is called "The Old Woman Who Lost Her Dumplings." I honestly think I have lost my dumplings. But I will not be called, as Anne Lindbergh's grandchildren call her, Granny Mouse.

Max Beerbohm wrote my epitaph (in a copy of W. J. Turner's *Paris and Helen*):

> O glen, grove, dale, vale, glade, grove, glen,
>   Right good are ye to dwell in;
> But when is Paris coming—when?
>   And where the Hell is Helen?

Harry Reasoner, news commentator on ABC, says of the Bicentennial, "It's a wonder we've *lasted* two hundred years." You would think by the hoopla that, engaged since 1776 in the pursuit of happiness, we have achieved it, along with equality, independence, liberty, civil rights, and peace. We have a Bicentennial Minute every night on CBS, courtesy of Shell gasoline. Each crossroads and cow pasture in the country plans its parade. One idea is to drape the Statue of Liberty in red, white, and blue. Another is to have the Queen of England come over and congratulate us.

February

Margaret Church, a professor of English at Indiana University, sent me a list of questions on one of their Ph.D. examinations. The student was to identify and explain the significance of the following items:

1. Castiglione
2. *Hero and Leander*
3. Thomas Dekker
4. Roger Ascham
5. *Amoretti*
6. Nicholas Udall
7. David Bevington

I think I could answer satisfactorily all but #7. That's a stickler.

March

I flew to Chicago because Bob Cromie asked me to appear on his television program "Book Beat." Peggy drove me to North St. Louis Street to the studios of PBS where we met Bob Cromie fifteen minutes before the taping, and he hugged me as if we were old friends (he used to review my books in the *Chicago Tribune*. Once he wrote, "The lady is a lady," a comment I never understood but appreciated). Bob had just arrived and was headed for the lunchroom. "What would you like to eat?" he said.

For twelve years he has talked with writers, the Bookman of the Air. By now he has lost count of the numbers listened to—except on the rare occasion when an author in a state of shock falls mute and Bob amiably fills in the half hour by asking a question and answering it himself. While he enjoyed a belated lunch in obvious serenity of spirit, I sat wordless, clutching a cup of black coffee, waiting to be briefed or whatever the procedure was, to be told for goodness sake what to do. The minutes passed while he chatted comfortably on. It was clear there would be no briefing. Far from unfolding a plan of action, Bob had no plan of action. The performance would be spontaneous, unrehearsed.

At the thought I froze. As a teacher who talks most of the time, my way of being spontaneous is to prepare beforehand with the care of a tightrope walker; I also carry notes to avoid falling on my face. We took a short unnerving stroll to the broadcasting room. Bob held my hand, an unruffled man. "That's a good shade of blue you're wearing," he said. "I'm windblown," I said and he laughed, relieved I could open my mouth.

Heaven knows what we went on about, except that Bob remembered the contents of my book better than I did. Peggy in the control tower said afterward the crew found us funny. I recall dithering on about Bertrand Russell, his despair of the human race and prediction of the end of the planet. "Russell kissed you once, didn't he?" Bob asked suddenly. "Yes," I said, "but not while he was predicting the end of the planet."

April

Wallace Stevens was asked by Ronald Latimer which poem of his own he preferred. He looked into *Ideas of Order* and answered, in a letter of November 15, 1935: "It seems to be 'How to Live. What to Do.' I like it most, I suppose, because it so definitely represents my way of thinking."

How to Live. What to Do

Last evening the moon rose above this rock
Impure upon a world unpurged.
The man and his companion stopped
To rest before the heroic height.

Coldly the wind fell upon them
In many majesties of sound:
They that had left the flame-freaked sun
To seek a sun of fuller fire.

Instead there was this tufted rock
Massively rising high and bare
Beyond all trees, the ridges thrown
Like giant arms among the clouds.

There was neither voice nor crested image,
No chorister, nor priest. There was
Only the great height of the rock
And the two of them standing still to rest.

There was the cold wind and the sound
It made, away from the muck of the land
That they had left, heroic sound
Joyous and jubilant and sure.

The man and his companion are travelers. Having left the muck of the land in quest of faith, seeking "a sun of fuller fire," they stop to rest from their journey and find only a bare rock—*not* a crucifix or haloed image but a rock, *not* divine but massive and real, replacing the setting sun they left behind. They hear no voice of chorister or priest, only the cold wind's actual sound, which, being real, is joyous and jubilant and sure.

Instead of crying for help to God or one of the gods, Stevens said, we must accept the reality of the rock that is only rock in an unpurged, unsponsored world. A strong spirit stands free and ungrieving in a world without God. This is accommodation. This is how to live and what to do. He called it "the version of the thing." I call it victory.

How to Live. What to Do

The title (borrowed from Wallace Stevens)
Reminds me of other useful How-To formulas—
How to grow waterlilies or 25,000
Kinds of orchids, how to end despair
Or make love in bed. How to abolish termites.
You have but to follow the written instructions
Which, since somebody's found the perfect answer
(In this instance, Wallace Stevens),
Will explain—if you know how to read the directions—
How to Live. What to Do. What the poem *says* to do.
The only question is, *how to?*

May

The Democrat peanut farmer of Plains, Georgia, Jimmy Carter (still called Jimmy Who?) says, "The next President, I believe, will be myself." We have a new verb, *to carterize*. He has a toothy smile and a strong sense of being the Lord's chosen. A good old Southern Baptist who has been, he says, reborn, "As President, I will be willing to help those who help themselves." Isn't it the Lord who does that? Carter, says Eric Sevareid, is too close to God in his remarks.

President Ford, on his way to campaign in Nebraska, bumped his head again as he entered the helicopter. Photographers are forbidden to take pictures of him beaning himself. A movie actor, Ronald Reagan, is running strong against Ford for the nomination, each good at putting his well-shod foot in his mouth. At the diminishing morale, Ford asks, "What has gone wrong?"

From F. Scott Fitzgerald's *Note-Books*: "It grows harder to write, because there is much less weather than when I was a boy and practically no men and women at all."

W. H. Auden, pretending to quote a social worker: "We are here on earth to help others. What on earth the others are here for I don't know."

The Worrywart

Why worry because
There is dust on the credenza,
Or that the golden apples of the Hesperides
Were probably hard and bitter quinces,
Or the apple tree in the Garden
Grew forbidden figs instead, with fig leaves?
Nine frail young quail this morning
Led by their mother in parade formation
Are marching to their doom past my own dooryard,
Stalked by a yellow cat.
I worry about that.

June

Fifty years ago I stood outside Hutchinson Commons at the University of Chicago, waiting with a crowd of students to greet Edward, Prince of Wales, who was invited to lunch on chicken à la king. As he walked smartly to the door escorted by an honor guard, we yelled and cheered the dashing heir apparent and he smiled wickedly at us as if being royalty was, take it from him, a joke.

Today I was invited to lunch at Hutchinson Commons on beef stroganoff. Seven of us received the Professional Achievement Award, but I was the unlucky one who made the acceptance speech, as the Prince of Wales hadn't been obliged to do. It was my *nunc dimittis*. Now let thy servant depart in peace.

I told them that, in my day, women were not treated at Chicago as the weaker sex. We believed in equality of the sexes, strictly fifty-fifty, a single standard that meant one behaved like a gentleman and paid one's way on a date to a movie or for a hamburger. I told them I had lived emancipated and free, taught the knightly virtues of "fredom and curteisye" by a few wise professors, all of which was meant to sound plausible, impossible to prove or deny fifty years later. Nobody asked me if I was trying to be funny.

At the end, Mr. Nayer, Director of Alumni Affairs who conducted the ceremony, came to the lectern and kissed me. That was the best part, like receiving an Oscar as a Hollywood star. The Bevingtons walked home, and I made a large pot of potato salad for the English department picnic this afternoon.

July

I picked up a book whose title astonished me: *Journal of a Landscape Painter in Albania and Illyria*, by Edward Lear, *the* Edward Lear. He was a sober Victorian who gave drawing lessons to Victoria, with one serious ambition all his life to be a landscape painter in the grand style. It must have hurt when Ruskin praised not his landscapes but his verse. Even so, I believe he was better than Landseer, of whom Lear wrote, "Landseer has a huge canvas full of slosh."

A contrary man, Mr. Lear. The twentieth of twenty-one children of a wealthy London stockbroker who was ruined and went to prison, from boyhood Lear was sickly, ugly, with a shapeless nose and tiny nearsighted eyes. An epileptic who adored children, he suffered deep melancholy, considering himself "more or less hideous," morbidly conscious of his looks. He had a horror of noise, was terrified of dogs, untidy in his dress, a poor, misfortunate, frightened creature who could be funny even about despair:

> Cold are the crabs that crawl on yonder hills,
> Colder than cucumbers that grow beneath . . .
> Such such is life—

I thought he invented the limerick but he merely adopted it in *The Book of Nonsense*, 1846, and never used the word. Nonsense, pure and absolute, was his aim, which meant making no sense about owls and pussycats, easy for a child to follow.

August

Last week the world's first International Symposium on Humor met in Wales. Robert Benchley once said, "There seem to be no lengths to which humorless people will not go to analyze humor." E. B. White: "Humor can be dissected as a frog can, but the thing dies in the process." In Wales it was analyzed, dissected, and died in these addresses:

"Humor *in situ*: The Role of Humor in Small Group Cultures."

"Ethnic Humor as a Function of Social-Normative Incongruity on the Basis of Multiple Dependent Variables."

"Phylogenetic and Ontogenetic Considerations for a Theory of the Origins of Humor."

A member of the congress proposed establishing "designed unifunctional anxiety-release centers in a community situation."

Seven years after the first man walked on the moon, the Viking set down on Mars in a search for life. The Viking, not a man but a robot, sent back disheartening pictures of a red desert with pink sky. The little planet is lifeless as the moon, a barren place of no giraffes, green Martians, trees, or canals. Man couldn't live there unless it rained. Ironically we go on hoping we're not alone in the universe, while we prepare to destroy the only planet we've got. A project called "The Search for Extraterrestrial Intelligence" is under way at the Jet Propulsion Laboratory in Pasadena, a search among four hundred billion stars in our galaxy for something we call human.

> The human races
> All live where time and space is;
> Their nature uniformly base is.
>
> —R. P. Lister

September

I retired from the classroom and the university this month, no longer on the muster. The gong rang, the chalk dust settled, and all I've got is a Duke parking sticker to show for it. The conflict is resolved: the love of teaching and the doubt when a student said, "You have changed my life," and I didn't know whether it was for better or worse.

At least I outlasted the movements I talked about, whose day was briefer than my own—the Georgians, Imagists, Symbolists, Dadaists, Surrealists, Existentialists, Beats, Activists, Projectivists, Objectivists, Angry Young Mania, and a movement called The Movement. One dependable fact of life is that no movement lasts. In thirty years of college teaching I had in mind to convey three skills, all of which I have yet to learn myself:

how to read
how to write
how to grow up

The question now is how to rest on one's laurels, for lack of something livelier to do. The laurel, worn by the victor at the Pythian games, was always a crown. It fitted the brow, a wreath of laurel, or at the

Nemean games a wreath of green parsley. You weren't supposed to *sit* on it.

Isaak Walton retired from his ironmonger's shop at 125 Chancery Lane, London, at the age of fifty with only forty years left to live. These he devoted to living. With fishing rod he wandered upstream and downstream before he died at ninety and at peace. Having learned to be free, Walton gave advice on the way to go about it—how to catch a carp, how to treat a frog ("Use him as though you loved him"), how to achieve longevity. He recommended river journeys. He endorsed pleasure, however short the excursion, and patience, however small the day's catch. "I have laid aside business," said Isaak Walton, "and gone a-fishing."

Projects for future scholarly research:

Why are lions in front of public libraries? Why not lionesses, as at the gate at Mycenae?

When was pubic hair introduced into art? In Greece the female figure was precariously draped at the hips. In the Middle Ages came the fig leaf and the saints clad in billowing clouds. The Three Graces, whether painted by Botticelli, Correggio, Andrea Appiani, or Renoir, were bare and beautiful. I conclude from them that goddesses don't have pubic hair.

What has become of the aspidistra? At every front window in working-class England there used to be dingy lace curtains and an aspidistra, a national emblem, symbol of gentility. In 1955 I heard Gracie Fields sing at the Palladium, "It's the biggest aspidistra in the world." George Orwell wrote *Keep the Aspidistra Flying* that he said should be on her coat of arms instead of the British lion.

In his novel the hero Gordon Comstock lives in Mrs. Meakin's boarding house, which reeks of cabbage, bedroom slops, and aspidistras. Upstairs in Gordon's room is a mangy specimen that he hates and tries without success to kill—the cast-iron plant, the tree of life, too tough to die.

"You talk a great deal about aspidistras," says Ravelston.

"They're a dashed important subject," says Gordon. He goes to her bedroom with a whore, "And, by Jove! on the bamboo table by the window, positively an aspidistra!"

What proof has England now of respectability?

Today the hawks are circling the sky. It occurs to me that I may view them as I please this year with no poet to act as interpreter and guide.

Hopkins looked at the windhover, a small hawk, with ecstasy, marveling at its shining glory, possessed of Christ's own beauty, pride, valor. "My heart in hiding / Stirred for a bird."

Dylan Thomas saw the hawk as predator over Sir John's hill, the fiery executioner calling to the blithe, unsuspecting sparrows, "Come and be killed," silly birds like ourselves forgetful that the hovering hawk is death.

Robinson Jeffers wanted to be a hawk himself. In *Give Your Heart to the Hawks,* he brooded with revulsion on the human race from his tower in Carmel and gave up mankind as a hideous job, crying, "Cut humanity out of my being / that is the wound that festers."

Ted Hughes imagined he already was one, a merciless bird of prey. In "Hawk Roosting," the arrogant destroyer speaks of ways to kill and devour: "I kill where I please because it is all mine / . . . My manners are tearing off heads— / The allotment of death."

Poets seldom agree about hawks.

October

Now the baths at Bath are closed after 1,900 years. What will become of the Pump Room, opened in 1706 in charge of The Pumper, the Assembly Rooms for balls, routs, gaming, and dalliance that brought London society flocking? Beau Nash, a lowborn gambler and dandy, reigned as Master of Ceremonies and forbade the ladies of quality to wear aprons. The balls began at 6:00 p.m. with a minuet, observed, Goldsmith wrote, with precedence and decorum of the utmost exactness. Nash died in 1761; the century ended with Bath no longer a center of fashion and frivolity.

When B. and I visited Bath in the 1960s the Pump Room attracted dodderers hobbling about on canes. Though the baths had lost their reputation for curing leprosy, they were believed good for the gout. B. and I dutifully drank the nasty stuff, after which we bathed in the Royal Baths, after which I was sick. B. deplored this inelegant conduct, a disgrace to the memory of Beau Nash.

Luckily on hand was Philip Thicknesse's *The Valetudinarians Bath Guide.* Thicknesse lived in Bath, a fickle friend of Gainsborough whom he hounded out of town. Given to malice, he spoke ill notably of the Bath waters, which injudiciously used produced grievous and fatal consequences: "It is true that the Bath waters sometimes kill." The safest way to health was to breathe in the breath of young virgins, but if one chose the waters he advised merely soaking each foot in a bucket and taking two five-grain cathartic pills each night. "Should the use of these pills bring on, as they frequently do, piles, so much the better."

Thicknesse himself lost a beloved brother Ralph who, after drinking a large quantity of Bath water and eating a hearty breakfast of Sally Lunns, dropped dead while playing the fiddle at Sir Robert Throgmorton's.

I'm surprised I lived through the experience.

November

I woke this morning not knowing who was the next president of the United States. The newspaper didn't know, since the race between Carter and Ford was too close to call. I turned on the 7:00 a.m. news in time to catch smiling Jimmy arriving home a hero in Plains, Georgia (pop. 683), having spent the night in Atlanta awaiting shaky returns. President Ford had gone to bed. I hope Carter will grow from a little man to a big one. I hope he will keep smiling when the loaves and fishes prove to be beyond his multiplying.

December

Virginia Woolf's letters are to reach six volumes. She was obsessive about letter writing, compulsive as Richardson's Pamela who whipped out pen and paper wherever she was, generally in her daily plight when Mr. B. chased her with ravishment in mind. Instead of fleeing her seducer, Pamela appeared to crawl under the nearest bush to inform her parents with immense relish how close she had come this time to being raped. Clarissa Harlowe too suffered from a fantastic urge to write letters when they could never be delivered. This epistolary disease attacked Virginia Woolf. "Life would be split asunder without letters," she wrote in *Jacob's Room*.

Her most mocking words were reserved for a spinster lady I knew well and used to visit in her old age in Fordingbridge, England—Virginia's first cousin Miss Dorothea Stephen, daughter of Leslie Stephen's brother Fitzjames. "Dear dobbythings," she called her, "a fat religious cousin, very red in the face," "a cumbersome square footed cousin" whom she despised. I liked Miss Dorothea, who was definitely fat, religious, and red in the face. She was a marvelous Stephen, I thought, durable (outliving them all, dying in 1965 at ninety-four) and tough-minded, a loyal descendant of the Clapham Sect, permanently distressed by Uncle Leslie's agnosticism and his two daughters' loose and scandalous behavior. But then she wasn't my cousin.

Since I read in bed every night (cursed with insomnia, like the writer Peter Fleming who said he counted not sheep but weasels), I like volumes of letters because I can lie on my left side and read the right-hand pages straight through without lifting the book. Next night I turn over and start again, though after years of experience my belief is that the right-hand page makes better reading than the left. Admittedly, the plot may thicken and both sides need attention, but generally not, not in letters, dictionaries, poems, diaries even. This costs 4¢ a night under an electric blanket.

I reach for Richard Steele's diverting letters to "Dear Prue," the name he called her after they were married. She liked it better than her real one, Molly Scurlock, whom Steele had tempestuously courted from whatever tavern held him to swear he was tenderly, passionately, faithfully hers and would live in her heart and die in her lap. Molly was nearly twenty-nine, a handsome Welsh girl with auburn hair, blue eyes, scrappy temper. For the last three years she had lived in Swallow Street, London, with her maid for companion. She had attended the funeral of his first wife the previous December and was much in love with the adoring Steele, quite ready for marriage. But as a dutiful daughter she wanted first her mother's blessing. When the anxiously awaited letter from Wales failed to arrive on the day of the wedding, the bride refused to go to bed with her husband.

For a week Steele waited on her doorstep, protesting, pleading, raging to no avail. He wrote three times to his mother-in-law, who maintained a frosty silence. Another week passed and another while the hapless bridegroom implored Molly to relent. After a month of it and still no word from her mother, suddenly on October 8 the begging tone of the correspondence changed. Richard Steele's note that day began "My Dear Wife."

Luckily she saved his letters, though he asked that they never be seen save by her. During the eleven years of marriage till her death, the notes would arrive, instead of him, any time of day or night. "Dear Prue," he wrote from the Old Devil Tavern, Temple Bar, "I can't come home to dinner. I languish for yr Welfare and will never be a moment carelesse more." "Dear Wife I honour, I love, I doat on you." "Dear Prue Sober or not, I am Ever Yours Richard Steele."

He sent her a packet of tea at four in the afternoon ("This is my second letter today") or walnuts, "which is the greatest proof I can give you at present of my being, with my whole Heart, yours." Below the address he added, "There are but 29 Walnutts."

He was a trying husband—affectionate, faithful, tender, sweet-tempered, generous—and very seldom at home.

1977

January

Rosa who cleans my house goes to meetings of a Golden Age Club, where the older you are the more you are congratulated. At a recent celebration, whoever was the oldest in the group was asked to stand up and state his or her age. A spry old lady jumped to her feet and said, "I'm 98." Everybody clapped.

"That's fine," said the leader. "Especially since last year you were only 100."

The old lady's daughter explained that her mother actually is 101, but she prefers to lie about her age.

"And she got the dash to do it," said Rosa admiringly.

The Durham Academy had a book fair, at which I was asked to autograph my books. Since it was held in the gym of the Lower School, many young children were on hand, staring greedily at the juvenile works on display and staring at me as at a female monkey not up to interesting tricks. A handmade sign said, "Come and meet a real author," but they were sensibly cautious. Even the book title *Along Came the Witch* didn't fool them or maybe it did: one little girl ventured near and, when I smiled, ran off and burst into tears.

I remember my first autographed book, *A Daughter of the Samurai*, by Etsu Sugimoto who lived downstairs in my rooming house at Columbia. I had no more than a bowing acquaintance with her, but the signature was precious to me for years. Then I reread the book and gave it away. I had outgrown author-worship.

David writes that a new book by A. L. Rouse has the following correction: "The caption for the illustration on p. 461 is incorrect. It should read 'Winston Churchill in the bombed-out House of Parliament,' instead of 'Winston Churchill bombed-out in the House of Parliament.'"

February

I'm amazed that E. B. White should allow his letters to be collected and published in his lifetime. They're edited by Gus Lobrano's daughter Dorothy (686 pages), not only with the sanction of the author but with his notes and comments. Maybe he welcomed the chance to read them over.

As a writing man, Mr. White says about writers, "They always give themselves away sooner or later." This is his way of doing so. The letters are his autobiography, memoirs, confession, and full-length portrait of, he says, a "nudist." I'm glad to make his acquaintance. There were the puzzling contradictions before.

I thought him a simple man, and so he wants to be but isn't—"My dream (unfulfilled) is to keep my life simple." I thought his sense of humor was able to offset his tragic sense of life. It isn't. He is modest but not simple, a private, separate man, "an easily discouraged fellow," edgy, panicky, hypersensitive, neurotic. He winces a lot. He makes one wonder how so funny a man can be so sad. Or the other way round, so witty about woe.

"A doctor last spring told me that I would be all right if I quit writing. He said most writers were neurotics—if they weren't neurotic they wouldn't go to the trouble, the enormous trouble."

That leaves only Mr. White of Selborne, the one simple man I have left. And even he, if the truth were known . . .

March

When I saw him again after thirty years, he was walking across the platform of Page Auditorium at Duke. Except for a slight limp, a loss of hair, and being at seventy-two patently older, he looked himself. Here was the same dignity I remembered in a friend of my youth in New York, the same courtesy of a kind and cultivated man.

Alger Hiss spoke tonight, as the students requested, on "The McCarthy Era," a shameful time in our history. He talked knowledgeably with anecdotes and a few sickening facts, but objectively and it seemed wearily. I was sorry he didn't delve into the personal meanings that came to mind, how the witch hunts had affected him. In the question period his answers were polite, brief, noncommittal until one would-be orator began, "I

think you were framed," and Alger instantly flared up, "I was framed!"
For three days at Duke before he came to my house, he attended with
good grace every seminar, interview, reception the students arranged, and
they grew fond of him. His reason for this speaking tour is to earn money
to defend his case, after twenty-seven years still seeking to clear his name,
grown old with trying, bitter at those who assume he is guilty or no longer
care—a fearfully long time for a man to fail to prove his innocence. He
has a name nobody forgets.

Epistle to Horace. I

"I find all men are like all men; and how can
one be angry with everybody?"
—from a letter of Horace Walpole

Being a man, then, being like other men,
Could you be angry, Horace, with yourself?
Was it compassion for the human lot,
No man your enemy—yourself included—
That kept you tolerant of all men, just,
And sweetly reasonable? (The other Horace
Said he was reasonable except whenever
He had a head cold.) Or was it scorn instead,
Indifference to the fact men *are* alike,
Marked by the toad of venom, swelled with pride—
As some found you to be. Which way it was,
How angry were you, Horace, with yourself?

Epistle to Horace. II

"I once read a silly fairy tale, called *The Three Princes
of Serendip*: as their highnesses travelled, they were
always making discoveries, by accidents and sagacity,
of things they were not in quest of." —from a letter
of Horace Walpole

One should be looking for some other thing
Like paradise, or the seven golden cities
Coronado went in search of
(And came upon New Mexico instead),
Yet cultivate the happy faculty
Of settling, in one's quests and travels, not
For the mythical kingdom (which is seldom there)

But for the chance domain that serves as well—
Since to look for heaven and wind up in hell
Is hardly serendipity, is it, Horace?
The gift lies in the accidental choice,
Unsought for but a fitting compromise.

Epistle to Horace. III

Horace, I have it on the authority
Of a Miss Hawkins, daughter of Sir John,
How finical you were, with an affected delicacy
Of entering a room on tiptoe, knees bent, mincing
("The march of a dabchick," you described it)
As if you were afraid of a wet floor.
She mentions too those lavender suits you wore,
The waistcoats worked in silver, frilled with lace,
And the excessive hauteur of your face,
Which fits the image frankly of a bore,
A fop, a prig, a humbug, a poseur—
Not of the Horace who survived his vanity,
Till now his portrait as a man of sense
Makes him so real he seems a memory.

April

People As Sights. I saw Pearl White in 1916, when my mother took me on a sightseeing trip to New York. Though I pleaded to go to the Ziegfeld Follies, my mother said I was too young for follies and led me one night to a nickelodeon on Broadway where episodes of mayhem and slow torture were showing of "The Perils of Pauline." My friends in the fifth grade and I loathed and despised Pearl White, queen of the serials, but my mother who seldom went to movies thought her appealing as a wo-man wronged. Her heart went out to any female left in dire peril every week.

As my mother was buying the tickets, in walked Pearl White. She was there to make a personal appearance. Swathed in furs, her pretty face white with powder, she had the look of a woman who had met with foul play. Pushing my mother aside she yelled at the stupefied cashier in her cage, "What the hell is going on here? Where's the goddamn manager? Where in hell am I supposed to go?"

My mother charged forward. "You will kindly watch your language in front of my daughter," she said, silencing the silent-film star as we marched out of the theater.

Woodrow Wilson lived in Washington, D.C., in 1922 when my mother conducted another of our yearly pilgrimages. On a rubberneck bus we were stopped by traffic on Pennsylvania Avenue next to an enormous black limousine.

"There's the president," shouted the guide through his megaphone.

We craned to look. A voice in the bus said, "Don't you know Warren G. Harding is president? That's nobody but Woodrow Wilson."

Mr. Wilson didn't turn his head. He was wrapped in blankets, his shrunken face and pince-nez visible under his silk hat. Mrs. Wilson sat statuesque beside this humped old man. Since my mother hadn't voted for him and he hadn't saved the world for democracy, she didn't consider him much of a sight.

I said, "I think he is going to die."

When we were seniors at the University of Chicago, my boyfriend Bob took me out to Cicero one night to a hangout of Al Capone's, who had his headquarters in the suburb of Cicero. Bob, a Chicago boy accepted at Harvard Law School, wanted to study the racketeer criminal type in the flesh.

"They won't let us in," I said.

"I can get us in," said Bob, today a criminal lawyer in Chicago. By mentioning the name of some big shot and submitting to being searched he got us in.

It was a tough dance hall, with lantern-jawed bouncers and girls so brassy I was afraid to leave Bob to go to the ladies' room. The jazz deafened, the couples danced in the dark glued together. I had on a tight black dress and high heels, but I knew I couldn't pass for a moll. Even so we aroused the suspicions of a bouncer, who lounged over to our table when I held up my compact to powder my nose.

"What yer doing there, quit it or get out."

Al Capone sat a few tables away, surrounded by hoods wearing black fedoras, overplaying the part. Al drummed his fingers, staring glumly about. Suddenly he jumped up and moving fast came down the aisle toward us, accompanied by his bodyguards. As we looked the other way, he paused beside Bob, then quickly moved on and left the hall. I had seen enough to know him for life, old Scarface with a scar visible in that light, the razor slash he got in a brawl. Capone had been a bouncer himself in a whorehouse in this district. Now he was a killer who eliminated people in broad daylight. He was a gorilla, and I was scared out of my wits.

"He's got our number," I whispered to Bob. "I think he's going to rub us out."

We sat absolutely still for ten minutes. Nobody stopped us at the door, and in the parking lot nobody gunned us down.

When I was a graduate student at Columbia, I took the subway at 116th Street one September morning and sat all the way to 34th Street opposite Amelia Earhart. She was leaning back, alone in an almost empty car. Her brown curly hair was short like a man's. She was thirty years old and plain, no makeup, big hands and feet. Her body was lean and unfeminine, dressed in a nondescript white blouse and dark skirt. You might take her for an underpaid schoolteacher instead of a daring pilot or aviatrix. I liked her, especially when, as I gazed at her closed eyes for three subway stops, she opened them and her smile broadened to a grin. "Hello," she said shyly and glanced away. "Hello," I breathed.

A few months later Amelia Earhart flew the Atlantic solo. In 1937 she was lost in the Pacific. I think of her often, not so much of her courage as of her smile.

At New York University—the uptown college in the Bronx—B. and I lived across the street from Brown House, the elegant mansion built by Stanford White before he was murdered in 1906. Though a white house by Mr. White, it was called Brown because Chancellor Brown lived there. After his death the house, by this time a white elephant, was inherited by the English department, with offices installed upstairs and the two drawing rooms used sparingly for an occasional tea or a passing poet. The larger room had a grand piano on a raised platform, red velvet hangings, and space for thirty straight chairs set in close rows. We of the department gathered to listen to writers like Middleton Murry and Jan Struther, poets like Archibald MacLeish and Robert Frost, who made do with a small honorarium and small audience.

The evening I like to remember was graced by Ford Madox Ford, who came in November 1938 to tell us about "The Literary Life" as led by his friends Joseph Conrad and Henry James. Ford, accompanied by his young wife, Janice, was a stout, lumbering man with a pale yellow mustache, watery, goggling eyes, thin hair. (Hemingway said he looked like an upended hogshead.) From his huge bulk came a voice barely above a hoarse whisper. In the trench warfare of World War I he had been gassed, now at sixty-five left a wheezing, gasping old man.

Since he was obliged to lecture sitting down, a stuffed wicker chair had been placed in front of the piano on the tiny platform, and I had placed myself on the front row in the optimistic hope of hearing what he had to say. Slowly he moved down the aisle, heaved himself up the step, and lowered himself gingerly into his chair. At that moment one foot of the chair slipped off the edge of the platform and dumped Ford Madox Ford, author of 81 books, into my lap. It took us both by surprise, a tornadic event, as his body enveloped and buried my own. My lap felt permanently squashed. He was said to have a susceptibility toward women, but this was breathtaking.

Knocked out by the plunge, neither of us spoke. Finally, his dignity somewhat restored, Mr. Ford assisted by several aghast professors got himself unscrambled and back to the platform into his wicker chair. After a quiet wheeze or two, he began to talk in his strained whisper, while I kept one eye on the chair leg to see it didn't slip again. I couldn't look him in the face because of a wild desire to laugh.

This incident led to the Fords inviting B. and me to their New Year's party in their Manhattan apartment. It was a large, noisy affair with dancing, at which I have no memory of antic behavior by Mr. Ford. If after forty years I think of him as a man who fell in my lap, he would understand, for he professed a contempt for extraneous facts. Inaccurate as to facts he claimed to be but dependably accurate as to impressions.

I danced most of the evening with Alain, a cartoonist with the *New Yorker*, an Alsatian or maybe Luxembourger with red hair.

"Where did you come from?" he asked me.

"The Bronx."

"*The Bronx*! Who will get you home again?"

"My husband."

Ford Madox Ford sailed with Janice to France in May, and in June he died in Normandy. Sometime later I read in the *New York Times* that Janice was married again, to an artist named Alain.

May

"Somebody's boring me," Dylan Thomas said, "I think it's me." It was time to leave town and spend the next three months in New Mexico with Phil, to cure myself of what ails me—solitude. Our first stop was Chicago, where the journey of the week took us back three thousand years to King Tut, the most popular tomb in town. In the simulated Valley of the Kings, we speculated on how much precious gold had been returned to the earth, pondering the afterlife that requires such fuss and an awesome clutter of belongings to take with you—roast duck, for example. King Tut's needs were immoderate: jewels to wear, cooking utensils to use, seeds to plant, beds, boats, mirrors, fly swatters, 3,059 items in all for his everlastingness. In the burial chamber we accompanied the boy to his death—Tutankhaton, who abandoned the worship of the sun, Aton, and changed his name to honor the restored god Amun with the curled horns of a ram.

The gold death mask is believed to be an exact likeness. That's how beautiful he was. During the excavation, everything had been removed to the Cairo Museum except his body, which was left in the tomb where it still is. Separate coffins contained his mummified viscera, lungs, liver. The heart remained in the body, though nothing was said of the genitals —one as useful as the other, you'd think, throughout eternity. The mummification ritual said, "You live again, you live again forever."

(Christiane Desroches-Noblecourt in *Tutankhamen*: "Between the legs they [the embalmers] replaced the bandaged genital organ in a state of erection.")

You can attend the Charisma School in White Rock or take a Women's Practical Firearms Course in Basic Gun Handling. Instead I go to the Los Alamos library for my observables, especially its book section labeled "Genuine junk." Today I learned to say in Spanish *grillos en la cabeza*, meaning crickets in the head. E. B. White said he had mice in his subconscious. Kafka had bats in his soul.

On the new-book shelf was an unappetizing volume, *Lewd Food*, instructions in dietary lechery, how to prepare lascivious dishes and a seven-course aphrodisiac dinner. What happens if you overeat?

I looked up the lovely word *contrails*, those streaks in the New Mexican sky made by the jet planes. When the white filament changes to a band of fleece, you can't tell it from a cirrus cloud. Sometimes two contrails make a sign of the cross. Not that it worries anybody.

From there I got sidetracked into reading about the Fall of Man. Till now my theory was that Adam would have fallen anyway with no help from Satan, being Adam, flesh and blood. Give him a woman to love and an apple to leave alone, and he is on his way. A new version (new to me) of the loss of Eden was held by an early Gnostic sect: Adam and Eve wanted to eat of the tree of knowledge so that *they would know their true identities* (Gen. 3:5). Here is the beginning of the identity crisis—adopted by the confessional poets, the walking-naked movement—that tempts everybody to write his memoirs and find himself. The despairing cry of Lear, "Who is it that can tell me who I am?" got its start in Eden. The question is eternal. It arises, Renata Adler observes, even when one is faced with a self-addressed envelope.

Listening to Anne Lindbergh being interviewed tonight by Eric Sevareid was a dismaying experience. She is a figure of my time, living alone in her house in Darien, Connecticut. Too shy to face interviewers, this is her first appearance on television; it may well be her last. She kept her poise while Sevareid, a naturally courteous man, asked intimate, prying, heartless questions that the media require—about Lindbergh's mistakes as a tool of the Nazis. ("Yes, he made blunders. Yes, he was used.") About her murdered child, if she thought Hauptmann guilty. ("I have not read the recent book. No, I shall not read it. That happened, you know, more than forty years ago.") About her husband's death, their last conversation after he asked to be flown to Hawaii to die. About the dire failure of her book *The Wave of the Future*, which opposed America's entry into World War II, and her quick agreement that it was bad. ("I didn't know what I was talking about.")

I can't understand these grillings, or how Mrs. Lindbergh could keep her voice steady. I was proud of her, also ashamed. What kind of listeners do we make?

Here is the book I was waiting for. Till now it didn't exist except in manuscript, though Eleanor Jette wrote it thirty years ago about life in Los Alamos when the bomb was created. She called it *Inside Box 1663*, the only address they had. It might be called *The Wives of Los Alamos*. I grieve that Eleanor Jette is dead; I think she would be glad her words exist in print.

Her husband, Eric Jette, was a professor of metallurgy at Columbia's School of Mines when Oppenheimer asked him to help make a nuclear bomb. Eleanor went to New Mexico with him and their ten-year-old son to find herself uprooted, isolated on a remote mountain mesa, and not told why she was there. The wives named themselves the Lost Almosts. They endured primitive living conditions that sent Eleanor to the edge of lunacy. The barracks in a sea of mud were such firetraps that, from the Jettes' upstairs quarters, the only means of escape was by fifty feet of rope Eleanor hastily bought and tied to the bedpost. By 1944 the population reached 5,700, though Oppenheimer had anticipated thirty scientists and their families. General Leslie R. Groves ordered the C.O. to halt the flood of babies who seemed to be born at a phenomenal rate.

While the men raced with the calendar, tensions mounted that they communicated to their wives. Eleanor Jette's son, turned eleven, asked one day, "What goes on in this Tech Area, Ma?"

"Oh, Roosevelt's bound to be elected for a fifth term. They're making campaign buttons."

In April 1945 Roosevelt died. On July 15, a Sunday, Eleanor's husband left home hurriedly with the words, "You might see something if you stay up all night." At 5:30 a.m. the wives saw from mountain lookouts an unearthly sunrise. They made the V for victory sign. As their husbands returned, exhausted, safe, there was at first elation before, shortly, other feelings took over of depression and grim anxiety.

Two weeks after the war ended, the Association of Los Alamos Scientists was formed on The Hill to urge international control of the bomb for keeping life on the planet and world peace. It became known as ALAS.

Twenty-five years later, in 1970, Dr. Eugene Rabinowitch, editor of the *Bulletin of the Atomic Scientists*, wrote: "The most one can say of mankind in the age of the atom bomb is that it has so far survived." Harold Urey, who helped create both the A- and hydrogen bomb, said, "I'm afraid there may be no life left at the end of the century."

The sky was lurid, filled with billowing smoke like a mushroom cloud. It came not from the laboratory setting off a thermonuclear bomb but from a tremendous raging fire out of control in the Jemez Mountains, the kind of disaster the physicists used to dread and still do.

Day after day we heard the crackling roar and found it hard to breathe. Spreading rapidly down the mountain, by Thursday the fire had jumped over Frijoles Canyon four miles away and at one point crossed the road to the laboratory in an area marked Explosives. The towns of Los Alamos and White Rock waited, ready to evacuate. Phil stayed at work with his computer; at home I walked the floor. For six days the fire blazed and 1,500 men fought while no rain came, while thirty-eight miles of fire left behind a blackened forest.

When it was over I got in the car and drove straight up the mountain to look down on skeleton pines. What a place Oppenheimer chose to make the bomb!

June

Imagine flying to Vancouver, across the Canadian border in British Columbia, without mishap, loss of luggage or each other—a miracle of noncatastrophe. So if Phil suffered panic, as he did, it wasn't the fault of the Canadian Pacific Airlines but the fact he had been invited to speak at the Second International Conference on the Nucleon-Nucleon Interaction, the subject of his paper being "Single and Double Pion Production Experiments," which seems justifiable cause for panic if not terror.

We rented a Ford Granada at the Vancouver airport and found the University of British Columbia tucked away at the tip of Point Grey overlooking the Pacific. In the confused manner of academe they tried to put Phil and me into a one-bedroom suite, then sensing the impropriety of that arrangement transferred us to a fourth-floor quad in Gage Towers, the student center, where instead of one bedroom we had six with a bathroom meant to accommodate any number up to twelve.

Before I was whisked away on the daily Tour for Ladies, arranged by the university to keep us from under foot during the four-day meetings, I heard Phil's paper, a lucid explanation of the pioneer work of his group, of which I understood not a word. My son spoke in the amphitheater with a pipe organ at his back, the pipes framing him and the projection screen as if heaven itself bestowed approval and blessing on this outrageous peering into the mysteries of the universe.

Ladies, as we know, are partial to visiting botanical gardens and museums, gratified by being fed sumptuous buffet luncheons, though the plates are always too small. At the Quarry Restaurant in Queen Elizabeth Park, by sampling the banquet of fifty dishes of British Columbia salmon, caribou meat, octopus, herring, mussels, knobs of fiddleback fern, and twenty-six kinds of relish, one walked away with a many-splendored, many-layered thing that tasted like nothing at all. Desserts offered the same concoction of watermelon on top of fudge cake and strawberry mousse.

Certainly the Burnaby Art Gallery provided the most striking entertainment, so far from the ordinary that an old lady (not a member of our sturdy group) asked a stranger at the door to take her by the hand and lead her inside. "I'm afraid to go in by myself," she said. The Canadian artist Badanna Zack, aged forty-four, from Toronto, was exhibiting a special collection in this elegant gallery.

The art on view consisted entirely of vulvas and penises, erect and erected on pedestals, hung on walls or from the ceiling, in marble, bronze, bone, wood, ceramic, nickel (looking like water faucets). At one end of the room stood the rear ends of three horses, titled "A Trio of Great Canadians."

Miss Zack has concentrated on this preoccupation of hers for the last three years. The ceiling was full of great Canada geese flapping through the sky. Where the head and beak should be, each bird was pointing a phallus, reminiscent somewhat of Picasso's Artist and Model series with its flying penises.

Some pieces in smooth white marble consisted of a vulva or an idealized penis emerging from the stone, like Rodin's emerging sculptures—so innocent that my impression was Miss Zack was fantasizing and had not studied firsthand what she so repetitiously created. But she said in an interview that, though she never works from models, she depends on memory. As a result of this obsession, she is sternly criticized in Canada, censored in Winnipeg, accused of being vicious, obscene. I assume she is merely being modish, following the current fashion like the poets and novelists. The exhibit probably appealed in its way to us ladies much as did the discussion of protons to the physicists. In the end I found it stirring but monotonous.

July

Santa Fe used to be a little mud village of Holy Faith, Spanish then Mexican, to which the first settlers came before the Pilgrims landed at Plymouth Rock. For sixty years of the nineteenth century it was the end of the Santa Fe Trail, where the lines of wagon trains were unloaded in the Plaza after a journey of a thousand miles from Independence, Missouri.

The trail began in 1821, the only link between the Mississippi and the Southwest. It was not a route for homesteaders in covered wagons; they took the Oregon Trail. Santa Fe was Mexican till 1846 when after our war with Mexico it became insecure American territory. This route was for teamsters carrying cargoes of merchandise from dress goods to hairpins, perfume to guns, bartering them for Mexican mules and buffalo hides to take back to Missouri. Josiah Gregg wrote of traveling with a caravan of 28 wagons, 2 cannons, 47 men, 200 mules, 300 sheep and goats. In 1828 a returning wagon train lost 1,000 mules to Indians.

They were tough bullwhackers cracking a ten-foot whip over three span of oxen, or muleskinners with heavy loads drawn by struggling mules, men of violence and endurance who survived, or did not survive, attacks in Indian country by roving Apaches and Comanches, the perils of cholera, herds of stampeding buffalo, quicksands, lashing storms, prairie fires that caused their kegs of gunpowder to explode, or worst of all, prolonged thirst in the desert of the Jornada. Their destination after months of travel was the Plaza at Santa Fe. A mile outside town they fired off guns to announce their arrival in proper style and were met with trouble—Mexican authorities who taxed and sometimes confiscated their goods. It might take a year for the round trip, since nobody dared venture homeward in the winter snows.

In 1880 the Atchison, Topeka, and Santa Fe Railroad reached Santa Fe, the days of the trail were over, though not till 1912 did New Mexico become the forty-seventh state. At the Plaza under the portal of the Governors Palace, Indians from nearby pueblos now spread their goods, where from the portal once hung not ears of Indian corn but strings threaded with the ears of Indians.

We have a new pet shop in the White Rock marketplace with two skunks on display in the window, fullgrown and beady-eyed, price $149.90. I know this is true from having gone inside to inquire the price of roadrunners, which as the state emblem cannot be hunted, captured, or sold. The store sells boa constrictors, prairie dogs, and iguanas, under a prominent sign, No Refund on Live Animals. You can't get a medical doctor for love, money, or last rites in White Rock. But you can receive a house call from a doctor at the Plant Clinic for your sick philodendron. This service is advertised as "available to everyone regardless of race, color, or national origin."

July 7. Two neutron bombs have been exploded in Nevada to test their efficiency in killing people. They kill by twice the radiation of a nuclear bomb—the Pentagon terms it "radiation enhancement"—100 percent effective against human beings, leaving structures intact. Our relations with Russia are at their lowest depth, what with Carter's insistent desire for human rights. The final joke will be annihilation of life on this planet in defense of human rights. One right should be not to be killed by a neutron bomb.

I feel the usual foreboding. The risk of war increases as the four winds choose.

August

The sudden journey into death of Philip, young Philip, on the night of July 18 put an end to anything in this world but grief. Bitter, sudden, merciless grief. He died of a raging strep infection that destroyed his heart. It is a makeshift world, reduced to making do without him, a poor dodge never to be countenanced, accepted, believed.

He was fourteen, and he said, "It is dark, it is getting dark," and he died.

O dark, dark, dark, amid the blaze of noon.

September

Every hour it's true—Philip lost the chance to live this hour, this day. He is gone out a door, no reason given. The sun still shines, the birds still sing and I hear them but he does not. What does grief do to the mind? As usual I look to a library to find words. Is curiosity enough to keep one going? Curiosity about what? About words on a page, generally written by dead men, those who were "dressed in a little brief authority."

George Orwell wrote in *Burmese Days* of bitter sorrow and loneliness, "which is felt in essence to be the subject's own fault." Flory is a middle-aged bachelor in Burma, isolated by circumstance. "To talk, simply to talk! . . . The need to talk is the greatest of all needs." So he is doomed. He shoots himself through the heart, and that's one way to end a novel.

George Santayana noted what people will put up with: "There is nothing to which men, while they have food and drink, cannot reconcile themselves. They will put up with present suffering, with the certainty of death, with solitude, with shame, with wrong, with the expectation of eternal damnation. In the face of such things, they can not only be merry for the moment, but solemnly thank God for having brought them into existence."

September 13. Robert Lowell died yesterday. He died in a taxicab in New York, returning from Ireland, where he parted with his third wife, to the home of his second wife, Elizabeth Hardwick.

It seems he didn't want to live. His new book of poems, *Day by Day*, says, during one more racked stay in a mental hospital, "I wish I could die." The final poem "Epilogue" asks, "All's misalliance. / Yet why not say what happened?" I like that question. I often ask it myself.

Why Not?

Yet why not say what happened? To say all
Or half of all, or even what might have been,
Is only trying—as it's been tried before
By the confessors like Jean Jacques Rousseau,

Saint Augustine, Cellini—to say again
With words made clearer through transparency,
"This is the way it was," and "This is I."
And nothing to be gained by never saying.

October

In the Duke gardens is a tree I love, the ginkgo, a native of Chinese temple gardens. A small pyramid with fan-shaped leaves, in the fall it turns gold as a maiden's hair—the maidenhair tree. I saw it this afternoon at the instant when all at once it drops its leaves. Turner should have painted the ginkgo tree as a great gold sunburst, yellow mist and glory.

But Howard Nemerov writes a poem about the leaf of the ginkgo that filters "a urinary yellow light." I hate forced images like "urinary yellow" that make one visualize what the poet affects. John Ashbery strains his neck to see "wadded tissue paper clouds." James Schuyler says, "the sky on the horizon is oily bilge."

It's high time someone wrote a biography of Anonymous, who has been around these centuries without acclaim except, say, in the seven-volume *Dictionary of Anonymous and Pseudonymous English Literature*, by Samuel Halkett. Willard Espy has concocted a *Life and Works* that graciously leaves room for more searching biographers to praise immortal writings like the old English ballads, Christmas carols, Norse sagas, *Beowulf*, "Lady Greensleeves."

Espy claims to be the one living man to have known Anon. personally. His death was announced prematurely in 1856 by *Punch*, where he was called the only author who could compete with Ibid. Espy, in a factual account of his own life, has Mr. Anonymous turning up in Espy's home-town of Oysterville, Wash., sixty years ago accompanied by a yellow dog Author Unknown. Anon. resembled a drawing by Dr. Seuss: a huge fellow with dewlaps, a fat belly, derby hat, spindly legs like asparagus stalks. Plucking a mandolin, he presented himself as Great-Uncle Allie, who had disappeared in the Klondike in 1879, though his habit of reciting authorless verse identified him to his nephew, aged six—"the optimum age," says Espy, "for a human being." He may be right, and this book should have a special appeal for readers that old.

Uncle Allie lingered in Oysterville, while the boy Espy memorized the verses that filled the air. "They are friends," Uncle Allie said, "orphans of the storm." The rascal's pursuit of the widow Calder allowed for quoting

of amorous lyrics ("Sweet Cupid, ripen her desire"). His thirst brought
forth paeans to alcohol ("God, in his goodness, sent the grape"). He
denied that off-color limericks attributed to him were his. He said there
had never been a Miss Anonymous. (Untrue. What about the author of
nameless works by "A Lady," or "One of the Fair Sex"?)

After years of training for it, the mantle fell to Espy, since, we're told,
from the first Roman invasion of Britain it has passed from man to man.
In 1976 Uncle Allie, nearing death at 116, chose his successor. "In fact,"
Espy admits, "I had begun to take on certain of his characteristics." As the
present Anon., his canine Author Unknown at his side, he continues
prolific, corny, and well. I think highly of his contribution to anonymity
in these lines:

> The womb's a fine and private place
> In which to propagate the race.

November

Harvey Shapiro sent me Margaret Halsey's book to review, *No
Laughing Matter*, and I came smack up against one of my strongest aver-
sions—the acronym. Her second title, *The Autobiography of a WASP*,
to most readers will be crystal clear. To me she could be a member of the
Women's Airforce Service Pilots or the Westinghouse Advanced Systems
Planning group. She could mean she is a recognized authority on
Wordshape Analysis and Scheduling Procedure.

The use of acronyms is as old as the Roman Empire (SPQR), but the
word itself is new. It appeared in dictionaries as late as 1947 to define the
habit, peculiarly American in this age of technology, of using initials to
create a new language. By the 1920s these telescope words were everywhere from Nabisco to AFL. In the Second World War they swamped us:
Nazi, GIs, radar, snafu, awol, WACs, WAVEs, and WASPs.

Margaret Halsey means, of course, White Anglo-Saxon Protestant,
which she grew up being, one of a self-appointed elite that no longer
dominates our culture, having lost caste, been cut down to size, dis-
credited. Miss Halsey calls Nixon her fellow WASP. Her chapter "How to
Raise a Prig" describes an education in intolerance and rigidity in Yonkers,
New York, where her parents were conformist middle-class Episcopalians,
though the god they worshiped was Respectability. "We reveled in all the
standard prejudices of the Calvin Coolidge era against Jews, Negroes,
Catholics and the foreign-born." When she married Henry Simon of the

publishing firm of Simon and Schuster, her mother's reply to the announced event came sharply over the telephone: "Well! You know what I think about Jews!"

In 1936, a year she and Henry spent in England, Margaret wrote the irreverent bestseller *With Malice Toward Some*, witty and malicious in showing up the English as bona fide WASPs in their complacent superiority. But her writing turned serious in attacking hatred and intolerance, prejudice, bigotry, discrimination with what Thomas Mann called "the true Protestant's passionate, relentless sense of personal responsibility." In the McCarthy era, her volume *Color Blind* on racism was removed from some public libraries as obscene; she was accused of being a Communist. She became obsessed with the injustice of the Alger Hiss trials that she is convinced created a wrong turning, a climate of fear that prepared the way for subsequent disasters—McCarthyism, Vietnam, Watergate, the breakdown of morality in American life. For her, for us all, it is no laughing matter. "When I look back over my life," she says, "it seems to have been about equally divided between rage and happiness." Since, come to think of it, I too am by definition a WASP, I thank her for the redeeming claim that one may live happy half the time between the rages and catastrophes.

Peter Schrag, who wrote *The Decline of the WASP* in 1971, claims the WASPs have had it, an endangered species. World War II brought an end to their rule when the country moved away from them. "For 150 years the politicians, the writers, the poets, the social theorists, the men who articulated and analyzed American ideas, who governed our institutions, who embodied what we seemed to be, or hoped to be, nearly all of them were WASPs"—the Adamses, Lowells, Rockefellers, Roosevelts, Carnegies, Mellons. The American mind was the WASP mind.

Jean-Paul Sartre, in an interview "Self-Portrait at Seventy," faces old age. Nearly blind, unable to read or write and robbed of reason for existing, he sees no cause to be upset.

Interviewer: "Does it bother you when I ask you about yourself?"

Sartre: "No, why? I believe that everyone should be able to speak of his innermost being to an interviewer. I think that what spoils relations among people is that each keeps something hidden from the other, holds something secret. . . . I think transparency should always be substituted for secrecy."

He too believes in confession, a walking-naked existentialist.

December

A couple are driving on the turnpike, and the wife, brooding about the problems of life, wonders aloud, "What are we coming to?" "Connecticut," says her husband.

—Peter De Vries

Like Sandburg's poem:

I am riding on a limited express, one of the crack trains of the nation.
Hurtling across the prairie into blue haze and dark air go fifteen
    all-steel coaches holding a thousand people.
(All the coaches shall be scrap and rust and all the men and women
    laughing in the diners and sleepers shall pass to ashes.)
I ask a man in the smoker where he is going and he answers,
    "Omaha."

One Goes Abreast

You ask me where I am going.
Quoting from *Don Quixote*,
I answer modestly,
"That is as it may turn out."

I leave the matter hopeful,
Like the man in Sandburg's poem
Who, asked the unfathomable question,
Answers, "Omaha."

Yet in a strait so narrow
(Quoting now from Shakespeare)
Who knows the destination
Where one but goes abreast?

President Carter, on a visit to Poland, took with him an interpreter who told the Poles that Carter was saying, in response to their warm welcome, "I have erotic desires for you."

He is referred to lately as our nation's most baffling president.

1978

January

Losers

Elizabeth Bishop said it in a poem,
"The art of losing isn't hard to master,"
Words that have leaped and chirped all day tuning
Like crickets in my head, a charming villanelle
To say that loss is no disaster—
Since everyone carelessly loses things, mislays
A door key, car key, credit card, finds missing
A friend lost track of, places left behind,
One's world, one's faith, one's squandered love. And who's
To say it's never too late to lose?
With every hour the less, faster, faster.

February

Then someone will remark, "I only look at the cartoons in the *New Yorker*. I don't *read* it." What began as a magazine of humor mingled with a little seriousness is hard pressed to stay in tune with the world seen from West 43rd Street, where things look worse and worse. Nobody can read an issue today and keep smiling. But the cartoons are funny.

The editors must fret when on the same page with a barren story of unhappy people or a bleak poem of loss will appear a cartoon amusing enough to cut out and fasten by Scotch tape to the refrigerator.

This week a piece titled "From the Journals of a Poet" consists of excerpts from the diary Louise Bogan kept before she died in 1970, identified as "tragic reverberations"—the memory of pink roses in her dying mother's hospital room, the pain of rereading her former husband's letters, a complex of suffering. "Casting back," she wrote, "what we get is (often) the faces of fools and madmen."

The adjacent cartoon shows a husband in a fool's face, the mask of a happy clown, peering over the back of his wife's chair, while she shouts in fury, "And stop trying to cheer me up!"

Today I went for my yearly checkup with Dr. Wysor to see what good counsel he would give that he wouldn't take himself. Since my body so far causes us no concern, and the list he reads of common ailments takes no time to cross off, one nonafflicted organ after another, Dr. Wysor turns with obvious reluctance to my mind. There he knows we are in trouble.

"Do you have nightmares?" he asks. "Hallucinations? Insomnia? Do you suffer from depression, distraction, anxiety, fear, worry, stress? Do you stumble? Is your mind disturbed?"

"Yes," I say.

"May I recommend a psychiatrist?"

"No."

(Louise Bogan, from a sanitarium in Connecticut, "My God, what was the crime? Did I deserve / Therapy, out of possible punishments?")

Each year we run through the routine. Dr. Wysor is a family man, with pictures of his four children on his desk. He has never visited a psychiatrist for his emotional problems, if any. Moreover, he admits nobody could drag him near one. But as a doctor he seeks a cure.

"Have you tried pastoral help?"

I said, "If you mean have I gone out to dance in the meadows? Or sought greener pastures among happy shepherds? No."

Today, after the usual round of symptoms, Dr. Wysor gave some advice he has actually taken himself. "It works," he said. "Seriously, I've tried it, and I think it's just the therapy you need. I recommend it as a cure for the soul."

"What is that?"

"A trip to Disneyland."

Granted, I need to have my head examined, but preferably on the outside by a phrenologist. After the science was originated by Franz Gall and became the rage in the nineteenth century, phrenologists by exploring bumps on the skull were able to define one's talents and aptitudes, one's capacity for love, hope, piety, self-esteem, instead of one's tensions, fears, neuroses, and general havoc in the head.

Walt Whitman kept a chart of his bumps. Thomas Hardy had his bumps felt. So did Sydney Smith, who after examination was declared to be a naturalist. Smith modestly replied, "I don't know a fish from a bird." The only temptation to see a psychiatrist would be to try to analyze the analyst, uncover his load of ills the same as one's own. E. B. White played with that idea in "The Second Tree from the Corner." As the visits progressed, his character Trexler began to identify with the doctor, gradually transferring himself to the doctor's seat. He found him incurable, "a poor, scared overworked bastard." "Scared as a rabbit," Trexler said.

According to J. B. Priestley, who had several talks with Jung though not as a patient, Jung did not encourage writers or artists of any kind to consult him. The reason he gave was that creative work provided its own therapy. I can think of other reasons for avoiding such a confrontation. Both therapists and poets are notoriously unstrung with a high suicide rate. An analyst might recognize the risk of being exposed by an expert. "The poor, scared guy," thought Trexler.

After reading Joyce's *Ulysses*, Jung remarked, "Good. If he hadn't been able to write that he might have gone mad." Apparently Jung didn't read *Finnegans Wake*. He would have said, "Poor man. So he went mad after all."

In Sunday's *New York Times*, the Dutch-American abstract expressionist painter, Willem de Kooning, was interviewed about his work because eighty-four of his paintings and drawings go on view this week at the Guggenheim. As to his work, de Kooning wants only to get on with it, left free to live as a recluse in East Hampton and spared the interruption of pests who ask questions. He says, "I don't think artists have particularly bright ideas."

Now in his seventies but undaunted ("You get old, you get used to yourself"), he has no trouble starting a new picture. A big interior with figures is the project currently in mind, on one enormous canvas. His figures are generally frontal, garish females with extra arms and legs furiously askew or dismembered, it's not clear which since he splatters his brush about like a tempest, one layer of paint dripped and splashed on another. This is called headlong art, ferocious in intent (like Soutine's paintings of mutilations), outrageous to some viewers, messy to others, authentic to the experts.

"I see the canvas, and I begin." He may begin by closing his eyes or by writing words on the canvas such as *hope* in large letters across the top, *man* across the bottom. Thus de Kooning attempts to write pictures by sheer intensities of color that collide and explode—bold pinks turning to golden yellow, shimmering reflections of *hope*, terrifying shades of *man*.

The colors he mixes in salad bowls. The message he mixes in his head. "I have an attitude," he says. "I have to have an attitude." And he adds, "My interest in desperation lies only in that sometimes I find myself having become desperate. Very seldom do I start out that way."

The Painter

The arrogance is beautiful. Had he said
The shades of light, the changing hues of love
In wild distorted eyes, the color of stars
("The stars I think about"),
All in one big interior of space,
Then one might know he held these in his mind
As Turner saw the sun and Monet saw
Reflections in the waterlily pool.
Or if he meant the tinctures and the dyes
Of summer. . . . No, it's with the arrogant
Intrepidity of the artist that he speaks—
"I'd like to get all the colors in the world
Into one single painting." And he stands
Before the empty canvas. And begins.
But is it fair to ask how one would gather
Into a single poem all the words?

March

William Gass has written a "philosophical inquiry," as a professor of philosophy, into the color blue. Calls it *On Being Blue*. This amazing color, he says, is so versatile it means a state of mind—as do all the colors? white with fear, red with shame, green with envy, purple with rage. Blue, he says, means contradictory states: erotic, moral (Puritan blue laws), and celestial (Mary's color).

On his mind is blue language, which I should call off-color. He sees no improvement in life through the four-letter words that are so impoverished and should be used sparingly since there aren't enough to make a vocabulary. (Harold Pinter in an interview: "There are very few [obscene] words—you shouldn't kill them by overuse.") We might adopt some from the more inventive past: *bung*, as Doll said to Pistol, "Away, you filthy bung." Gass concludes that people who can't speak decently have nothing to say anyway.

To the Man with the Blue Guitar

Blue is the sound of it, bright as air.
I twang it out and leave it there.
Blue is the tune for it, ai-yi-yi,
Blue is my color too. Blue am I.
Here's blue in your eye.

"Except a man be born again," Jesus told Nicodemus, "he cannot see the kingdom of God." The latest style is to be reborn, from President Carter to Muhammad Ali, a transformation more complete than being revived in what preachers used to call revival. Billy Graham announces periodically his rebirth. He has written a book of instructions, *How to Be Born Again*, and says he is going to a literal heaven where he will play golf and see Elvis Presley.

I thought Father Divine started the movement in the twenties. He was born again or rebegot, though he couldn't recall how or when—a divine birth that turned him into God Almighty, and his followers chanted, "He is God, God, God!" I knew one of Father Divine's angels named Heavenly Grace. She worked as a maid for a friend of mine on 72nd Street and would greet you at the door, "Peace, it's truly wonderful!" She lived in heaven up in Harlem.

These days the renaissance is available to everybody, even in a secular world. Francine du Plessix Gray in her autobiographical novel *Lovers and Tyrants*, a book on the pleasures of sex for women, sums up her new existence: "We can all be reborn. I am better off now, much better off. I am total, complete."

How to Look at This and That

It's after all the way you look at things
That everyday is birdsong (well sung, bird),
Or else it isn't, and the cold sets in,

Though this too may be viewed indulgently,
With tolerance as Eskimos look at snow.
"How many snows," they'll ask you, "have you seen?"

And you reply by quoting Villon, "Where . . . ?"
Or possibly "*What* snows of yesteryear?"
Since living in the South you miss a few.

I went tonight to hear the Alban Berg Quartet play Berg, averse ever again to listening to the "Lyric Suite," one atonal movement of which sounded like tiny insects scratching one's back.

As my mind wandered from Berg, I gazed around the Music Room at East Duke where I've spent hundreds of hours listening to chamber music, guest speakers, occasionally myself on that platform. Eudora Welty spoke from there on "Place," meaning Mississippi. Her voice was very small, yet when she stood at the microphone and opened her mouth, what issued forth was an outburst of rock music. Somebody had plugged in the band by mistake, and the effect was thunderous. Afterward when I thanked her with honest admiration and said good-bye, she shook my hand but forgot to let go. We stood unable to break apart, while "Good-bye, good-bye," she murmured and hung on, caught in another predicament that had befallen her like the rock music. I love writers. They do funny things like that. Robert Lowell came to the Music Room and growled his poems under his breath, inaudible from the front row; James Dickey came blandishing; Randall Jarrell came obliterated by a beard. I introduced Elizabeth Bowen one night with her nearly unmanageable stutter that obliged her to hold both arms tight around her body as she talked. At the reception at the Pattons later, she rushed into the house crying, "B-b-b-b-b-b-bourbon!"

April

James Agate was a London drama critic (died 1947) who wrote a nine-volume diary called *Ego*—the perfect title, an egoist who recognized himself. He started the diary in his fifty-fifth year after reading Arnold Bennett's *Journal* and, as befits an egoist, felt inspired to perpetuate himself in a last ditch of expression.

Somebody described him as a wit who poured vinegar on troubled waters. Edith Sitwell said, "I absolutely *hate* Agate, and would stick at nothing to do him in." I admire a man who objected to the word *poetess* —"Surely a woman is a poet or nothing"—and found a striking difference between a land flowing with milk and honey and a land swarming with cows and bees.

A play he saw in March 1933 and damned as dull appeared as "Gay Love," when gay was a usable adjective and men were gay deceivers. The title made me laugh to remember a verse I wrote once about John Gay, "The Poet Gay"—the first line of which commands briskly, "Poet, take the poet Gay." Write Gay's name lowercase and you have a worthless piece of advice.

This spring afternoon on East Campus was like a fiesta—two separate groups dancing to stereos blaring disco and country rock that shook the trees, young male athletes stripped to the waist throwing Frisbees, girls lying in the sun in bikinis, and two barking dogs. It was hot and flowery with April.

I picked up a copy of the Duke *Chronicle* to read on the library steps. It had these notices:

Special seminar: How to be filled with the Holy Spirit.
Duke Democrats will show a film "Minister of Hate." Refreshments.
Gay Alliance (a member of the National Gay Task Force) will hold a
    potluck supper.
Ken Feit will lead a workshop in clowning and sidesplitting.
Come join a Runathon around East Campus wall. Beer and music.

The Upstart Mole

While squirrels and rabbits fling the earth about
To make a fitting festival of spring,
The upstart mole works furiously in the dark
Throwing up molehills, casting wide and deep
As if Olympus to a molehill should
In supplication nod. As if by burrowing
Among the earthworms he would dig my grave.
Well done, old mole, old excavator!
Who said, old beady eye, that you were blind?

May

I'd hate to try to hide family secrets from Robert Gittings, the latest biographer of Thomas Hardy. In *Young Thomas Hardy* and *Thomas Hardy's Later Years*, he has taken pains to document the lowdown trick Hardy played, a literary imposture resulting from vanity, snobbery, hunger for fame, and an obsessive need to live in strictest privacy—a hoax that finally didn't work. The irony, for a man haunted by life's ironies, is that Gittings is the kind of biographer Hardy wanted to avoid, who would track him down and find him out. Secretly, in his late seventies, he wrote his autobiography, as much and as little as he wanted the world to know, a flattering, inaccurate portrait in the third person that Hardy pretended his second wife, Florence, had written. She not only agreed to the lie but typed the manuscript and helped him get rid of the evidence.

After Hardy's death in 1929, the first volume of the *Life* appeared under her name as author, the second in 1930. For years the deception went on. A half-century later Gittings shows how Hardy almost succeeded in effacing the records, with bonfires to destroy letters and diaries, conceal his humble origins, deny his cold treatment of both wives, hide his infatuation with other women. Hardy's mother had been brought up on parish charity. His family and relatives in Dorset were poor working people, laborers, cooks, servants. He was ashamed of them. And he betrayed them all.

B. and I spent a week once in Dorchester because Hardy had lived there. It was Casterbridge to us and to the woman in whose house we stayed—6 shillings for bed and breakfast—a worshiper of Hardy. Her name was Mrs. Major but I think of her as Mrs. Yeobright, her favorite role in the productions of the Hardy Players she acted in over the years. Proudly she led us about the market town with a copy of *The Mayor of Casterbridge* in her hand, stopping to read aloud passages describing Henchard's world in the 1830s when he was mayor of the village. Packing our lunch, Mrs. Yeobright sent us to the hamlet of Higher Bockhampton three miles away where Hardy was born in a thatched cottage on the edge of the heath. We went to Puddletown where his relatives lived, we wandered through furze and heather on desolate Egdon Heath, mindful of the "tragical possibilities" of *The Return of the Native*. By the end of the week we were steeped in Hardy country, over our ears in Wessex. The only place Mrs. Yeobright failed to mention was Max Gate, but we went anyway. Florence still lived in the house Hardy designed and built for Emma, his first wife, who like the house depressed him—a fudgy mansion. Mrs. Yeobright had a low opinion of Florence, a snubber giving herself airs. Mrs. Yeobright's hero was Thomas Hardy.

June

There had to be a last survivor of the Bloomsbury group, and he died the other day at ninety-three—Duncan Grant, the postimpressionist painter. Everybody loved him, including myself. He was a beautiful small man, boyish and slender, self-effacing or perhaps elusive, with sultry gray eyes, full warm lips, dark coloring. In fact, adorable.

When B. and I visited Charleston in 1950, he met us at the train in Lewes in a ramshackle two-seater we could barely squeeze into. He appeared happy to see us in his shy, amused way, but I had no idea who this shabby fellow was. Vanessa Bell had invited us down for the day, and we hurried from London to meet her and her husband Clive, unaware of Duncan who had been her lover for many years, the father of Angelica. In 1916 Vanessa had found a primitive farmhouse, Charleston, on the South Downs in Sussex. There she went to live with her two boys and Duncan, apart from Clive. Having married in 1906, by 1914 he and Vanessa had amicably gone their separate ways, though he wrote her, "I far prefer your society and Duncan's and the Charleston atmosphere to any other." For forty-five years Vanessa clung to this house that she and Duncan decorated with fanciful screens and panels, whose walls were hung with their pictures. Their child was born upstairs on Christmas Day 1918. Vanessa died there in 1961. Duncan died there alone.

The two men, Clive and Duncan, were startlingly unlike in appearance and manner. I was sure, especially by the second visit to Charleston in May, this was the perfect ménage à trois. Clive, who appeared to live there, was plump and jovial, a showman full of roars, a large, gleeful man with a pink face and some wisps of ginger hair. His relish for gossip made him garrulous. Over martinis before lunch, he questioned B. and me about so many literary figures of whom we knew far less than he did, such as Rebecca West and her affair with H. G. Wells, that as we sat down to the table I said, "I'm abashed to tell you, but you haven't descended yet to my level of acquaintance." Their son Quentin burst into laughter and winked at his mother. Clive laughed but turned the talk to partridges. Though he had coined the phrase, he didn't mention Significant Form. Vanessa told me eagerly that she and Duncan would soon go up to London to their studio, painting from the same model. He was six years younger than she, the better artist—with pride she said so. I couldn't tell their paintings apart.

I had a letter from her on our return to America in June: "May I say to you both that I am only too happy that we may count you as two new friends. I hope you will let us know when you come to England next year or whenever it may be." But we never saw them again. Ten years later it was Quentin who had become a dear friend.

Virginia Woolf often referred to Duncan in her diary and letters. ("I can't help loving him in spite of all.") She called him wayward, mellifluous, and androgynous, and wondered how he ever got through life, "but as a matter of fact he gets through it better than any of us." After *The Waves*, she knew she must start a new book to keep her sanity and thought of a life of Duncan. She told Vanessa, "I should like to write a book about

Duncan. Are you the only person who is really acquainted with him? intimately profoundly? I dare say."

"Kiss that adorable man for me," she wrote. "I often wonder how we should have done married."

July

Personal Intelligence (or Glad Tidings): The city of Durham has a "courteous and professional" cathouse. It's for boarding cats.

Last night the question on a radio program was "Do hippies still exist?" People drawn in from the street answered with spontaneous relief, no. Hippies had had their day. They were defined as unwashed, hairy, beaded, spaced-out flower children, who attended rock festivals and invented love-ins, claiming love as the solution no one else had thought of. "Hippies were far out," someone said. "Now everybody is far out."

I have a friend whose favorite reading is Longinus "On the Sublime." That to me is far out.

August

Thoreau taught me what to do—to renounce possessions, the acquiring of them and being possessed by them. Accumulating dross, he called it, cluttering one's life, wearing fetters. "Simplify!" he cried. Like him I'm not a collector but a rejector. A friend, shocked by my penury when I refused to buy a carrot peeler at Woolworth's that she found indispensable to gracious living, offered to pay the 25¢ it cost. "I hate gadgets," I said. While writing a thesis on Thoreau at Columbia, I was accused by friends of being the Salvation Army's main source of supply. I made lists of things I didn't want: a cuckoo clock, a wolfhound, an enemy. When we moved to a house in the Bronx with an incinerator, B. predicted I would throw him in as well. I rid myself of books, conscious of Thoreau's gesture of throwing out the limestone at Walden because it accumulated dust. Books gather dust.

Sir Kenneth Clark, in his autobiography *The Other Half*, calls the opposite way of life nimiety, or excess, redundance, too-muchness—from which he has suffered all his life—too many possessions, too many books, too much to eat and drink. Coleridge said you find this too-muchness in all Germans.

Yet in 1853 Thoreau wrote in his journal, "I have now a library of nearly nine hundred volumes, over seven hundred of which I wrote myself." These 706 were *A Week on the Concord and Merrimack Rivers* that the printer returned to him. Today I received fifty copies of *Beautiful Lofty People*, a book I wrote and have no need of, having already read it.

September

A TV awards program for excellence in acting was interrupted tonight, September 17, while a set of abler actors took the stage in a theatrical scene in the East Room of the White House. Sadat of Egypt, Begin of Israel, and between them Carter of the U.S.A. sat at a table midcenter and, while the world watched, exulted. "It is a great moment," said Begin.

After thirteen days at Camp David that Franklin Roosevelt named Shangri-La, the Middle East summit meeting appeared to end disastrously, though Carter had taken Begin and Sadat on a tour of Gettysburg to reflect on our own scenes of bloodshed. Then the three came glowing in an accord, with pats and embraces. Before our eyes they signed two treaties to bring an end to a thirty-year Arab-Israeli conflict, five wars in three decades and the immediate threat of more to come.

Carter's face was drawn with fatigue after close to total breakdown of negotiations, after daily prayers for enlightenment and an even break. A Christian, a Jew, and a Muslim, each a man of deep religious faith, sought together for peace. For a brief moment they dared to hope.

October

In her book *Speedboat*, Renata Adler says, "I have led several lives, and I still lead some of them." Whether one leads one's lives or is led by them, they disappear along the way. Like Orpheus and Lot's wife, I tend to look behind me, proving as they did no good can come of it.

I walk too much in my childhood, which is not there. There is no village of Worcester, New York (pop. 800), with its dirt road Main Street, Tabor's blacksmith shop, and a family named Goodenough. At the yearly victory beanbake, the Grand Army of the Republic—a few white-bearded old men in blue uniforms—squatted around an artificial campfire singing "Tenting Tonight," while we ate cold beans and hardtack on tin plates.

I return to my mother's house, which is not there. It has three rooms and nothing in it, nothing but her lace curtains, upright piano, Singer sewing machine with foot pedals, the yellow hammock on the stoop, her dim shadow and mine. You would think by seventy years later one should be old enough to recognize

> It is an illusion that we were ever alive,
> Lived in the houses of mothers, arranged ourselves
> By our own motions in a freedom of air.
>
> Regard the freedom of seventy years ago.
> It is no longer air. The houses still stand,
> Though they are rigid in rigid emptiness.

> —from Wallace Stevens, "The Rock"

November

I've asked Ben Crabtree of the service station to tune up my car for a 3,000-mile trip, without specifying the direction. I've requested passage on the Delta Queen down the Mississippi. I've polished my house for immediate departure to Tibet. I've started to pack my bags.

Instead of going anywhere, I sit at home and read the life of Lady Hester Stanhope, one of the greatest travelers of her day, certainly the maddest. Daughter of the earl of Stanhope, Lady Hester escaped him in her twenties and went to live with her uncle, William Pitt, where she ruled his household as well as London society with a high imperious hand till Pitt died in 1806.

At thirty-four she sailed for Gibraltar and never again set foot in England, traveling in the grand style through the Middle East accompanied by her English maid Mrs. Fry, her doctor Dr. Meryon, and her servants, all of whom she treated with harshness and contempt. She had a colossal ego, an unmatched pride, as Virginia Woolf says, "despised people without troubling to give them a reason for it."

From a boat in the harbor at Piraeus, she caught sight of Lord Byron gracefully diving into the sea, and for a few days in Athens at her invitation he paid her visits, ill at ease with a rude, disdainful woman who abused and browbeat him till he fled. "I think he was a strange character," Lady Hester remarked. "He had vice in his looks."

In Syria she emerged astride her horse, wearing Turkish male attire —purple velvet pantaloons, scarlet coat trimmed with gold—that she affected for the rest of her life. At Jerusalem she awaited the fulfillment of a prophecy, revealed to her years before, that she would be crowned Queen of the Jews. When she reached Palmyra, the first European woman to enter the city where Zenobia ruled in Roman times, the inhabitants crowned her with flowers. Thereafter she considered herself Queen of the Arabs. (Zenobia too was insolent, defying the Emperor Aurelian and declaring herself queen of Palmyra, a Roman colony. In her dark beauty pleasing to Aurelian, who confined her in gold fetters, she was likened to Cleopatra. Nobody said this of Lady Hester, who looked like Edith Sitwell.)

After years of wandering, the lady found an abandoned convent on the slopes of Mount Lebanon, later moving to a ruined monastery farther up the mountain. There she awaited the moment when she would ride into Jerusalem with the Messiah at her side, followed by a cavalcade of peoples to subdue the world. She kept two Arabian horses ready, Laila and Loulou, a milk-white steed as befitted the Messiah's bride. By now she wore a huge turban that seemed to Alexander Kinglake, who visited her, to be made of pale cashmere shawls. The barbaric Druses among whom she lived regarded her as a goddess and prophet, neither man nor woman but with her extremely white skin a sublime spirit.

Forty-eight hungry cats roamed the corridors of her mountain fortress, and sometimes she howled with them in fits of rage at the undue delay in her divine plan to deliver the Jews and redeem the world. Dr. Meryon, who after her death published six volumes of *Memoirs and Travels*, was packed off home where Mrs. Fry had earlier fled. Lady Hester died in 1839, robbed by her servants, friendless and alone, and was buried in her Syrian garden.

She has a point. She makes me content to stay becalmed.

"Lady Sackville was a most extraordinary woman. She led a most extraordinary life. But she is of no importance. Her history would never have been dug up without the present obsession with all things even faintly Bloomsbury."

So begins a review of a biography by Susan Alsop of Lady Sackville, mother of Vita Sackville-West. The heading identifies her as "Vita's Mother." I deplore the reviewer's impertinence. I deny her right to say of anyone, anywhere, *But she is of no importance.*

When she died at seventy-four, Lady Sackville left behind a fragment of a few pages unfinished in midsentence, "The Book of Happy Reminiscences for My Old Age." The illegitimate daughter of Lionel Sackville-West, distinguished British diplomat, and a Spanish dancer Pepita, she had led a charmed life ("Quel roman est ma vie!") that, aged sixty, she set herself in gratitude to praise. "Only happy thoughts are to be mentioned in these confidences," she wrote. "I want to have a golden old age ripe with happy reminiscences. . . . I have been so lucky all through life. Lionel [her husband and first cousin] gave me 10 perfect years of the most complete happiness and passionate love which I reciprocated heartily. I adored him, and he adored me." Who could read these words without wanting to leave behind a journal with that title?

Five years later, by 1928, so great a deterioration had occurred in Lady Sackville's fortunes that something snapped in her brain. Her beloved husband died after flaunting his mistresses and demanding a divorce. She turned on her daughter Vita, making infuriating scenes, so irrational and cruel that they were estranged. On August 3, 1933, Virginia Woolf wrote to Vita, "I'm delighted to hear that the old termagant your mother has turned against you again." Finally Lady Sackville died alone—blind, bitter, and mad.

December

You would think it was a man's world. I've been consulting book lists, diverted by the number of titles about A Man. He may be identified by an adjective: A Generous Man, A Single Man, A Certain Man, A Good Man, Available, Adaptable, Quiet, Married, or Invisible. He is a Man Called White or Cervantes, Intrepid or Peter, a Man Named John. He's a Man from Galilee, Nazareth, Maine, Mt. Vernon, New York, Main Street, Missouri, Monticello, Next Door, and Home. The Man in the Street, the White House, the Moon, the Sycamore Tree, the Gray Flannel Suit, in Black, in the Mirror, in the Iron Mask. The Man with the Hoe, the Pitchfork, the Bull-Tongue Plow, the Golden Arm, the Blue Guitar, and a Million Ideas. The Man of Destiny, Honor, Taste, Reason, Feeling, Passion, Principle, Property, Straw, and La Mancha. The Man Who Was Thursday, Who Would Be King, Who Came to Dinner, Married a Dumb Wife, Loved Children, Hated Sherlock Holmes, Knew Coolidge, and Understood Women. A Man for All Seasons.

So I bought a book titled *The Quotable Woman*.

I'm into fairies again. Now the spelling is different, *FAERIES*, as is the threatening tone. This is no book for children. Two Englishmen,

Brian Froud and Alan Lee, have taken from old sources the history of Faerie—a world of elves, pixies, sprites, leprechauns, a horrendous variety of banshees, bogies, kelpies, goblins and hobgoblins meant to fill one with hauntings and apprehensions.

It seems fair to ask: who besides children believe in faeries? You'd be surprised. Long a part of folk superstition, often objects of dread, they represent good and evil, especially evil in accordance with man's understandable tendency to fear unseen threats in the air around him. They hold a significant place in literature. Thomas the Rhymer in the thirteenth century met in a wood the Queen of Elfland dressed in green silk, was trapped by a kiss on her red, red lips, and lived for seven years in Elfland before he returned to write about it. In the sixteenth century the French word *faerie* replaced the Old English *elf*, so that Spenser and Shakespeare were inspired to create faerie queens. William Blake was surrounded by guardian faeries. Lewis Carroll made drawings of them that he said "you can't be sure don't really exist." In our day Yeats is closest in spirit to the little people, the Sidhe. He portrayed himself as "The Man Who Dreamed of Faeryland," who longed in vain to escape to an island "where people love beside the ravelled seas," and every lover is at peace.

The makers of this book, steeped in faerie faith, provide data that one may or may not need. Faeries with their powers are alien to human beings owing to their lack of heart or soul; through pranks, envy, spite they cause endless mischief. (In *Cymbeline*, Imogen asks the gods, "From faeries and the tempters of the night, guard me, beseech ye.") Some are malevolent —the Spriggens, dour, grotesque faerie villains who steal babies and cause whirlwinds. The world of Faerie is one to enter with extreme caution, and any mortal is wise not to fool around with it (Christina Rossetti wrote in "Goblin Market," "We must not look on goblin men"), or else learn to protect himself by turning his coat inside out while walking alone, carrying a Bible or fourleaf clover, ringing bells, praying aloud with honest zeal. Never eat faerie food (the nectar of primroses), accept a faerie kiss, or step inside a faerie ring to join the dancing and be made captive. Their favorite tune is "The Londonderry Air."

For centuries people believed in faeries; that is fact. The assumption here made that we still do, as part of a hidden spiritual world, is cause for skepticism, even alarm, when we read such words: "Common experience and clairvoyant sightings of faeries prove that the faeries of tradition are the faeries of fact." If this is so, then let him who dares venture forth at his own risk.

Some years ago Morris Bishop wrote a poem "How to Treat Elves." He tells how he met a wee elf in the woods sitting under a mushroom. After asking what it did all day and listening to its silly drool,

> I lifted up my foot, and squashed
> The god damn little fool.

I'm beginning to think I've had it with faeries.

1979

January

To face 1979 with a fitting slogan, the best I could find was James Reston in the *New York Times* saying "To hell with the old year." Writing from Paris, "But somehow life goes on," he added, "even without much visible evidence of support."

Time declares the whole decade to be a confused, decadent, exhausted patch of history shrugging off its crises, the apathetic age.

Hammacher Schlemmer advertises a post-Christmas sale of treadmills, useful for trying to stay where you are yet keep on going. The treadmill can be tilted upward if you feel like Sisyphus, forever climbing the same old mountain.

Last night, January 6, Eric Sevareid and Walter Cronkite had a friendly chat on CBS. Like two sages they sat back in overstuffed chairs before an open fire, crossed their legs, and talked comfortably, smiling often:

Cronkite: Quite a year. Are we better off? worse off? than a year ago?
Sevareid: A little worse off.

Cronkite: Is individual initiative really possible?
Sevareid: Bureaucracy is a kind of tyranny in our lives.

Cronkite: What is it in our democracy that keeps us from tackling the great problems of our time?
Sevareid: Ours is a spoiled country in some ways. Very big businesses, mergers, whole chains bought up, absentee ownership. . . . Somehow these things must be altered.

Cronkite: Where is the leadership to come from?
Sevareid: It's a pretty unrewarding life now. A trivialization is going on. A lack of leadership. Are there any heroes around?

Cronkite: Has Carter a hold on affairs?

Sevareid: He must get inflation under control. He must stop *boring* people. Everybody is scared. Inflation is frightening. It is the big problem. How will we trust each other, get along with each other?

Cronkite: A year of considerable turmoil ahead.

February

Virginia Woolf heard sparrows singing in Greek. Joan of Arc heard heavenly voices, and the Lord commanded her to listen. In Shaw's *Saint Joan* she told Baudricourt, "God is very merciful, and the blessed saints Catherine and Margaret, who speak to me every day. I hear voices telling me what to do. They come from God."

The voices I hear telling me what to do come from television. Inside my head they are perpetually singing, "Have a Coke and a smile." "You deserve a break today." "What's the best tuna? Chicken of the Sea."

March

An editor and friend, Dan Wickenden, who keeps me posted on this news item or that, sent a clipping from the *New York Times* on the stupidity of butterflies. Seems they forget everything, even the little they learned as caterpillars. A lady in Northampton, Massachusetts, trains caterpillars to crawl in the direction of delicious leaf pudding instead of turning the other way to receive an electric shock. This bit of education they promptly lose the minute they become butterflies. Either they fly away on heedless wings or if restrained fail to head for the pudding.

Karel Čapek wrote a play, *The Insect Comedy,* that revealed the shallow nature of the butterfly brain. His brilliant satire had a profound effect on me, especially Act I, the scene of the giddy butterflies dancing in a mad social whirl till one of their number drops to earth and the others flutter and soar over the body, blithely indifferent to his fate. Iris, the frivolous, vacant heroine, cries to her lover, "Chase me! Catch me if you can," as a bird flies by and eats him up.

In simple contrast, the characters Mr. and Mrs. Cricket (Act II), domesticated insects happily awaiting offspring, move into a tiny cottage where they put up gingham curtains, singing to each other, "Cricket, Cricket, Cricket, will you always love me?" A doting ichneumon fly comes along and murders them to feed his larva. A pair of greedy dung beetles guarding their pile of manure ("Our capital! Our gold! the gift of God"), and an army of ants make up the cast, all closely resembling humankind, our futile lives and our fate. A passing tramp says, "Thank heaven, man's different."

B. and I saw the play one night in New York, entertained by its fantasy but not greatly overcome by its message. Afterward we went to the Waldorf to dance at the Starlight Roof, where gradually, insidiously, the plot began to sink in. Over B.'s shoulder I looked around and, lo, the place was full of butterflies flitting about the dance floor. I was wearing a gray dress with no bright markings, and I felt inferior and depressed. I didn't chirp like a cricket, I felt like a slug. B., a slow dancer, said he felt ignoble like a snail, adding that Crates, the philosopher, wanted to regulate his life with the humility of the snail.

In a poem called "Money," Philip Larkin declares, "You can't put off being young until you retire." Little he knows. By his credulity it's clear he hasn't set foot in Florida. I've returned from Fort Myers on the Gulf of Mexico where, surrounded by white-haired youngsters, Larkin would have to swallow his words. He blew it that time.

My friend Edie, recently retired from a career in advertising and vigorous as Charlie's Angels, has bought into a golden-age village, an invention of the 1970s, where the ticket of admission is to be in the bloom of health and rich. No children or pets are allowed. On the lookout as usual for paradise, casing Florida for the fountain of youth, I went with an open mind. I found an Eden of sorts, streets lined with royal palms, a state of eternal spring. Far from accepting crabbed age or repose, the residents race about on bicycles, play golf without motorized carts, compete fiercely at shuffleboard—a game that originated in Florida and spread to ocean liners—or whack away at their garden plots. Indefatigable to banish care, they are the funmakers, where bridge is a mania, scrabble a tournament, Bingo thrives. They join classes in bodybuilding or reshaping, create works of art from seashells, never miss a baseball game at Terry Park, where the crowd is Medicare.

At the entrance gate guarded as in Eden is a sign appropriate to paradise, "For the best of your life," which also translates into making the best of it—the ultimate solution to family life, the end of the journey. I noticed in the luxurious apartments an abundance of framed pictures, a daughter in wedding dress, a son in cap and gown, a dog that had to be disposed of, a home that had to be sold. And a collection of seashells.

Occasionally when one of her children telephones, Edie weeps. But she'll survive by what it takes: vitality, an acceptance of the inevitable, a fast hold on a sense of humor, a few tears.

April

The first thing I did when I got home from Florida was to join a class in aerobic dancing at the Y, before the salubrious effect of the trip wore off. Under young Beverly's instruction, a dozen women over twenty-one, eager to shape up and shake off age, heft, arthritis, slouch, heartache, a tendency to list and droop, become airborne to dance music. Our romps take place in the basketball court of the gym, where the time clock is stopped at 0:00, the wall signs say, "Proper language and conduct expected," "15 laps equal a mile," and "No dunking" (I don't know yet how to dunk). She leads us in the Cha-Cha, Bossa Nova, Charleston, Teaberry Shuffle, Stomp, Hustle, Alley Cat, something called Slop, a bit of the Can-Can. These are choreographed into songs like "Boogie Fever," "Salty Dog Rag," and "Fancy Pants." I wish John Travolta could see me now.

Around the edge of the gym floor while we dance are fat guys and old guys jogging, panting, churning along. A bald man with a paunch had his picture in the paper with 800 miles to his credit, or 12,000 laps. The most enticing of the wall signs recommends "Date a Gymnast."

Lord Chesterfield to his son: "Dancing is in itself a very trifling, silly thing; but it is one of those established follies to which people of sense are sometimes obliged to conform."

May

William Carlos Williams made himself famous by writing reams of objectivist poems, simple little notations about seeing a red wheelbarrow beside some white chickens ("so much depends/upon/a red wheel/barrow"), or a red firetruck with the number 5 on it ("I saw the figure 5/in gold/on a red firetruck"). Today I had a like experience:

> I saw a sign
> on a red
> pickup truck
> of the Pickard Roofing Co.
> It said
> "Roofers need love too."

June

Woody Allen tells us we are all Woody Allens. In his new film *Manhattan* everyone is a loser, everyone hurts others, and there is no solution. The solution would be to love and be loved on a permanent basis.

After writing the story, Woody Allen directed the film, casting himself in the role of romantic hero, Isaac Singer—a skinny, big-nosed, pint-sized guy of forty-two who is losing his hair and having an affair with a seventeen-year-old, six-foot adolescent named Tracy, presented as being in love with him. She is in high school. "I care for you," she says. "We have great sex" (when her passion is for an ice cream soda?). Though she buys him a harmonica, he throws her over, hurts her, then tries to return to her after a doomed affair with a pseudo-intellectual from Philadelphia, a divorcée who goes on about Kierkegaard and Van "Gawgh." Isaac has two ex-wives, one a kindergarten teacher into drugs, the other a lesbian who has published a confessional book about marriage with Isaac, exposing his weird fantasies.

The scrubbiness of human lives, the misery, pain, insecurity, are shown against a background of Manhattan—a place never ugly or dirty, never defeated. The meaning is, with music by Gershwin, a beautiful city is filled with confused unhappy little people who live unbeautifully in it. The love they give or receive is sooner or later betrayed.

As in real life, Woody Allen can be comic or sad, with an owlish face that looks perpetually alerted. Since this is the world as he sees it of neurotics like him, the ending of the tale seems peculiarly poignant. Young Tracy, the only uncomplicated one (but give her time to grow up), says in farewell to Isaac, "You've got to have a little faith in people." What has been made abundantly clear is that it does no good to have faith in people. There is nobody to be faithful to. You always lose.

July

We waited for the sky to fall on the date set, July 11, each of us naturally assuming Skylab would fall on himself. A woman I know said, "I'm going to hide in the house with the curtains drawn." Across America we made an occasion of precrash parties, Chicken Little T-shirts, tin hats, survival kits, insurance policies with Lloyd's of London. Spivey's Corner, N.C. (pop. 40), prepared its football field for the crash. In Switzerland they rang churchbells. The odds were 1 in 600 billion of any one person being hit.

Skylab was launched six years ago, the heaviest manmade object in space, with no plan to return it to earth. Three separate crews lived in the laboratory, the third for eighty-four days, to see how long man could exist at home in the sky. Scientists at NASA expected it to stay in orbit, then break up beyond the earth's atmosphere. Suddenly they warned us the thing was a goner, about to hurtle to earth. They urged us to stay calm. A *New York Times* editorial recommended not jumping into a car and racing down the highway. Nobody would have time to dodge.

The day came, the hour as predicted, 12:30 Wednesday. I kept a date with the dentist. It fell—a fizzle in a shower of sparks, plunging into the Indian Ocean and an uninhabited part of Australia. Survivors of Skylab, our nerves a bit more taut, we returned to the real hazards of living.

August

"Is it ideas that I believe?"—Wallace Stevens
There is E. M. Forster's idea of the undeveloped heart.

Forster made dominant the theme of immaturity (an idea that obsessed him), the inability of most of us to grow up. He wrote about England's problem of the eternal adolescent—callow schoolboys passing for men, snobs of the privileged class sworn to schoolboy honor and loyalty. They live, he said, in the world of the undeveloped heart. (Virginia Woolf wrote in some doubt of Forster himself: "He is limp and damp and milder than the breath of a cow.")

To me T. S. Eliot's most poignant poem is "Animula," the small soul that finds life too complex and so remains a perpetual child in a man's body,

> Irresolute and selfish, misshapen, lame,
> Unable to fare forward or retreat,
> Fearing the warm reality, the offered good,
> Denying the importunity of the blood. . . .

Life for him is a process of dying after the security and wonder of childhood.

Ford Madox Ford's idea of relative truth.

Ford, a cheerful and extravagant liar, explained the virtue of relative truth over the absolute kind. To communicate with others, one has to heighten one's remarks to catch their wandering attention and limited imagination. One pitches the note too high, overstates lest the listener hear nothing. (William Carlos Williams wrote his friend Ford: "Thank God you were not delicate, you let the world in and lied! damn it you lied grossly sometimes.")

"The worst of me," said Mark Twain, "is that I exaggerate so; it is the only way I can approximate to the truth."

Montaigne's idea of modesty.

Before learning anything else, Montaigne said, "We must master the elementary lesson of modesty," we must rid ourselves of self-love and self-importance. What do I know? he asked, and found no reason to be vain. "I do not find so much good in myself that I cannot tell it without blushing."

"Pull down thy vanity, / I say pull down," wrote Ezra Pound in the *Pisan Cantos*. But Pound was momentous to himself, so relentlessly vain he betrayed his craft by caprice. When he fell, he crumpled to earth with an overburdened sense of his self-important failure as man and poet.

Yeats's idea of memory.

He said, "People do not invent. They remember." Yeats scorned those who write out of anything but real experience. After he accepted his naked role as poet, he wrote of friends, relatives, ancestors, the headlong affairs of Ireland, his love for Maud Gonne, and called it *the reality*. It was not invention, it was autobiography. The language of poetry must be kept, but the facts themselves, what he saw, heard, felt, had to be true.

Wallace Stevens' idea of order.

Because like other men he was a connoisseur of chaos, Stevens sought a necessary order in a chaotic world. Only by using the imagination, he said, can one restore order to the mind. The dismal failure in us is a failure of the imagination, to understand others, to understand ourselves. Literalists see merely a literal green world, when the only way to perceive life *as it is* is neither to distort reality nor change it into fantasy but to see it more consciously through the imagination—that is, to live in a blue-green world. Or try to.

What is there in life except one's ideas,
Good air, good friend, what is there in life?

September

Our aerobic dancing class has moved to the Duke gymnasium, where we're enrolled in the School of Continuing Education. Three mornings a week at 9:00 I hike across East Campus, dressed in warm-up suit and jogging shoes. Former colleagues whistle when they see the outfit. "You *dance?*" they cry in solemn amaze, reproach in their voices. I used to dress like a lady professor.

I jog past Carr Building where in September I taught Chaucer at this hour. We should be meeting the Wife of Bath this morning, whose company I miss with autumn in the air. She was a lusty oon who loved to dance,

"Wel coud I daunce to an harpe smale,
And singe, y-wis, as any nightingale."

October

Leon Edel, in his new book about Bloomsbury, *A House of Lions*, remarks, "Virginia was making literature out of Vanessa." That is what Edel has done to the Bloomsbury figures, fast fading into legend. He set himself the amusing task, he says, of telling it "as if it were a novel." He has taken nine people now dead—Roger Fry, Lytton Strachey, Maynard Keynes, Clive Bell, Leonard Woolf, Duncan Grant, Desmond MacCarthy, and two women: Virginia Woolf, Vanessa Bell—and made them into storybook characters, a little larger than life. His title calls them lions, his chapter headings identify the book as fiction: "Clive in Paris," "Leonard in Ceylon," "Love Among the Artists."

Time, as usual, let it happen. They who are "beyond living confrontation" had a measure of fame before they receded into the past like the Pre-Raphaelites or the Sitwells. Edel's scrutiny is at a chilling remove. Biography as he understands it is an art, not a two-volume memorial. But must it be a novel?

I'm glad I knew some of them, lunched with Leonard Woolf, listened over the teacups to his sisters praise Lytton Strachey, sat in a modest farmhouse with Vanessa, Duncan, Clive, and heard their voices. Though far from ordinary people even then, they lived and breathed. Yet this is how it goes.

> For Time is like a fashionable host
> That slightly shakes his parting guest by the hand,
> And with his arms outstretched, as he would fly,
> Grasps in the comer.
>
> —*Troilus and Cressida*

November

Subject: birds resort to churches.

Recently in a small parish church in the English village of Brant Broughton, a sparrow flying about during a music recital got itself caught in the rafters and burst into song. The offended rector asked the congregation to leave and had the bird shot. The story spread quickly, arousing all England to shocked protest and newspaper headlines. The *Daily Mirror* said in an editorial, "You never know, vicar. The next one might be carrying a harp."

From *A Jacobean Journal*, April 28, 1605: "Dr. John Milward, preaching at St. Paul's, in the midst of a sermon a cuckoo came flying over the pulpit (a thing never heard of before), and very lewdly cried out at him with open mouth."

In R. P. Lister's travel book on Turkey, *A Muezzin from the Tower of Darkness Cries*, he tells of visiting in Istanbul the Blue Mosque of Sultan Ahmed, which I remember for the flock of white pigeons flying around inside the celestial blue cupola. Lister stood awestruck in his stocking feet on the priceless Turkish carpets of the mosque and gazed at a blue heaven of Muhammad full of pigeons. With acuity he put two and two together, which is more than I did. Why hadn't the birds befouled the carpets and the prayer rugs turned toward Mecca? He consulted a man at the Ministry of Tourism and Information, who suggested that the pigeons were good Muslims, unwilling to desecrate a mosque.

R. P. Lister is another great traveler. He will go anywhere, just say the word. A while ago a friend asked if he was going abroad for a summer holiday.

"I thought of going to Lisbon," he replied.

"Go to Lapland."

Without ado Lister went. Though he had no idea why he or anyone else should visit Lapland, he saw no way of avoiding it. Actually he liked the place and went twice. Lapland is a virtually uninhabited country north of the Arctic Circle, containing a few nomadic Lapps who drift about following their herds of reindeer. As a traveler British to the core who abhors sightseeing, Lister found little temptation to do any. He walked for weeks through a monotonous scenery of mountains, glaciers, rocks, boulders, and birch trees. He went to a good deal of trouble to suffer from hunger, exposure, mosquitoes, and the shortening of his expectation of life. His diet, when spasmodically he had one, was reindeer or whale meat plus some packaged Mother's Milk that he put on the native cloudberries.

I thank him for setting me straight about lemmings, which live in these polar regions. In his travels Lister came across a lone lemming and took its picture, a fat round rodent of solitary habits, closely resembling a mouse. While the lemming is known to join other lemmings in periodic mass migrations in search of food, Lister explodes the popular myth that it has a tendency to plunge into the sea like the Gadarene swine and drown itself. Lemmings don't die on purpose. They don't even like to swim. "In fact," he says, "the lemming is almost alone among the inhabitants of Scandinavia in possessing no suicidal impulses whatever."

> Westward, until the salt sea drowns them dumb,
> Westward, till all are drowned, these lemmings go.
>
> —John Masefield, "The Lemmings"

December

The Marquis Publications want to send me a diary to enter a new decade. On a burgundy cover with a morocco grain it says in full capitals, "Who's Who," followed by my name embossed in 22 karat gold. Price $35.

Each day of a two-page week begins with the formidable heading "To Be Done" (no room for remembrance of things past, what's left undone). Whether I'm a detailed planner or a fast jotter, they say, this will accommodate my style. Actually I'm a detailed jotter and no planner at all.

"Who am I?" is a question I need no longer ask. Now it is "Who is who?"

The words of the Ayatollah Khomeini would look strange in a diary of what is To Be Done. What in an international crisis is to be done with him? A fanatic calls on Muslim nations to rise up and defend Islam against the infidel. President Carter warns Iran of grave retaliation if harm comes to the fifty-two hostages held captive in the U.S. Embassy at Teheran. It is like the Crusades, a threat of Holy War, where we are the infidels, the pagans, enemies of God.

What does one learn by taking a journey, any journey? I've taken a shaky trip through a decade (to Russia, to the mailbox, to bed) to the end of the 1970s, about which uncomplimentary and increasingly anxious remarks were made by us all—you, me, and the media. This was the Me Decade, the age of overexposure with its quests for self, mania for soul-baring confession, narcissism—defined by the experts as a time out of whack, a time of personal survival (all other kinds proving untrustworthy) in which by means of jogging, disco, astrology, being born again, having orgasms, swallowing vitamins and proteins, we sought to escape with our lives.

The 1970s were short on heroes. This was the Age of Diminishing Expectations and the crunch—the energy crunch, gasoline crunch, inflation crunch. Now that predictions are tossed about for the 1980s, we are promised not more of the same but fewer certainties, heavy weather ahead in the storms of tomorrow. Already a book has appeared, *The 80's, A Look Back at the Tumultuous Decade 1980-89,* in which the worst came to pass: England was taken over by Disneyland; people rode in rickshaws or migrated to Mexico because of oil shortages; colleges went bankrupt; children divorced their parents; with growing food costs fat women appeared lovable.

We squeaked through the seventies without fighting another war but with increased tensions between the U.S. and U.S.S.R. World War III is predicted for August 1985 (a war of inadvertence quickly becoming total), but before that we have Orwell's 1984. President Carter says, "The danger of holocaust hangs over us." Our best hope seems to be to move to another planet.

You have to humor the hellgazers, keeping a sharp lookout for a sole rejoicer, himself a cause for rejoicing. E. E. Cummings said fifty years ago,

Me: "Being funny doesn't help."
Him: "Neither, he inadvertently answered, does being tragic."

Though the Equal Rights Amendment wasn't ratified in this decade, women gained the glorious right in 1973 to be addressed as Ms. Some say the horse and buggy, along with woodburning stoves and marriage, is due back as a way to go, wherever we're going. William Safire says, "We're embarking up the wrong tree." Some say the chances still are.

The hellgazer: "It's a cold, cold world you're walking through, my friend" (from a popular song of 1979).

The rejoicer (from another popular song): "Just pick yourself up, dust yourself off, and start all over again."

Helen Bevington has published many books, including *Doctor Johnson's Waterfall, Nineteen Million Elephants, A Change of Sky, When Found, Make A Verse Of, Charley Smith's Girl, A Book and a Love Affair, The House Was Quiet and the World Was Calm, Beautiful Lofty People,* and *Along Came the Witch*. She has written regularly for the *New York Times Book Review,* has published light verse in the *New Yorker,* and has contributed to *Atlantic Monthly* and *American Scholar,* among other periodicals. For many years she taught at Duke University, as did her late husband, Merle. She is now Professor Emeritus of English at Duke.